AF606046

THE UNMAKING OF HOME IN CONTEMPORARY ART

CLAUDETTE LAUZON

The Unmaking of Home in Contemporary Art

UNIVERSITY OF TORONTO PRESS
Toronto Buffalo London

© University of Toronto Press 2017
Toronto Buffalo London
www.utppublishing.com

ISBN 978-1-4426-4982-8

(Cultural Spaces series)

Library and Archives Canada Cataloguing in Publication

Lauzon, Claudette, 1969–, author
The unmaking of home in contemporary art / Claudette Lauzon.

(Cultural spaces)
Includes bibliographical references and index.
ISBN 978-1-4426-4982-8 (cloth)

1. Dwellings in art. 2. Dwellings – Social aspects. 3. Art, Modern – 21st century. I. Title. II. Series: Cultural spaces

N8217.D94L39 2017 704.9'496431 C2016-905731-3

An earlier version of chapter 3 previously appeared in "Giving Loss a Home: Doris Salcedo's Melancholic Archives," *Memory Studies* 8, no. 2 (April 2015): 197–211.An earlier version of chapter 4 previously appeared as "Reluctant Nomads: Biennial Culture and Its Discontents," *RACAR (Revue d'art canadienne/Canadian Art Review)* 36, no. 2 (Fall 2011): 15–30. Portions of this book previously appeared in "'Relics from the Mansion of Sorrow': Melancholic Traces of Home in Recent Art," in *Breaking and Entering: The House Cut, Spliced and Haunted in Contemporary Art*, ed. Bridget Elliot (Montreal: McGill-Queen's University Press, 2015), 19–32.

This book has been published with the help of a grant from the Federation for the Humanities and Social Sciences, through the Awards to Scholarly Publications Program, using funds provided by the Social Sciences and Humanities Research Council of Canada.

University of Toronto Press acknowledges the financial assistance to its publishing program of the Canada Council for the Arts and the Ontario Arts Council, an agency of the Government of Ontario.

Canada Council for the Arts
Conseil des Arts du Canada

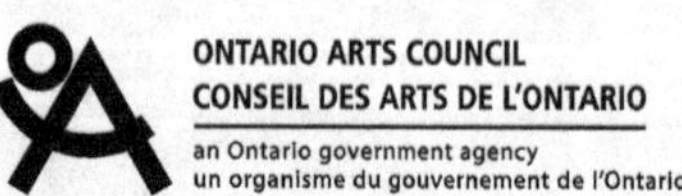

Funded by the Government of Canada
Financé par le gouvernement du Canada
Canada

Contents

Illustrations vi

Acknowledgments viii

Introduction: Unmaking Home 3

1 An Unhomely Genealogy of Contemporary Art 26

2 The Art of Longing and Belonging 69

3 Unhomely Archives 104

4 Biennial Culture's Reluctant Nomads 137

Notes 177

Index 209

Illustrations

I.1 Mona Hatoum, *Mobile Home*, 2005. 4
I.2 Donald Rodney, *In the House of My Father*, 1996–7. 5
I.3 Petrit Halilaj: *The places I'm looking for, my dear …* 2010. 6
I.4 Akram Zaatari, *In This House*, 2005. 8
I.5 Petrit Halilaj: *I'm hungry to keep you close …* 2013. 15
I.6 Mona Hatoum, *Interior Landscape*, 2008. 18
1.1 Krzysztof Wodiczko, *The Homeless Projection*, 1986. 35
1.2 Martha Rosler, *Knife* from *Semiotics of the Kitchen*, 1975. 36
1.3 Martha Rosler, *Homeless*, 2015. 38
1.4 Martha Rosler, *Cleaning the Drapes*, ca 1967–72. 41
1.5 Gordon Matta-Clark, Documentation of *Splitting*, 1974. 46
1.6 Gordon Matta-Clark, *Splitting 32*, 1975. 51
1.7 Gordon Matta-Clark, *Untitled*, 1974. 53
1.8 Paulette Phillips, *The Floating House*, 2002. 55
1.9 Gordon Matta-Clark, letter to *"The Meeting,"* 1973. 57
1.10 Acconci Studio, *New World Trade Center*, 2002. 58
1.11 Martha Rosler, *Photo-Op*, 2004. 65
1.12 Martha Rosler, *The Gray Drape*, 2004. 67
2.1 Krzysztof Wodiczko, *Dis-Armor*, 1999–2001. 71
2.2 Santiago Sierra, *Covered Word*, 2003. 72
2.3 Krzysztof Wodiczko, *Ægis*, 1999–2000. 76
2.4 Krzysztof Wodiczko, *Tijuana Projection*, 2001. 83
2.5 Santiago Sierra, *3000 Holes*, 2002. 89
2.6 Santiago Sierra, *Lighted Building*, Mexico City, 2003. 91
2.7 Alfredo Jaar, *Lights in the City*, 1999. 92
2.8 Krzysztof Wodiczko, *Homeless Projection*, 2014. 93
2.9 Santiago Sierra, *Workers Who Cannot Be Paid …* 2000. 95

2.10 Santiago Sierra, *Submission*, 2007. 98
3.1 Doris Salcedo, *Untitled*, 2003. 107
3.2 Wafaa Bilal, detail from *And Counting …*, 2010. 112
3.3 Doris Salcedo, *Untitled*, 2008. 115
3.4 Doris Salcedo, *La Casa Viuda I*, 1992. 119
3.5 Wafaa Bilal, detail from *Domestic Tension*, 2007. 120
3.6 Doris Salcedo. *Tenebrae: Noviembre 7, 1985*. 1999–2000. 124
3.7 Doris Salcedo, *Noviembre 6 y 7*, 2002. 126
3.8 Doris Salcedo, *Neither*, 2004. 129
3.9 Emily Jacir, *Memorial to 418 Palestinian Villages*, 2001. 131
4.1 Alfredo Jaar, *One Million Finnish Passports*, 1995/2014. 144
4.2 Ursula Biemann, *Contained Mobility*, 2004. 146
4.3 Tony Labat, *Day Labor: Mapping the Outside*, 2006. 157
4.4 Tony Labat, *Day Labor: Mapping the Outside*, 2006. 158
4.5 Yto Barrada, *La Contrebandière (The Smuggler)*, 2005. 160
4.6 Yto Barrada, *Autocar – Tangier, Figure 1*, 2004. 165
4.7 Yto Barrada, *Autocar – Tangier, Figure 2*, 2004. 166
4.8 Yto Barrada, *Autocar – Tangier, Figure 3*, 2004. 167
4.9 Yto Barrada, *Autocar – Tangier, Figure 4*, 2004. 168
4.10 Ursula Biemann and Angela Sanders, *Europlex*, 2003. 169
4.11 Ursula Biemann and Angela Sanders, *Europlex*, 2003. 170
4.12 Ursula Biemann and Angela Sanders, *Europlex*, 2003. 171
4.13 Dean Ayres, *Dancing on the Edge*, 2007. 175

Acknowledgments

Several years in the making, this book is the product of more conversations, collaborations, and unexpected convergences than I could hope to fully acknowledge here. First, my thanks to the scholars who have motivated and mentored me through my academic career. I am extremely grateful to Christine Ross, whose support and wise counsel saw me through the early drafts of this text and whose own rigorous and thought-provoking scholarship has been nothing short of inspirational. Thanks also to the many friends, colleagues, readers, and interlocutors who contributed to this work in so many ways over the years, including Jenny Burman, Erin Campbell, Robyn Diner, Bridget Elliot, Jennifer Fisher, Sean Gauthier, Shelley Hornstein, Alice Jim, Hajime Nakatani, Carol Payne, Kirsty Robertson, Sharon Rosenberg, Imre Szeman, Tamar Tembeck, and three anonymous reviewers whose comments challenged me to produce an ever stronger manuscript. Others have engaged thoughtfully with various versions of the papers that would become chapters of this book, and I am especially grateful for the comments and input of audience members at several venues where I have presented portions of this work – including the Breaking + Entering: The House Split, Cut and Haunted symposium hosted by the Department of Visual Arts at Western University in London, Ontario (2011), the Universities Art Association of Canada annual conference (2007 and 2010), and the Visible Memories Conference in Syracuse, New York (2008).

This book would not have been possible without generous funding from the Social Sciences and Humanities Research Council of Canada and the Centre de recherche sur l'intermédialité (Montreal). I also thank the Centre for Canadian Architecture in Montreal, which provided both material and intellectual resources during a research residency in 2009, and the Department of Art at Cornell University for warmly welcoming me into their community, especially Renate Ferro, Patricia Phillips, and Jolene Rickard. For their support of this project, I am grateful to the University of Toronto Press, particularly my editor Siobhan McMenemy, whose thoughtfulness and rigour I have come to admire greatly, and Jasmin Habib, editor of the Cultural Spaces series, whose enthusiasm for this book has been invigorating. Thanks also to acquisitions editor Mark Thompson, managing editor Frances Mundy, marketing coordinator Luciano Nicassio, and copy-editor James Leahy for helping to bring this book to fruition. I also thank my invaluable research assistant, Marianne Fenton—truly one of the best. I am grateful to the artists, gallery directors, curators, and assistants who have made their artworks available to me for this publication – with special thanks to Ursula Biemann, Wafaa Bilal, Petrit Halilaj, Mona Hatoum, Alfredo Jaar, Tony Labat, Paulette Phillips, Martha Rosler, Doris Salcedo, and Krzysztof Wodiczko, who made the challenging but crucial process of acquiring reproduction rights a little more human(e). These are also some of the artists whose practices I've had the remarkable opportunity to think with and about during the writing of this book. Thank you for inspiring me every day to remember the unique power of art to respond to what Okwui Enwezor calls the "multiple mutinies" of the contemporary condition.

Finally, my deepest gratitude to my family. To Eldritch, for his unwavering commitment to intellectual enquiry and equally steadfast support of mine. To my mother Connie, who knows first-hand both the agonies and joys of exile and migration. Without her, this book would simply not exist. And to Penelope, who has been by my side since the inception of this book. May she never know trauma, may she always find her way home.

THE UNMAKING OF HOME IN CONTEMPORARY ART

Introduction: Unmaking Home

Picture two steel barricades, the kind you might expect to see blocking access to a street or public area during a political rally. The barricades are approximately twenty feet apart, and strung between them are two rows of twelve cords, one row at calf height and the other about four feet off the ground. The first impression might be of an enormous institutional cot whose frame and mattress have ominously disappeared, except that the cords are festooned like clotheslines with everyday household objects connoting a kind of itinerant domesticity (dish towels, a rug, a stuffed bunny, battered suitcases, a bedroll, an inflatable globe, a kitchen table set for one with camp dishes). The environment in its entirety also seems caught between the sedentary and the nomadic. The cords are attached to a motorized pulley system that slowly transports the objects from barricade to barricade and back again, and so, while the assembled objects appear permanently trapped in this manufactured cobweb of sorts, their constant state of flux renders them troublingly precarious. As the table, for instance, makes its way across the room, the cup and bowl atop it teeter unsteadily, seeming ready to topple at any moment. This juxtaposition also creates a disorienting experience for the viewer: the movement of the objects, so slow as to be almost imperceptible, creates the perception that the ground is moving under you. Alluding to both the grinding repetition and confinement of domesticity and the precariousness of the migrant condition, Mona Hatoum's 2005 installation *Mobile Home* evokes a complex set of tensions related to the possibility of making oneself at home in the world. This set of tensions, and the strategies that contemporary artists employ to address them, is the subject of this book.

In the early years of the twenty-first century, artists have turned increasingly to the trope of home as a fractured, fragile, or otherwise

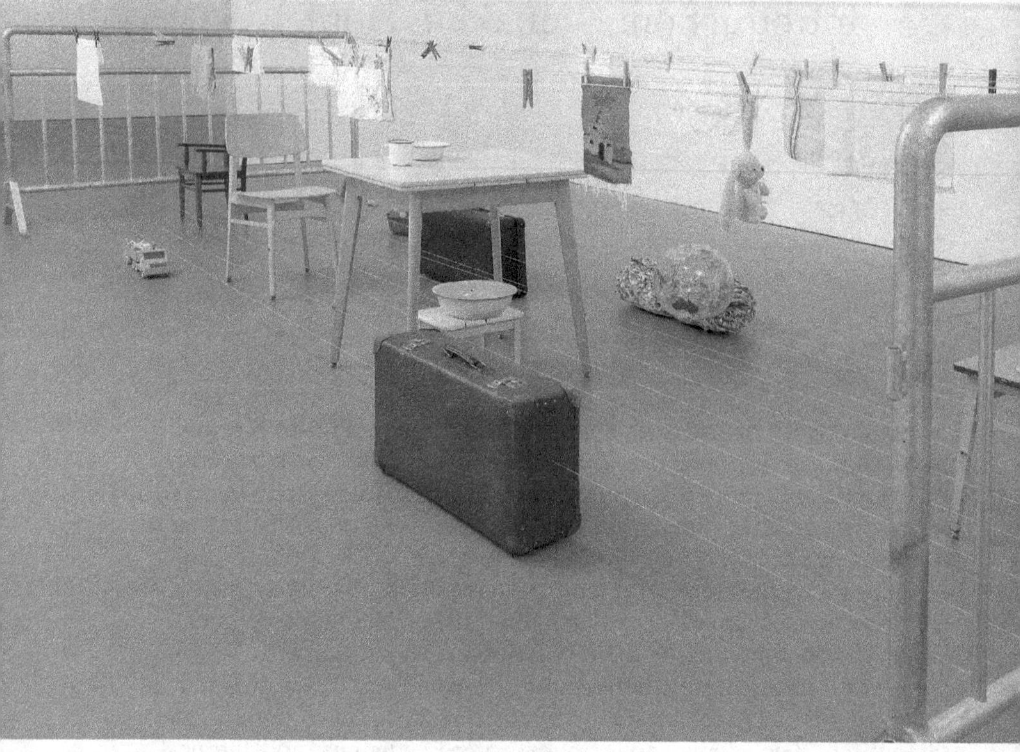

I.1 Mona Hatoum, *Mobile Home*, 2005. Furniture, household objects, suitcases, galvanized steel barriers, three electric motors and pulley system, 47 × 86½ × 254 in. (119 × 220 × 645 cm). Photo: Jason Mandella. © Mona Hatoum. Courtesy of Alexander and Bonin Gallery, New York.

unsettled space of impossible inhabitation. In their practices, home figures as a silent, incomplete, and unstable witness to loss – a "mansion of sorrow," to recall Mahmud Darwish's evocative phrase – that nevertheless conveys an insistent desire to shelter human memory, however imperfectly. This study argues that these artists – including Krzysztof Wodiczko, Santiago Sierra, Doris Salcedo, Alfredo Jaar, Paulette Phillips, Emily Jacir, Wafaa Bilal, Ursula Biemann, Yto Barrada, and Mona Hatoum – convey loss as an unhomely experience, wherein the often-elided links between what Homi Bhabha identifies as "the traumatic ambivalences of a personal, psychic history" and "the wider disjunctions of political existence"[1] are brought to life. This fragile figuration

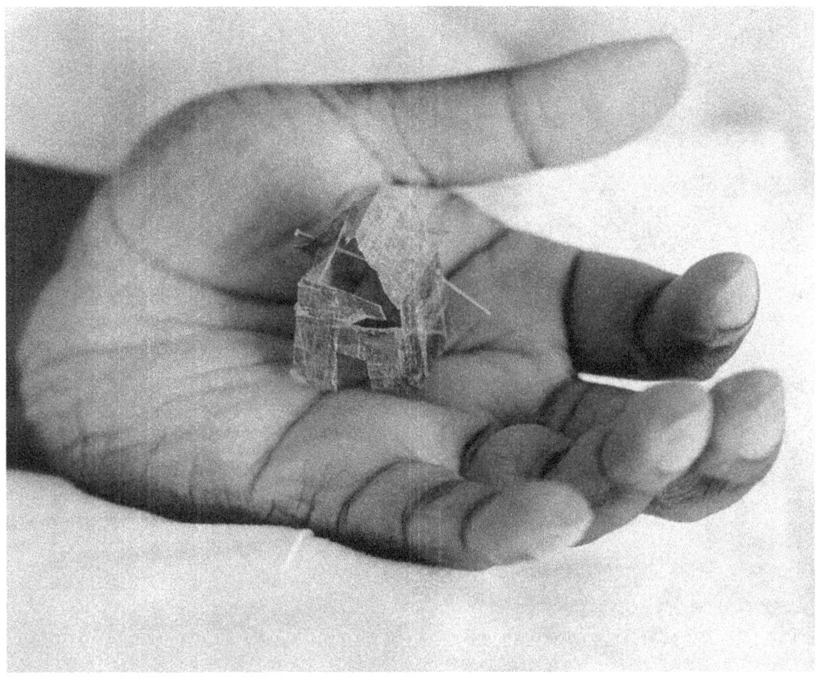

I.2 Donald Rodney, *In the House of My Father*, 1996–7. Colour photograph on paper mounted onto aluminium, 1,220 × 1,530 mm. Presented by the Patrons of New Art (Special Purchase Fund) 2001, © The Estate of Donald Rodney. Photography © Tate, London 2016.

of home in contemporary art, I propose, functions in two ways: first, to construct (literally or figuratively) a scaffold or structure around loss that both reflects and makes space for its palpable materiality (a materiality, I will argue, that is often occluded by the foregrounding of trauma's psychic dimensions); and second, to imagine this structure as a liminal space that articulates the fragility of self–other relations through the motif of home, a concept that has itself become as fragmented, disillusioned, and fragile as the concept of self in contemporary society. These art projects, which in a certain sense endeavour to give loss a home, transform this home into a potential site for intersubjective encounters based on shared acknowledgment of what Judith Butler calls the "universality of human precariousness."[2] In the process,

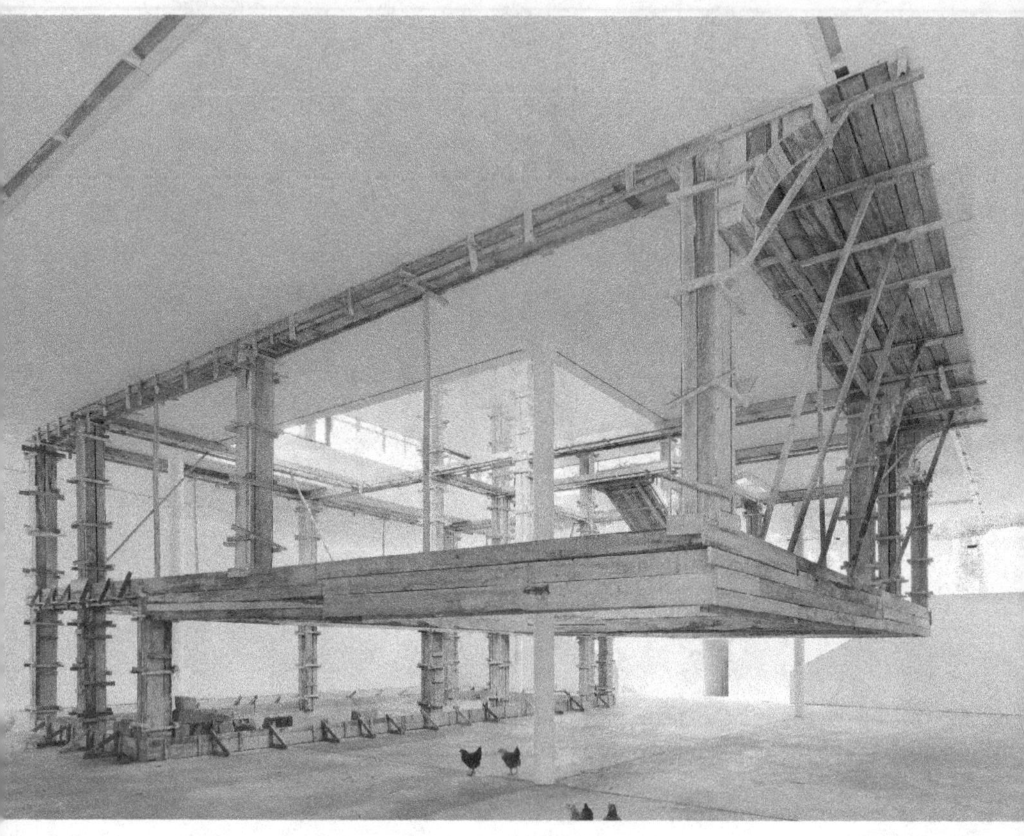

I.3 Petrit Halilaj: *The places I'm looking for, my dear, are utopian places, they are boring and I don't know how to make them real*, 2010. Installation view, 6th Berlin Biennale. Photo: Uwe Walter. Courtesy of the artist.

these artists enable critical insights into how we might bear witness to the suffering of others, and how contemporary art might be uniquely positioned to facilitate such an experience.

To properly frame my objectives, let us briefly consider a few more artworks, all of which point to contemporary art's engagement with home as a sort of tattered reliquary, carrying the precarious materiality of the past into the present. The first is Donald Rodney's *In the House of My Father* (1996), a close-up photograph of the artist's outstretched hand cradling a miniature makeshift house. Barely held together with pushpins, the walls of the tiny structure are sections of the artist's own skin that were removed during surgery to treat sickle-cell anemia (an inherited disease that would take Rodney's life the following year). The second is Petrit Halilaj's *The places I'm looking for, my dear, are utopian places, they are boring and I don't know how to make them real*, installed at the 6th Berlin Biennale in 2010. An oversized replica of the scaffolding of the artist's family home in Kosovo (built to replace a house destroyed during the Kosovo War), the installation's skeletal form suggests a vision of a stable future ("*the places I'm looking for*") that is clouded by difficult recollections of a precarious past ("*I don't know how to make them real*"). The third artwork is Akram Zaatari's 2005 *In This House*, a two-channel video installation documenting the artist's search for a letter that had been buried in a backyard in southern Lebanon by a soldier who occupied the home in 1978, during that country's protracted civil war. The letter's excavation, accompanied by interviews with prior and present occupants, reveals a tension between the desire to unearth the past and the equally strong impulse to bury its painful memories. Finally, and perhaps most saliently, is an earlier work, Rachel Whiteread's 1993 public installation *House*, which saw an entire terraced house in London's East End cast in concrete in situ. The resulting sculpture was an inverted and petrified domestic interior at once disturbingly sealed and unnervingly revealed. Offering prosaic traces of past occupancy, from wallpaper patterns to the imprints of worn doorknobs, *House* stood as a silent monument to the lives that define a sense of place and the places that mark their inevitable absence. In all of these works, home is figured as a fragile space whose anticipated capacity to shelter its human inhabitants is radically compromised. But the works also point to home's tenacious function as a site of belonging and a locus of memory. Whether it is evoked as a metaphor (in Rodney's work) for the body's own fragility, a re-enactment (in Halilaj's and Hatoum's installations) of the instability of our structures of inhabitation, or an archive of sorts (in Zaatari's and Whiteread's projects) in which memories of belonging and attachment exist as silent relics, home in contemporary art figures as a tangible site of memory whose fractured remains serve as melancholic traces of a lost but not forgotten past.

It has become a truism to observe that we live in an age of trauma. While the condition is conventionally linked to the seismic sociopolitical shifts (large-scale mechanized warfare, mass atrocity and annihilation, and alienating processes of urbanization, industrialization, and colonization) that characterize the modern age, it is undoubtedly the contemporary period that has embraced the culture

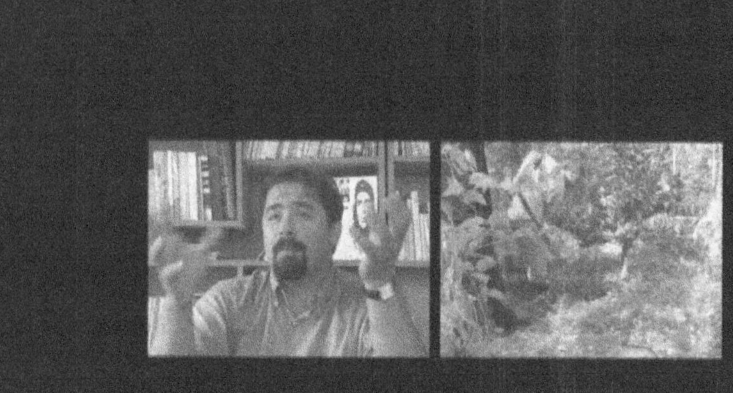

I.4 Akram Zaatari, *In This House*, 2005. Video, colour, sound, 30 minutes. Film still. Courtesy of the artist and Sfeir-Semler Gallery, Beirut/Hamburg.

of trauma as its own.[3] Indeed, the early twenty-first century seems to be "haunted by trauma"[4] – a spectre that appears ever more frequently in discourses surrounding everything from slavery and apartheid, to AIDS, to child abuse and family violence, to the September 2001 attacks in the US, and, more recently, the 2015 attacks in Paris. From a global perspective, however, any effort to understand how traumatic experience marks the present must also recognize ours as the age of mass migration – a period of unprecedented mobility, often involuntary and often involving oppressive and alienating experiences of exile, asylum, immigration, internal displacement, and statelessness. A snapshot view of United Nations statistics from 2013 – 51.2 million forcibly displaced persons, including 11.7 million refugees and 1.2 million asylum seekers, constituting a record level of displacement[5] – lends credence to political philosopher Giorgio Agamben's hypothesis that the refugee "is perhaps the only thinkable figure for the people of our time."[6] But while for Agamben, the refugee marks a radical crisis in the anachronistic concept of nation that will enable the advent of new forms of political community unmoored from the "originary fiction of [state] sovereignty,"[7] the lived realities of the refugee (and, to varying degrees, the immigrant, the exile, the asylum seeker, the stateless, and the urban homeless) also demand recognition of the daily struggles, humiliations, and sense of desperate alienation experienced by those whose lives have been upended by war, famine, ethnic cleansing, poverty and, increasingly, climate change.[8] Home, for the millions of displaced and disenfranchised citizens of the world, is inextricably linked to loss.

Nor is the West immune from the twenty-first century's increasingly unsettled relationship with home. The 2008 sub-prime mortgage crisis and ensuing global economic meltdown, coupled with already increasing levels of poverty and destitution, saw millions of American individuals and families lose their homes in subsequent years. Furthermore, at a collective level with global consequences, the attacks of 9/11 represented – as many have noted – a shattering of the North American illusion of safety and security. As I argue in chapter one, if the promise of home (or homeland) as a safe haven from the troubles of the world has always been a myth screening out more brutal realities both within the home and just beyond its borders, then that myth is simply no longer sustainable.[9] Furthermore, America's collective sense of homeland insecurity had international ramifications that only exacerbated the precarious state of contemporary global society following 9/11. Various levels of response to the attacks – the formation of a federal department of Homeland Security, heightened restrictions on entry into the country, and countless reports of hostility towards, even violence against, Muslim Americans – saw the US quickly transform into an "unhomely" place of fear, suspicion, xenophobia, and what Susan Buck-Morss rightly calls the "post-September 11 brave-new-world of surveillance,"[10] while the ensuing so-called war on terror led to massive refugee crises in both Afghanistan and Iraq.[11]

The question this book asks is: In what ways can contemporary art respond productively to "the aftermath of displacements, migrations, enslavements, diasporas, cultural hybridities and nostalgic yearnings" that art historian Irit Rogoff rightly identifies as the conditions of contemporary subjectivity?[12] Taking as a starting point Rogoff's assertion that art, which can no longer presume a transcendent position vis-à-vis the world, instead acts as an interlocutor that "chases [us] around and forces [us] to think things differently, at another register,"[13] this study proposes that contemporary art, which conveys home as a place of unmaking where longing is also a kind of belonging and absence also a kind of presence, offers new models of intersubjectivity that recognize the embedded vulnerabilities of memory, inhabitation, and indeed human existence. At the same time, this book intervenes in recent efforts to valorize home as a mobile concept and idealize precariousness as an aesthetic category of contingency and risk. Indeed, contemporary art has for several years been identified as a privileged site for explorations of home, with art exhibitions, symposia, and books of the past decade strongly indicating the art world's fascination with the increasingly charged and fluid concept of home in what we clumsily term the contemporary globalized world.[14] More often than not in these investigations, contemporary art is treated as a space for the expression of a new kind of globetrotting cosmopolitanism, wherein artists form part of an increasingly mobile international citizenry that must learn to be at home everywhere.[15] Nicolas Bourriaud's neologism for one such genre of practice is "radicant aesthetics," which he advocates as a strategy of "replacing the question of origin with that of destination. 'Where should we go?' That is the modern question par excellence."[16] Likewise, art historian Jennifer Johung proposes a paradigm for understanding "being in place" as an "ongoing process of replacing home."[17] For Johung, contemporary art practices that privilege a mobile concept of home (from Rafael Lozano-Hemmer's relational architecture to Lucy Orta's body architecture) allow us to "continuously move into and out of place; we can resituate and replace our experience of belonging at home in a variety of sites."[18]

To a certain extent, both Bourriaud and Johung propose useful, even necessary, tactics for coping with the multiple pressures of neoliberal globalization. As Bourriaud puts it:

> On the basis of a sociological and historical reality – the era of migratory flows, global nomadism, and the globalization of financial and commercial flows – a style of living and thinking is emerging that allows one to fully inhabit that reality instead of merely enduring it or resisting it by means of inertia. *So has global capitalism confiscated flows, speed, and nomadism? Let's be even more mobile than global capitalism ... So the global imagination is dominated by flexibility? Let's invent new meanings for flexibility.*[19]

There is certainly something alluring about Bourriaud's manifesto for cultural practices that will somehow beat global capitalism at its own game of flow, speed, and nomadic flexibility. But as cultural geographer

Doreen Massey already observed in 1994, mobility is allotted and enforced according to complex vectors of power relations – not all of which originate with capital: "Different social groups have distinct relationships to this anyway differentiated mobility: some people are more in charge of it than others; some initiate flows and movement, others don't; some are more on the receiving end of it than others; some are effectively imprisoned by it."[20] I will return to the notion of differentiated mobility in the fourth chapter, which takes up the theme of the artist as nomad in greater depth. For now, it will suffice to point out that this book stakes an entirely different claim vis-à-vis the concept of home, which begins with recognition of the contingencies of emplacement, but insists nevertheless on maintaining a productive relationship with a politics of location. The unhomely aesthetics of contemporary art imagine home as neither a stable site of belonging nor an anachronism to be abandoned to the logic of nomadic deterritorialization, but instead as a complex sign (symbolic, metonymic, and indexical) of the stark materiality of traumatic dispossession. But to better understand what is at stake in the theorization of unhomely aesthetics, it is necessary to lay out the book's three central themes, namely: melancholy as a source of political agency; witnessing as dispossession; and the unhomely as both contemporary condition and aesthetic strategy.

Melancholic Agency

In current investigations of the ethics and aesthetics of mediating difficult knowledge,[21] some key questions have emerged. First, to what extent does the contemporary fascination with commemoration compel us to "over-remember" some events at the expense of others, and how can cultural producers intervene in the concomitantly "differential allocation of grievability"[22] in memorial culture? Second, do current approaches to trauma and testimony, largely rooted in psychoanalytic theory, provide a valuable framework for "listening" to trauma's fundamental inarticulability,[23] or do they instead minimize the political dimensions of historical violence and urgent questions of human rights by privileging personal narratives of suffering and recovery?[24] And finally, in what ways might contemporary artists be uniquely positioned to activate and respond to these urgent questions? Wary of the widespread mobilization of psychoanalytic theory in the context of trauma representation, this book argues that recourse to this model tends to neglect the material dimensions of loss, proposing a cathartic resolution that is all too often premature. To be sure, psychoanalytic theory has proven itself a compelling model for understanding the challenges of bearing witness to massive loss, including, most recently, the acknowledgment by one of the founders of trauma theory, Cathy Caruth, that trauma is "inextricably bound up with collective forces of power and control," its symptoms thus reflections "of the larger forces of erasure and witness that operate within society as a whole."[25] Nevertheless, significant questions remain regarding the extent to which a set of discourses rooted in Western practices of personal therapy (even in response to traumatic experiences that are inextricably linked to broader social forces) can be solicited to produce an ethics of bearing collective witness to historical atrocity as well as continuing contexts of traumatic suffering in contemporary global society. These questions are central to the present study.[26]

Social justice is a key concern in the unmaking of home in contemporary art, and in that respect, these art practices also find resonance in historian David Johnson's analysis of post-apartheid South Africa's Land Restitution Commission (the so-called "Cinderella of commissions" to the much better known, better organized, and better funded Truth and Reconciliation Commission). Drawing on the Freudian distinction between mourning (the therapeutic working through of grief) and melancholy (a pathological attachment to the lost object, or mourning without end), and wondering whether a justice process premised on the assumptions and goals of testimony and conflict resolution can adequately accommodate claims of rights and reparation, Johnson asks a powerful (and provocative) question: "Is it possible to mourn something you want back?"[27] His answer – that in cases of social justice where material redress is sought, it might be more productive to maintain a melancholic attachment to what is lost – is also crucial to understanding the workings of contemporary art's unhomely aesthetics. Reconceptualizing melancholy as a critical tool for engaging with histories of trauma without forfeiting the right to seek justice for losses sustained, contemporary artists deploy the trope of home as a fragile shelter for memories of lost belonging, thus attending to loss in ways that solicit what Judith Butler refers to as "melancholic agency" – the constructive "persistence of a certain unavowability that haunts the present."[28] From Rachel Whiteread's mute concrete memorial to a rapidly disappearing urban environment to Akram Zaatari's excavation of buried narratives of war and occupation, home becomes what I will theorize, in the third chapter, as a melancholically materialized archive that bears witness to absence by tracing its remains. In this introductory context, I will simply sketch out the salient issues raised in the theorization of melancholy as a critical methodology for bearing witness to the suffering of others.

Recall that Sigmund Freud identified two ways in which subjects respond to the loss of a loved person, object, or ideal. "Mourning" describes the laborious but vital process of de-cathecting or withdrawing libidinal attachment to the lost loved one in order to make room for the formation of new attachments. A "melancholic" response to loss, or "mourning without end," denotes instead a condition in which "the free libido was not displaced on to another object" but rather "was withdrawn into the ego."[29] The result, Freud postulates, is a state of dejection wherein "the shadow of the object fell upon the ego, and the latter could henceforth be judged ... as if it were an object, the forsaken object."[30] The melancholic subject, in other words, is unable to fully detach from the lost object, instead floundering in a self-annihilating state of identification with it. Clearly, Freud's paradigm privileges the process of mourning over what he terms the pathological state of melancholia, but recent efforts to theorize a politics of mourning *rooted* in melancholic attachment to the past have seized on the idea that Freud's understanding of melancholia as a refusal to transcend loss enables it to be retooled as a "creative process."[31] Of course, the association of melancholy with creativity is hardly new. Since the Aristotelian *Problemata* asked why it was that "all those men who have become eminent in philosophy or politics or the arts are clearly melancholic,"[32] melancholia has been understood as a double-sided condition of pathological dysfunction on the one hand and creative genius on the other.[33] What *is* new, and profoundly relevant to the present study, is the mobilization (and depathologization) of Freudian melancholy as both a methodology for attending to the socio-political contexts of loss and a source of collective political agency. Indeed, what literary theorist Leigh Gilmore describes as a "will to melancholia" (which she explains as "an embrace and extension of melancholia in which melancholia becomes a technique for knowing the relation of the present to the past")[34] must be understood as a key catalyst for critical encounters with pain and loss; in turn, this book proposes, contemporary art must be understood to be equipped with a unique set of resources for galvanizing such encounters.

Take, for instance, Petrit Halilaj's *The places I'm looking for, my dear, are utopian places, they are boring and I don't know how to make them real.* Raised in a small rural town near Pristina, Halilaj himself experienced a life-altering displacement at the age of twelve; during the Kosovo War that saw his house levelled during a bombing campaign, he was separated from his parents and deported to a refugee camp in Albania until the conflict ended a year later. Like many of the artworks analysed in this book, *The places I'm looking for, my dear, are utopian places, they are boring and I don't know how to make them real* suggests a twofold effort to convey personal history while connecting it to the "wider disjunctions" of the geopolitical realm – a connection that, for Homi Bhabha, signals a distinctly unhomely experience.[35] And it is the melancholic attention to the traces marking what Bhabha identifies as the violent incursion of the world into the home that renders Halilaj's work exemplary of the unmaking of home in contemporary art. Located in a main hall of Berlin's Kunst-Werke, the installation literally overwhelms its environment, the network of wood beams and steel girders jutting up through the ceiling of a room that cannot accommodate this larger-than-life structure. But the structure, a so-called utopian place, is indeed (in keeping with the etymology of the word) a non-place – unreal, uninhabitable, and itself only provisionally capable of accommodating the future to which it seems to beckon. A literal reference to the scaffolding that was used to frame the Halilaj family's new concrete house following the war, the installation (like its title) speaks to the uncertainty of a future in which even a house built of concrete cannot guarantee its promise of stability. But *The places I'm looking for …* also gazes towards the past, its skeletal form inevitably alluding to the bombed house of Halilaj's childhood. To that extent, the work resonates strongly with Butler's notion of melancholic agency insofar as the "melancholically materialized"[36] past becomes a political presence in the animation of what remains of it. In this case, furthermore, the animation of the past is also quite literal. For what appears, at first, to be a hollow, uninhabitable shell of a home is in fact inhabited – by a brood of chickens busily foraging for food, building nests, and laying eggs. And it is perhaps these chickens that most plainly embody the key claim made in this study. As noisy, smelly, unruly reminders of a past left behind (themselves exiles in a strange world), the chickens can be understood to exemplify contemporary art's capacity to register the messy, corporeal materiality of loss.

Halilaj's work articulates an unhomely aesthetics insofar as home here is conveyed as a fragile site of longing, belonging, and memory. Indeed, inasmuch as the idea of home as a precarious shelter for human memory is crucial to this book, it is also a key feature of Halilaj's overall

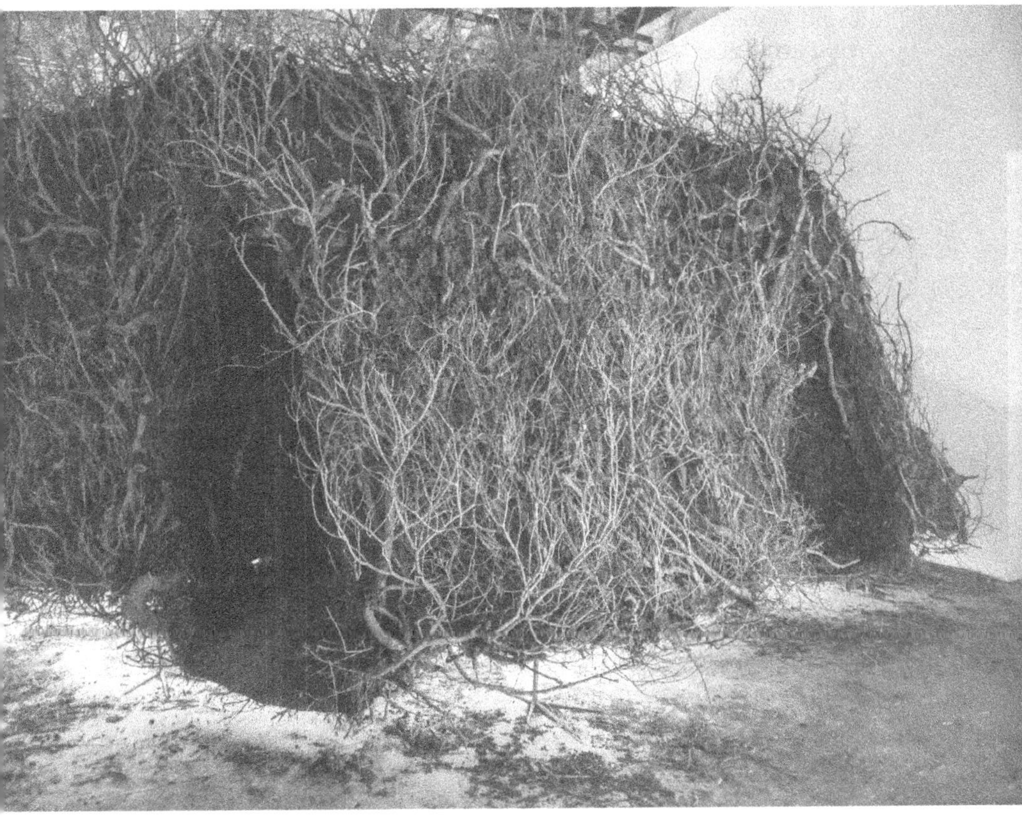

I.5 Petrit Halilaj: *I'm hungry to keep you close. I want to find the words to resist but in the end there is a locked sphere. The funny thing is that you're not here, nothing is,* 2013. Installation view, Pavilion of the Republic of Kosovo, 55th Venice Biennale. Photo: Atdhe Mulla. Courtesy of the artist.

oeuvre, including *I'm hungry to keep you close. I want to find the words to resist but in the end there is a locked sphere. The funny thing is that you're not here, nothing is,* his recent contribution as the first artist to represent Kosovo at the Venice Biennale in 2013. Here, the artist assembled personal objects and garments collected from friends and family members and installed them in a room-sized nest-like structure of twigs, branches, and soil – all, like the personal mementos, transported from Kosovo. The effect, as the pavilion's curator suggests, is of "a foreign body migrated from some subconscious and forgotten era or territory into a vicinity that is nothing less than a renowned icon of the historic western world's cultural and artistic achievements."[37] Then, like the Berlin installation, this structure is elevated (only slightly) on birdlike feet, again contributing to the ambiguity of Halilaj's gesture – as does the inclusion here of two live canaries. They animate the mementos with which they share the space, but also contribute to a sense of unease, perhaps owing to their implicit reference to the proverbial canaries in the coal mine. As capricious caretakers of memory in this large, cavernous, but nonetheless precarious place (nests being among the most ephemeral of shelters), the canaries read like an early warning system, alerting us to the embedded vulnerabilities of memory and inhabitation.

Thus foregrounding home as a fragile figure of longing, belonging, and memory, Halilaj's work emerges as a rich site of unhomely aesthetic, where traces of the past are materialized as melancholic reminders of the traumatizing consequences of dislocation. But how does melancholy become a conduit for ethical relations between the traumatized subject and the art audience? How do artists deploy representational strategies in such a way that the "will to melancholy" generates a field of commonality – the recognition, as Butler suggests, of the universality of human precariousness[38] – but acknowledges as well the differential distribution of precarity in human relations?

Witnessing (as) Dispossession

To bear witness, sociologists Roger Simon and Claudia Eppert suggest, is to bear an obligation to "translate stories of past injustices beyond their moment of telling by taking these stories to another time and space where they become available to be heard or seen."[39] One of the dangers, however, in the practice of witnessing is the assumption of a facile solidarity that solicits over-identification with the suffering other.[40] As Patricia Yaeger puts it, "How are we allowed to taste the deads' bodies, to put their lives in our mouths? How do we identify the proper tone, the proper images – for holding, for awakening, someone else's bodily remains?"[41] A major thematic question that emerges in this book therefore is the question of representation itself, as I observe in contemporary art practices a propensity to disavow the direct visualization of traumatic experience and instead proffer what Edouard Glissant terms the *opacity* of the other.[42] In particular, I am interested in the myriad ways in which the image of home is employed (for instance, in Donald Rodney's tiny skin house) as a metonymic stand-in for the suffering human body that defers the presumption of visual mastery over the body in pain while simultaneously evoking, as art historian Jill Bennett suggests, a "place transformed by pain." As spectators, Bennett observes, we are taken "into this place, not as witnesses shadowing the primary subjects of this pain, but in a manner that demonstrates, at the same time, the limited possibilities of either containing or translating pain."[43]

To better understand how contemporary art is equipped to take us into this "place transformed by pain," let us consider another work by Mona Hatoum, the 2008 installation *Interior Landscape*. In this small, sparsely furnished room (a steel bed without a mattress, a small table, and a coat rack) with a prison-like sense of comfort, the only elements that would indicate human occupancy are a map of Israel and Palestine cut up, formed into a makeshift purse and hung on the coat rack, and next to it a wire hanger also bent into the shape of the region. The installation's centrepiece, though, is a lone white pillow on the bed, onto which human hair has been laid out to trace, yet again, an outline of Palestine. Thus manifested in a melancholic, even obsessive, set of repetitions, Palestine in this installation emerges as a phantom state that exists only (at least in the experience of the artist) as a tattered set of relics; even this *lieu de memoire*[44] is uninhabitable and unhomely. Born in Beirut to a family of Palestinian exiles and later stranded in London during the Lebanese Civil War, Hatoum's own life has been marked by displacement, and much of her practice can be inferentially traced back to the plight of the Palestinian diaspora. But themes of exile and loss emerge in her practice less as autobiographical signposts than as perspectives from which to challenge the concept of home as a sanctuary from a troubled world. Home, in Hatoum's work, emerges as a place freighted with violent loss, fragile memory, and impossible return.

Like *Interior Landscape*, much of Hatoum's art production has sought to convey the unhomely nature of contemporary global society and its deeply unsettling consequences. It does so in ways that accord with Judith Butler's insightful observations around dispossession as both a condition of disenfranchisement *and* a basis for relationality – observations that merit rehearsing here. For the past decade, Butler has explored the degree to which one's own experience of loss can be a foundation from which to recognize and thus bear witness to the losses of others; her proposal for a radical reconsideration of vulnerability as proof of global interdependency and impetus for global solidarity is fundamental to the present study. Butler suggests that the "equivocation of

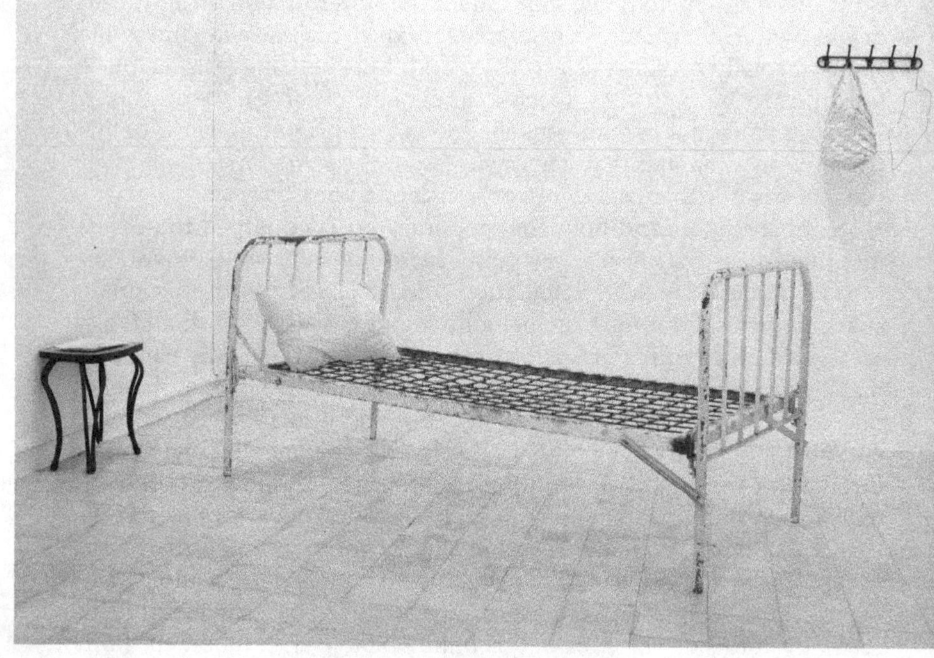

I.6 Mona Hatoum, *Interior Landscape*, 2008. Steel bed, pillow, human hair, table, cardboard tray, cut-up map, and wire hanger, dimensions variable. Photo: Fakhri N. al Alami, Darat al Funun. © Mona Hatoum. Courtesy of Alexander and Bonin Gallery, New York.

the human" – which was operationalized at the Nazi camps, and at military detention camps ever since – forces acknowledgment of the "geopolitical distribution of corporeal vulnerability," and thus a human rights discourse whose task is "to reconceive the human when it finds that its putative universality does not have universal reach."[45] This discourse, Butler argues, can be enabled by an attunement to the dual nature of dispossession – a term that necessarily refers to the loss of land, citizenship, shelter, protection, and/or rights, but which also, in its universal sense, marks our a priori interdependence:

> We are already outside of ourselves before any possibility of being dispossessed of our rights, land, and modes of belonging. In other words, we are interdependent beings whose pleasure and suffering depend from the

> start on a sustained social world ... Every life is in this sense outside itself from the start, and its 'dispossession' in the forcible or privative sense can only be understood against that background. *We can only be dispossessed because we are already dispossessed. Our interdependency establishes our vulnerability to social forms of deprivation.*[46]

According to Butler's conceptualization of relational dispossession, "we are dispossessed of ourselves by virtue of some kind of contact with another, by virtue of being moved and even surprised or disconcerted by that encounter with alterity." That this dispossession reveals a fundamental relationality – "we do not simply move ourselves, but are ourselves moved by what is outside us, by others, but also by whatever 'outside' resides in us"[47]– is crucial to the present study: it sustains the unhomely aesthetics of contemporary art as an ethical project. It also helps to clarify Mona Hatoum's critical intervention in works like *Interior Landscape* and *Mobile Home.* In both installations, we the audience are invited to occupy this precarious place, if only momentarily – to find ourselves in a state of dislocation that reveals both the universality of precarity and the inequality with which it is allocated in contemporary global society. In that moment of witness, ideally, we "move forward, awkwardly, with others, in a movement that demands both courage and critical practices, a form of relating to norms and to others that [opens us] to new modes of sociality and freedom."[48]

The multiple layers of witness that emerge in discourses of trauma and representation (the primary witness who experiences the event first-hand, the so-called secondary witness who is called on to record and convey that experience, the spectator who receives the mediated testimony and passes it on, etc.) – make it challenging to identify the witnessing agent in contemporary art's engagements with testimonial practice. As will become evident, the artists in this study take on the responsibility of witnessing with studied attention to the ethical and aesthetic implications of such a practice. However, while these practitioners certainly pursue what can be described as an art of witness, nevertheless they should not be understood to be using "witness" as an aesthetic strategy. Art, in other words, enables but does not itself bear witness; instead, certain aesthetic practices can be understood to *solicit* ethical modes of witnessing. In the art practices framed by this study, this interlocutory gesture is performed via the aesthetic strategy of the unhomely, whereby the material dimensions of dispossession are melancholically mobilized in order to unsettle conventional practices of witnessing. This brings us to the unmaking of home as both contemporary condition and aesthetic strategy.

The Unhomely

How is contemporary art uniquely positioned to convey trauma as an inhabited, political phenomenon, and in so doing to catalyze ethical practices of witnessing? This book proposes that to respond adequately to this question necessitates a shift from our understanding of *unheimlich* as uncanny to one which instead prioritizes the unhomely – a shift that I will briefly sketch in the context of these introductory remarks. An aesthetic sub-category of the Burkeian sublime related to a particular class of frightening encounters with supernatural beings, events, and forces (from doppelgängers to the undead), the uncanny was developed in psychoanalytic theory to identify a particular manifestation of the return of the repressed. In his 1919 essay "Das Unheimliche," Freud traces the etymology of the term to discover that *unheimlich* ("eerie, weird; arousing gruesome fear") exists not simply in opposition to *heimlich* ("intimate, friendlily comfortable; arousing a sense of agreeable restfulness and security as in one within the four walls of his house").[49] Instead, what gives it its terrifying power over the psyche is the fact that the *unheimlich* is actually a condition of the *heimlich,* insofar as *heimlich,* which denotes comfort, familiarity, and safe enclosure, always already contains within it connotations of withdrawal, concealment, secrecy, even danger. Thus *heimlich,* Freud concludes, "is a word the meaning of which develops in the direction of ambivalence, until it firmly coincides with its opposite, *unheimlich.*"[50] With this in mind, Freud comes to link the uncanny to his ongoing investigations of the repression of traumatic memories, and defines it as "something which is familiar and old-established in the mind and which has become alienated from it only through the process of repression." The *unheimlich,* Freud adds, is "what was once *heimisch,* familiar; the prefix '*un*' is the token of repression."[51]

Clearly, Freud's evocation of the uncanny as an aesthetic phenomenon that conveys home as a site of repressed trauma will have relevance to any study of art practices in which home is likewise figured as a place of trauma and estrangement. But an unhomely aesthetics of contemporary art would imagine home as a place haunted not by what has been hidden or repressed within its confines, but rather by unsettled memories of its own incapacity to shelter its occupants from the terrors of the world at large. I am therefore interested in a reading of the unhomely that levers it away from psychoanalytic thought and towards its application in and to an era increasingly characterized by war, exile, migration, and the socio-economic vagaries of global flow. Indeed, the unhomely is perhaps most usefully conceived as the underbelly of the uncanny: if the uncanny exposes the demons that haunt from within, therefore facilitating reflection on the limits of home's status as both site and source of domestic bliss and safety, the unhomely instead invokes the constant threat of external intrusion. The unhomely, to quote Homi K. Bhabha, represents that interstitial space in which "intimate recesses of the domestic space become sites for history's most intricate invasions."[52] A site of hybridity or inbetweenness that marks, especially for the diasporic subject, the displacement of the border between "home" and "world," the unhomely signals the moment at which "the private and the public become part of each other, forcing upon us a vision that is as divided as it is disorienting."[53]

This is not to suggest that the Freudian uncanny is entirely without geopolitical resonance. Certainly there is a spatiality implicit in the concept of the *unheimlich* (*heimlich* being etymologically linked to *Heimat* or homeland) that lends itself well to investigations of exile, foreignness, and xenophobia. For Julia Kristeva, the figure of the foreigner represents a "scar" between human and citizen – a scar that troubles the assumption of a unified national body, and thus demands a new model for self–other relations.[54] According to Kristeva, the Freudian uncanny provides exactly such a model (Freud himself observes that several European languages link the *unheimlich* directly to the idea of foreignness, but does not pursue this trajectory);[55] Freud "teaches us how to detect foreignness in ourselves," facilitating a way of being with others that does not depend on the integration or expulsion of the other, but instead "welcomes us to that uncanny strangeness, which is as much theirs as it is ours."[56] Kristeva's positioning of the Freudian uncanny as a way to rethink social relations from the perspective of a "paradoxical community"[57] of foreigners is richly apposite to the practices of several artists whose practices occupy this book, especially Krzysztof Wodiczko, whose own aesthetic strategies for unlocking recognition of the "stranger within" are addressed in the second chapter. But whereas the Freudian formulation maintains that the foreignness we perceive in our encounter with the uncanny is actually familiar but estranged or repressed, I am more interested in how the unhomely can be mobilized to understand encounters with those subjects who fall *outside* the purview of the homely – the stranger, the foreigner, the exile, the refugee and asylum seeker, the urban homeless. The unhomely in this way is less a psychological condition than a socio-political one (or, to be more precise, a psychological condition wrapped inside a socio-political one), in which the strange(r) is brought into proximity with the self. It is, to quote Homi Bhabha, "the shock of recognition of the world-in-the-home, the home-in-the-world."[58] For Bhabha, whose own theorizations of "the world and the home" simultaneously draw on and challenge both the Freudian uncanny and Kristeva's application of it,[59] the unhomely represents both a time and a space out of bounds, existing in an interstitial realm at the self's boundaries and the nation's borders. As such, it manifests as both a geopolitical condition and an opportunity to intervene in that condition. For in the space of the unhomely, as Bhabha suggests, the boundaries that define and limit stranger relations "may imperceptibly turn into a contentious *internal* liminality that provides a place from which to speak both of, and as, the minority, the exilic, the marginal and emergent."[60]

I will conclude this section with a brief return to Rachel Whiteread's *House*, which marks for me a pivotal moment in the paradigmatic shift from the Freudian uncanny to the unhomely aesthetics of contemporary art. Anthony Vidler has observed that the installation became the object of much anxious criticism that derided her "mutilation" of a home. *House*, Vidler suggests, appeared to evoke the horrors and anxieties of the uncanny, its entombed form seeming to suggest that it held "unaccounted secrets and horrors."[61] But, he continues – and this is key – *House* was less about the nightmare of *containment* than about the anxiety of *expulsion*; in turning the house inside out, the installation also turned the uncanny itself inside out. Vidler concludes: "Where even the illusion of return 'home' is refused, the uncanny itself is banished. No longer can the fundamental terrors of exclusion and banishment, of homelessness and alienation, be ameliorated by their aestheticization in horror stories and psychoanalytic family romances; with all doors to the unheimlich firmly closed, the domestic subject is finally out in the cold forever."[62] Like Whiteread's concrete cast, the art projects addressed in this book banish the uncanny, instead invoking home as a space of radical disjuncture where the private can no longer be presumed sheltered (or concealed) from the public. An unhomely aesthetics articulates home as neither a space of withdrawal from the Other nor a nomadic non-place where self collapses seamlessly *into* the Other, but instead as a dangerous, precarious, but nonetheless productive space of intersubjective relations.

The Parameters of the Study

The artworks in this book have all been produced in the past fifteen years, and indeed one of the study's central claims is that the early twenty-first century has witnessed a unique and global confluence of pressures circumscribing visual culture's capacity to respond to the challenges of geopolitical displacement. The book begins, however, with a short step back in time to trace a twentieth-century genealogy of Western art's troubled relationship to home, beginning with a critical look at the early avant-garde's rejection of the domestic realm in favour of an exalted state of existential exile. Identifying a paradigmatic shift in artists' attention to home during the late 1960s and early '70s, I focus on American artists Martha Rosler and Gordon Matta-Clark to establish the terms by which home is taken up as an unsettled space of social contest and repressed desire. Significant precedents for the unhomely aesthetics of contemporary art, Rosler and Matta-Clark's strategies of engagement with both the conceptual and lived realities of home show their work to have uncanny relevance to today's social and aesthetic contexts.

The second chapter examines the ways in which the unmaking of home in contemporary art conveys the unsettling impact of geopolitical dislocation, concentrating primarily on the practices of Krzysztof Wodiczko and Santiago Sierra. Both artists treat the themes of social alienation and geographical displacement through an uncanny aesthetic lens that reveals the condition of not-belonging to be deeply traumatizing, but rather than simply elucidating their commonalities, this chapter pivots on the salient differences between Wodiczko and Sierra's strategies of engagement. In works as diverse as *Ægis: Equipment for a City of Strangers* (1998), a wearable device that allows its user to address strangers via a prosthetic screen, and *Homeless Projection: Place des Arts* (2011), an audio video work that projected the stories of Montreal's homeless population onto a downtown building facade, Wodiczko draws explicitly on the psychoanalytic methodologies of Freud and Kristeva to make a case for art's capacity to facilitate testimonial acts that create opportunities for productive stranger relations. Compare this to Santiago Sierra's *Workers Who Cannot Be Paid, Remunerated to Remain inside Cardboard Boxes* (2000), for which Sierra hired undocumented Chechen asylum seekers in Berlin a minimal stipend to sit concealed inside boxes for four hours per day (the action was restaged in Busca, Italy, in 2010). Part of a series of actions that have seen the most precarious members of global society paid next to nothing to perform humiliating and/or degrading acts in gallery spaces, Sierra's work banishes the notion of art's therapeutic value, instead proposing that, at best, aesthetic practices have the capacity to draw dramatic attention to forces of marginalization and xenophobia by re-enacting them in settings where their traumatizing effects cannot be easily overlooked.

One of the chief claims made in this book is that the unmaking of home in contemporary art solicits reflection on the suffering of others, at the same time frustrating any inclination to over-identify with the suffering subject. The third chapter examines a range of artworks that treat empathy itself as an unsettling experience and the figure of home as a precarious, perhaps even impossible, archive of memory and belonging, and the archive itself as a fragile but fecund home for loss. Of special interest is Doris Salcedo's untitled 2003 public installation that saw hundreds of wooden chairs piled into an empty lot in a working-class neighbourhood of Istanbul, which, I suggest, demonstrates art's capacity to unsettle the assumption of collective access to the past while insisting nevertheless on bearing witness to suffering. In this and other works, Salcedo enacts a process of excavation and archivization that translates testimonies and experiences of trauma into haunting evocations of loss – spaces of contemplation and remembrance that, by failing to coalesce into sites of closure or redemption, disclose art's capacity to unsettle our collective access to the past while insisting nevertheless on ethical engagement with the suffering of others.

Chapter 4 expands the analysis of the unhomely as an aesthetic strategy in contemporary art to attend to the contemporary art world's own troubled relationship with both the conceptual and material realities of home. Since the mid-1990s, the embrace of so-called biennial culture has precipitated a series of questions connected to the ways in which international exhibitions interact with and intervene in global society's uneasy (and uneven) processes of neoliberal globalization. Addressing the biennialization of contemporary art in the context of geopolitical conditions of migration and exile, this chapter asks: Does biennial culture offer a utopian vision of transnational harmony, or does it simply epitomize the colonizing tendencies of global corporatism? If, I suggest, we can best understand large-scale international exhibitions as engaged in a kind of complicit critique whereby they participate in and profit from the "deterritorialization" of the global marketplace but are therefore also uniquely positioned to address its excesses, then how might we position those artists who challenge biennial culture's romanticization of itineracy and transnational mobility from within? These reluctant nomads, I suggest, subtly interrogate the assumptions of transnational mobility that attach to biennial culture, compelling us to consider the traumatizing realities of exile, emigration, and forced relocation that characterize the lives of those involuntary nomads whose travels are not similarly underwritten by a global art world. Thus figuring home as a charged space of unresolved trauma capable of fundamentally rethinking how we respond to the traumatic experiences of others, contemporary art enables an ethics of witness premised on recognizing both the universality of human precariousness and the limits of empathy.

1
An Unhomely Genealogy of Contemporary Art

The bomb which destroys my house also damages my body insofar as the house was already an indication of my body.

Jean-Paul Sartre, *Being and Nothingness*

Fifteen years ago, historian Kerwin Lee Klein issued a scathing report on what he termed the advent of the "memory industry" – the exponential growth of memory as a key vector of concern in the arts and humanities. And indeed, a collective turn to memory – variously referred to as an industry, a boom, an avalanche, and a crisis – undeniably began to materialize in both Western culture and critical discourse in the late 1990s.[1] As elaborated by Andreas Huyssen, this turn can be mapped along three trajectories: the rejection of modernity's blind trust in progress and development, the articulation of anxiety around the increasing flux of postmodern globalization, and an emphasis on minority rights and marginalized histories. Huyssen argues that the late modern memory boom – that is, everything from historical theme parks to Oprah-style confessional television – has reflected primarily a collective anxiety surrounding the disorienting postmodern condition of space-time compression, which generated an embrace of memory culture for both comfort and spatio-temporal anchoring.[2] At the same time, the ongoing memory boom has been complicated by a twentieth-century history of atrocities that "mars *a priori* any attempt to glorify the past,"[3] and thus the turn to memory has necessarily precipitated a crisis of memory. For Huyssen, the memory boom/crisis constitutes a double-edged sword. On one hand, contemporary memory discourses (particularly those that develop out of the language of trauma) tend to privilege personal narratives of pain and suffering in ways that risk obscuring both the political dimensions of historical violence and the socio-economic imperatives of reparation. Memory, Huyssen stresses, "can be no substitute for justice."[4] But the memory crisis has also revealed enabling dimensions, foremost among them the impossibility of treating the past – especially the recent past – nostalgically. We are required, instead, to write history "in a new key."[5] Huyssen concludes, "while the hypertrophy of memory can lead to self-indulgence, melancholy fixations, and a problematic privileging of the traumatic dimensions of life with no exit in sight, memory discourses are absolutely essential to imagine the future ... in a media and consumer society that increasingly voids temporality and collapses space."[6] Of course, any study that imagines home in its capacity as both metaphor and metonym for loss and the precariousness of belonging must guard cautiously against the "melancholy fixations" of nostalgia. Literally a longing to return home (from the Greek *nostos*, or return home, and *algia*, or longing), nostalgia, like melancholia, is an order of feeling that attaches itself to a lost object or ideal, specifically a home or homeland. An attachment, inevitably, to a fantasy (a fantasy rooted in personal memories, family lore, cultural narratives, and, frequently, political exigencies),[7] nostalgia often therefore accommodates, and is accommodated by, nationalist discourses that proffer a narrative of the "right of return" – a narrative which, as Irit Rogoff observes, is "problematic not only for the legitimation it provides for [contestable] territorial claims but also for the seamless naturalization of the concept of 'home' which it puts forth as a cultural metanarrative."[8] The challenge, according to Rogoff, is to eschew the naive assumption that there exists (somewhere) a "coherent site of absolute belonging" in favour of an approach to belonging and estrangement that recognizes the contingencies of emplacement.[9] In her study of the "unhomed geographies" of contemporary art and visual culture, Rogoff proposes a methodological approach to belonging and estrangement that recognizes the contingencies of emplacement but insists nevertheless on maintaining productive relationships with both the past and the politics of location, albeit relationships that are "permanently in flux."[10] Such an approach, she suggests, would "puzzle out the perils of the fantasms of belonging as well as the tragedies of not belonging."[11]

Advocating what he terms "critical cultural memory" practices (i.e., cultural practices that mobilize the productive potential of Western culture's memory crisis), Huyssen develops a correspondingly mobile approach to cultural memory. Huyssen points to a group of contemporary artists (among them Rachel Whiteread and Doris Salcedo) whose "memory sculptures" convey memory as a lived, corporeal experience that "activates body, space, and temporality, matter and imagination, presence and absence in a complex relationship with their beholder."[12] In these works, the past figures as a series of traces whose materiality constitutes the present as a palimpsest of experiences that resist consignment to the dustbins of history. Defying (or at least deferring) the politics of redemption, the spectacularization of memory, and the aestheticization of traumatic experience, memory sculptures instead operate as "inscriptions of time and displacements of space" that demand recognition of the "indissoluble relationship among space, memory, and bodily experience."[13] In significant ways, Huyssen's diagnosis of contemporary culture's "hypertrophy" of memory and his prescription for critical practices that challenge and complicate it reflect the socio-political issues and aesthetic concerns central to this book, which is likewise invested in contemporary art practices that unsettle conventional modes of witnessing those experiences to which most audiences have little to no access. But one claim in particular provides a useful frame for the present chapter. Introducing the emergence of memory sculpture in the international art world in the late 1990s, Huyssen suggests that artists who convey memory as a presentification of the past (as opposed to an ossification of the present or an idealization of the future) furthermore represent a challenge to the persistence of avant-gardism in the arts: "As opposed to much avant-garde practice in this century, then, this kind of work is not energized by the notion of forgetting. Its temporal sensibility is decidedly post-avant-garde. It fears not only the erasure of a specific (personal or political) past that may, of course, vary from artist to artist; it rather works against the erasure of pastness itself, which, in its projects, remains indissolubly linked to the materiality of things and bodies in time and space."[14]

Huyssen's emphasis on art practices that stave off the "erasure of pastness itself" is certainly pertinent to the artists and artworks associated with the unmaking of home in contemporary art, but it is also germane to the organizing principles of the present study. For at the same time as this book proposes that the post-9/11 cultural landscape in the West witnessed the emergence of a new aesthetic strategy that treats home as a haunted archive of longing and belonging, it also seems imperative to commit to a commensurately "post-avant-garde" analysis of such art practices in order to acknowledge and account for some of the historical and *art*-historical traces that haunt the works themselves. Thus, while this book proceeds with the conviction that the early twenty-first century has witnessed a significant shift in how and to what ends both the concept and material conditions of home are articulated in contemporary art, the artists who operate within the realm of unhomely aesthetics also practice within and contribute to – whether consciously or not – a lineage of twentieth-century art practices that represent home as a site of spatial, temporal, and/or affective disjuncture.

The lineage traced in this chapter begins in the early twentieth century, with modern art's renunciation of the domestic in its quixotic quest for a permanent state of existential exile (an elevation of the artist-as-wanderer that is echoed in the contemporary "biennialization" of contemporary art – a theme to which we will return in the final chapter). In the late 1960s and '70s, however, an interrelated set of conditions – the challenge to modernist (Greenbergian) orthodoxies of the artist as outsider, the rise of second-wave feminism, the ongoing suburbanization and consumerization of postwar families, the degradation (and then rapid gentrification) of urban centres (which generated, and then exacerbated, an epidemic of homelessness), and the American aggression in Vietnam – provoked among artists an unprecedented interest in exploring the intricacies of house, home, and domesticity. Two figures in particular, Martha Rosler and Gordon Matta-Clark, would come to exemplify this set of concerns. Both New York–based artists who achieved moderate success in the 1970s but whose works of that period have since become iconic, the two would otherwise appear to have little in common: Rosler was, and continues to be, a pioneering feminist photographer and video artist whose marriage of Dada-inspired agitprop and postmodern photo-conceptualism spoke directly and unflinchingly to the gender and class politics of the day. Matta-Clark, a member of contemporary art royalty (his father was Chilean surrealist Roberto Matta and his godfather was purportedly Marcel Duchamp) who trained as an architect, was conceptually indebted to land artists like Robert Smithson and Dennis Oppenheim; his investigations of site and non-site in the context of urban decay combined a sharp contempt for architectural convention with a playful sense of the radical possibilities of space and light. But as will become clear, in projects like Rosler's *House Beautiful: Bringing the War Home* of 1967–72 (a photomontage series that inserted documentary photographs of the Vietnam War into the opulent spaces of the suburban American home) and Matta-Clark's *Splitting* of 1974 (which saw a suburban house literally bisected), the artists disclose a common interest in investigating the contested nature of home, with all the psychological and political weight implied by such a contestation. But before exploring the stakes of such investigations, let us look briefly at early modernism's disavowal of the domestic realm, which puts the radicality of Rosler's and Matta-Clark's interventions into starker relief.

"Modernist Homelessness" and the Postmodern Unhomely

While the concept of domesticity as a social space separated from the public realm emerged during the late Middle Ages, it was during the nineteenth century that the domestic sphere became a site of social contestation, inextricably (and tensely) bound to the interrelated contexts of free-market capitalism, technological advances, and post-Enlightenment ideas of the (gendered, racialized, and classed) subject.[15] Also at that time, the development of avant-gardism in the arts – from Baudelaire to Greenberg, and from the brothels of Degas and Picasso to architect Adolf Loos's "distinctly unhomely ... cold storage warehouse cube[s]"[16] – was conceived as an escape from the confines of home towards the "landscapes of the great city."[17] There exist, of course, significant exceptions to early modern art's complex estrangement from home. William Morris's arts and crafts movement, for instance, engaged primarily and unapologetically with the aesthetics of the home.[18] Contemporaneously, the French impressionist painters Mary Cassatt and Berthe Morisot, who were rarely afforded the freedom to explore and record the emerging urban landscapes in the manner of their male flâneur colleagues, instead painted the domestic sphere as a rich but deeply fraught – and often paradoxical – place of freedom (from the objectifying gaze of the same ubiquitous flâneur) and oppression (within the home's narrow confines).[19]

Notwithstanding these exceptions, the theme of domesticity in modern art and architecture tended, as art historian Christopher Reed observes, to be "perpetually invoked in order to be denied."[20] For the most part, when home does make an appearance it does so as the return of the repressed. It is therefore not surprising that it was the surrealist movement, whose collective challenge to the rationalism of modernism and the modern world took the form of an embrace of the uncanny, that made it a mandate to investigate the psychological complexities of home in the early twentieth century.[21] Indeed one of the primary aims of surrealism in the 1930s was to challenge the modernist paradigm represented by Loos's warehouse cubes and Le Corbusier's "machines for living in."[22] The surrealist house, as art historian Jane Alison describes it, is instead "a convulsive theatre of the domestic; both a real space and a metaphoric space, inhabited, if not by the people, then by their ghosts."[23] Thus several prominent surrealists – including Tristan Tzara, Salvador Dalí, Leonora Carrington, and Roberto Matta – explored the irrational potential of domestic spaces, with Matta in particular creating hypothetical spaces with walls "like wet sheets that deform and marry themselves to our psychological fears."[24] Tzara termed such spaces "intrauterine": in response to modernist architecture, which, "as hygienic and stripped of ornaments as it wants to appear, has no chance of living … because it is the complete negation of the image of the dwelling," intrauterine architecture would manifest as soft, tactile, primitive constructions symbolizing "prenatal comfort."[25] At the same time, female surrealist artists were producing paintings of women confined in dark, disorienting, and claustrophobic domestic spaces that also, however, suggested powerful processes of alchemical transformation and hybridity. In works as diverse as Claude Cahun's *Self-Portrait (in Cupboard)* of 1932, which finds the artist nestled tightly into a shelf in a wardrobe, Leonora Carrington's *The Inn of the Dark Horse* of 1936–7, also a self portrait of the artist in a dreamlike domestic setting, and Louise Bourgeois's *Femme maison* drawings of 1946–7, in which headless female bodies are fused awkwardly with architectural structures to become, quite literally, housewives, the domestic realm is revealed in all its social, psychological, and physical complexity. As Katherine Conley puts it, "Representations of women in houses, women as houses, allowed [surrealist] women artists to question a woman's relation to a house as a safe haven and the inevitability of a woman's confinement to it."[26]

But while surrealists were exploring these multiple dimensions of the domestic realm, the prevailing tendency among Western artists in the first half of the twentieth century was to reject home in favour of what might be generously described as a kind of conceptual nomadism. In fact, the severed relationship between modernism and domesticity is reflected in Rosalind Krauss's vision of the twentieth-century avant-garde, which gives both conceptual and (to a lesser extent) geopolitical context to modernism's renunciation of home. In her 1979 essay "Sculpture in the Expanded Field," Krauss coins the phrase "modernist homelessness" to explain sculptural practices that exhibit formal markers of their "essentially nomadic" nature – in other words, their unmooring from any sense of historical, geographic, or cultural specificity.[27] Exemplary in this respect is the work of Constantin Brancusi, whose fetishization of the pedastal (insofar as the sculpture either becomes the base or enters into a symbiotic relationship with it) functioned as a "marker of the work's homelessness integrated into the very fiber of the sculpture," and whose fragmentation of body parts also signals "a loss of site, in this case the site of the rest of the body, the skeletal support that would give to one of the bronze or marble heads a home."[28]

What Krauss acknowledges only implicitly is the extent to which the "modernist homelessness" at play in sculpture's expanding field coincided not only with an avant-garde aesthetic sensibility of exile, but also with a period of mass displacement (both forced and self-imposed) between and during the world wars. This geopolitical condition (which saw a great number of Europe's leading artists transplanted to North America) underscored Martin Heidegger's well-known aphorism that homelessness was "coming to be the destiny of the world."[29] A salient example of this congruence is Marcel Duchamp's *La bôite-en-valise* of 1935–40, a series of suitcases outfitted with reproductions of the artist's own ready-mades that responded, as art historian T.J. Demos has suggested, to both the "uprooting tendencies of capitalism, artistic institutionalization, and photography" and "the transitory existence of the subject in exile"[30] – specifically, Duchamp's own experience of dislocation during the Nazi occupation of Paris. Demos, however, carefully distinguishes between the "modernist homelessness" identified by Krauss and its geopolitical cousin, acknowledging that a vast gulf separates Duchamp's playful suitcases (and equally playful wartime escapades across Nazi checkpoints) from, say, the suitcase of Walter Benjamin, one of a few items in his possession when he took his life after a botched attempt to flee Nazi-occupied France in 1940. And yet, as Demos argues persuasively, it is nevertheless productive to read Duchamp's aesthetics of exile in the context of an "ethics of exile"[31] that emerged during and after the war, fuelled first by the lived condition of displacement faced by many artists, and second by a disavowal of fascism's mobilization of "home" (*Heimat*)[32] to rouse nationalist sentiment, both underwritten by Theodor Adorno's maxim that it is "immoral to feel at home in one's own home."[33]

It was not until the 1960s and '70s that artists en masse began to turn their attention away from the aesthetics of exile and toward the domestic realm. Indeed, it can and has been argued that only during this period did Western artists – particularly American artists – begin to seriously consider home and the domestic realm as worthy subject matter. But even then this embrace, fuelled largely by a collective distaste for the modernist project, was troubled and equivocal. Conceptual artist Dan Graham's *Alteration to a Suburban House* (1978), for instance, was a proposal to replace the facade of a typical American home with a sheet of glass and bisect the open-concept interior with a ceiling-height two-way mirror that would reflect the increasing insularity and narcissism of middle-class families. Much of Vito Acconci's work, too (from *Seedbed* of 1972, a performance in which the artist masturbated under a raised platform in the gallery, quite literally exposing the seedy underbelly of the private sphere as a public spectacle, to *Bad Dream House* of 1984, an inhabitable but structurally disorienting and dysfunctional space) treats home as a metaphor for inner turmoil. But while Acconci revisits the domestic realm only to disavow it (a phenomenon that has been attributed to his own "modernist ethos of the singular, heroic, transgressive male, whose independence drives him from home"),[34] it was the advent of second-wave feminism that most compellingly inspired artists to reconsider both the stakes and perils of domesticity, and to contest both the avant-garde negation of home and more nostalgic visions of the domestic sphere as a space of comfort and security.

Like the surrealists in the '20s and '30s, many feminist artists in the 1970s figured the domestic sphere as a deeply uncanny space imbued with political resonance, reflecting home as a site of patriarchal power, sexual repression, and socio-economic oppression. These concerns already occupied Louise Bourgeois's *Femme maison* drawings of 1946–7 and would continue to permeate her art practice well into the twenty-first century.[35] Bourgeois's understanding of home as a fractured and fracturing place of shelter and confinement also animates several feminist art projects of the 1970s, including *Womanhouse* (1972), a collaboration of the Feminist Art Program at the California Institute of the Arts headed by Miriam Schapiro and Judy Chicago. For the month-long project, inspired by Bourgeois's *femme-maisons*, American feminist Betty Friedan's pioneering examination of the imprisoning dimensions of postwar suburban femininity,[36] and an emerging desire to celebrate women's experiences while developing alternative venues for the creation and display of art by women (which was largely absent from the mainstream art world),[37] a group of twenty-three artists occupied an abandoned mansion in Los Angeles and transformed it into a series of feminist installation and performance spaces. In its entirety,

Womanhouse reflected women's deeply ambivalent relationship with the domestic sphere, acting as a metaphor for what Arlene Raven described as the "isolation and anger that many women felt in the single-nuclear-family dwelling in every suburb of America,"[38] but becoming, at the same time, what Faith Wilding called a "repository of the daydreams women have as they wash, bake, cook, sew, clean and iron their lives away."[39] Thus Sandra Ogel's *Linen Closet* installation saw a mannequin literally embedded into her domestic context (a clear reference to Cahun's 1936 photograph), Karen LeCocq and Nancy Youdelman's performance-installation *Leah's Room* featured a young woman monotonously applying, removing, and reapplying makeup seemingly ad infinitum, and Judy Chicago's *Menstruation Bathroom* presented an otherwise pristine bathroom rendered abject by a trashcan overflowing with tampons and pads soaked in blood-red paint, an uncanny evocation of "everything that ought to have remained … secret and hidden but has come to light."[40]

But without discounting the revolutionary effects of *Womanhouse* and other early feminist interventions into the socio-politics of domesticity in the 1970s, it bears remembering the unacknowledged assumptions underlying this critique (i.e., the conflation of white, heterosexual, upper-middle-class housewives with a universal notion of "Woman"), which would soon be sharply scrutinized by African American feminist thinkers, including bell hooks, who argues that for Black women, "homeplace," far from a site of oppression, was traditionally a subversive space of critical consciousness and resistance.[41] Class-based feminist analysis would further call into question the presumption of a stable (and presumably well-appointed) dwelling that underwrote some critiques of the postwar American home, with Martha Rosler, for one, focusing instead on the concurrent onslaught of housing crises in cities across North America, especially New York City – where a fiscal crisis combined with poor city management saw parts of the city transformed into landscapes of dilapidated and abandoned tenements, and where rates of homelessness and inadequate housing seemed to multiply exponentially overnight.[42] It was in this context, as we will also see, that Gordon Matta-Clark produced several acerbic critiques of the architectural establishment's failure to respond to the housing crisis unfolding literally under its feet; it was also in response to New York's increasingly dire housing situation that German conceptual artist Hans Haacke produced one of his most acclaimed institutional critiques: *Shapolsky et al. Manhattan Real Estate Holdings, a Real-Time Social System, as of May 1, 1971*. A series of 142 photographs of tenement

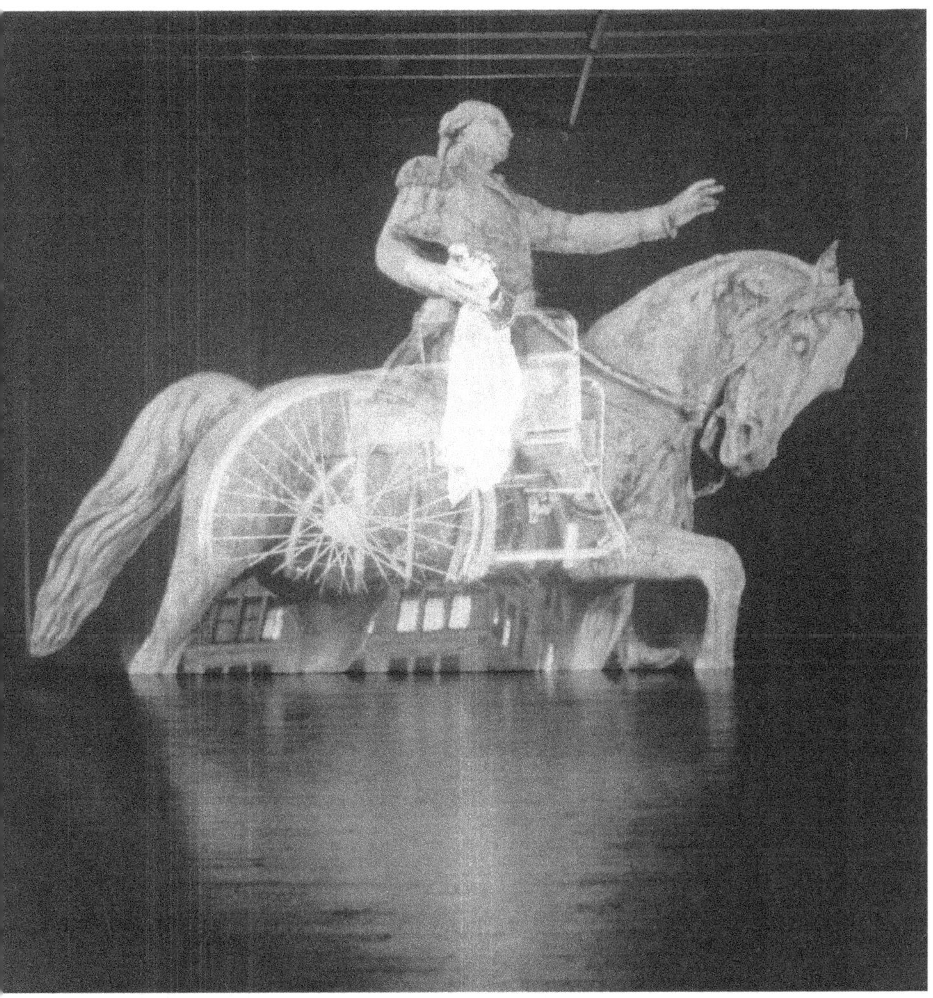

1.1 Krzysztof Wodiczko, *The Homeless Projection: A Proposal for Union Square*, 1986. Installation of four projected still images at the 49th Parallel, Center for Contemporary Art, New York. © Krzysztof Wodiczko. Courtesy of Galerie Lelong, New York.

buildings in Harlem and Lower East Side Manhattan accompanied by detailed documentation of their transaction histories, the installation unravelled a tangled narrative of one family's greed, wealth, fraudulence, and slum-dwelling mismanagement; at a more general level, it

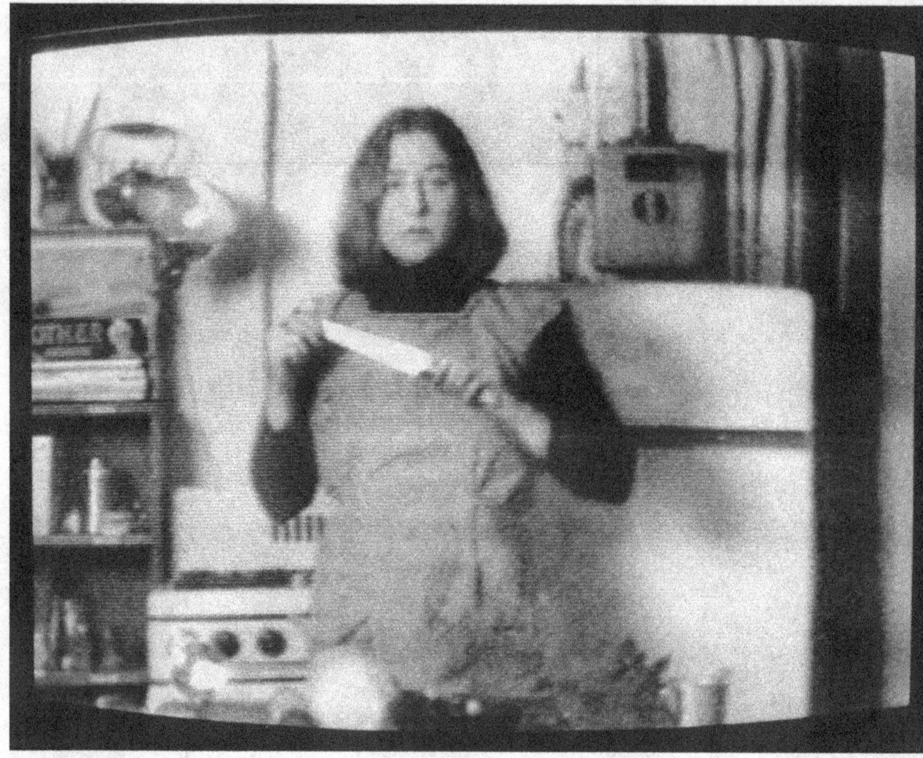

1.2 Martha Rosler, *Knife* from *Semiotics of the Kitchen*, black and white video, 1975. Courtesy of the artist.

furthermore sought to indict all upper-class Manhattan for turning a blind eye to the rapid deterioration of their city.[43]

The situation was only exacerbated in the 1980s, when regeneration and gentrification of America's urban cores combined with the regressive social and economic policies of the Reagan administration saw the housing situation in New York and other American cities reach a boiling point that was no longer possible to ignore – although near-Herculean efforts were made to do just that. As Rosalyn Deutsche puts it, "it had become clear to most observers that the visibility of masses of homeless people interferes with positive images of New York, constituting a crisis in the official representation of the city."[44] The "solution" was to make homelessness – or, more precisely, the homeless themselves – disappear by sweeping the poor and destitute off the streets and into underfunded shelters and marginalized neighbourhoods with inadequate infrastructure. And it was precisely the enforced invisibility of homelessness as a socio-economic issue that propelled artists like Rosler, Haacke, and Krzysztof Wodiczko to confront the crisis in ways that would "disrupt the coherent urban image that today is constructed only by neutralizing homelessness."[45] Thus, in 1988–9 Wodiczko produced the *Homeless Vehicle*, designed in collaboration with homeless men in New York City as a mobile shelter with compact compartments for sleeping, washing, and storage. Intended, according to the artist, as a "speech-act machine," the *Homeless Vehicle* was meant neither to simply symbolize homelessness nor to propose practical solutions. Instead, like Wodiczko's *Homeless Projection Proposal* of 1986 (a rejected proposal to project still images of homeless men and women onto civic monuments in Union Square), and the more recent *Homeless Projection: Place des Arts* of 2014 (an audiovisual installation that projected the bodies and voices of members of Montreal's homeless population onto the facade of a downtown theatre), the vehicle operated as what Dick Hebdige calls a "Trojan Horse" in increasingly fortified urban spaces – an uncanny instrument that, by "making strange our habituated ways of seeing" (or failing to see) homeless people, registers not so much the return of the repressed but rather, as the following chapter will elaborate, the return of the dispossessed.[46]

Bringing War Home: Martha Rosler

New York–based artist Martha Rosler has, since the 1960s, employed a wide range of media to investigate the social, economic, and political complexities of home from a class-based feminist perspective. First, and in allegiance with her feminist contemporaries at *Womanhouse*, Rosler's practice in the 1970s often cast a sceptical gaze on nostalgic notions of home as a place of respite and retreat, instead revealing it as a discomforting space of drudgery and confinement. Perhaps most incisive in this respect is the 1975 artwork *Semiotics of the Kitchen*, in which the artist "performs" the postwar suburban American housewife as part-automaton, part-renegade. A ruthless parody of the popular "Suzy Homemaker" stereotype of the period, the six-minute video sees a deadpan Rosler standing at a kitchen counter, mechanically itemizing an alphabetically sorted array of everyday kitchen instruments but wielding them like weapons and then flinging them disdainfully down. Here, home is revealed as a tense battlefield in the spirited gender politics of the day, as the work productively unites Foucault's analysis of the body as "the inscribed surface of events (traced by language and

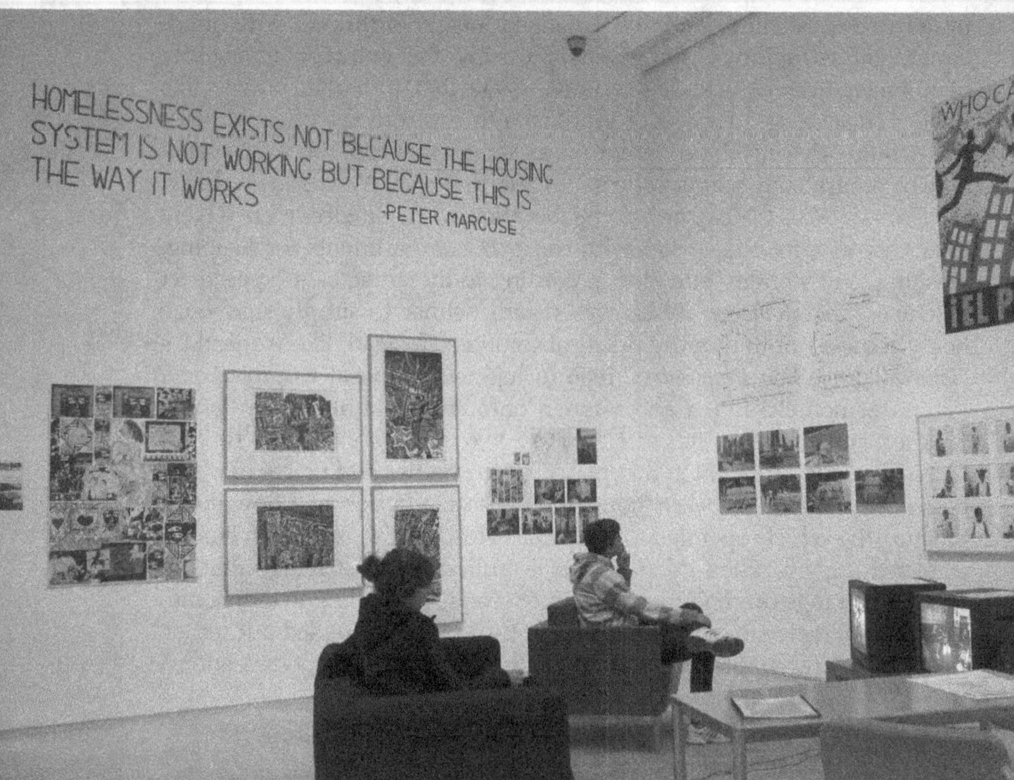

1.3 Martha Rosler, *Homeless: The Street and Other Venues*, Museo Nacional Centro de Arte Reina Sofia, Madrid, 2015 (partial reconstruction of *Homeless: The Street and Other Venues*, the second exhibition of the three-exhibition cycle *If You Lived Here …*, Dia Foundation, New York, 1989). Photo: Claudette Lauzon. Courtesy of the artist.

dissolved by ideas), the locus of a dissociated self (adopting the illusion of a substantial unity), and a volume in perpetual disintegration,"[47] with the feminist understanding of home as itself a contested locus of gendered subjectivity.

At the same time, Rosler's practice has agitated on behalf of the idea that housing is a human right, and this is in fact the title and message of a video billboard project in New York's Times Square that coincided with Rosler's 1989 exhibition *If You Lived Here ….* That project, actually a series of three group exhibitions and four discussion forums over a period of six months, concerned the interconnections of suburbanization, gentrification, and homelessness, particularly in New York City.[48] Like Wodiczko, Rosler implicated practices of urban renewal in the rapidly worsening housing crisis: the exhibition's title was borrowed from a popular real estate advertising campaign that sought to lure wealthy suburbanites back into the gentrifying core with the enticing promise, "If you lived here, you'd be home now." Drawing out the implicit message behind the advertisement and urban renewal writ large, a wall in the first of three exhibition spaces was stenciled with then-Mayor Ed Koch's infamous declaration at the onset of his war against New York's poor: "If you can't afford to live here, move!" Thus did both Wodiczko and Rosler solicit attention to the elided connections between gentrification, free-market capitalism, and homelessness, wherein, as Hebdige explains, "the homeless are revealed to be less the victims of their own inadequacies than of ... speculative property development, the suspension of planning controls, redlining, blockbusting, gentrification, soaring rents, the casualization and deskilling of manual labor and the drastic reduction of welfare and public housing programs [that] actively conspire to *produce* homelessness."[49]

Above all, Martha Rosler has maintained throughout her career that home – in all its social, psychological, and material dimensions – is a complex site of contestation and negotiation requiring nuanced, multidimensional responses that acknowledge that the comforts of the few are almost inevitably a product of the deprivations of many. But if the apparent comforts of middle-class domesticity during the second half of the twentieth century both concealed and exacerbated severe housing crises across the Western world, they were also deeply implicated in the emergent military-industrial complex, and thus in the late 1960s, another war drew Rosler to what she terms "the riddle of segregated representations of clean spaces and dirty spaces of human habitation."[50]

From 1967 to 1972, the US conflict in Vietnam compelled Rosler to produce a series of twenty photo-collages entitled *House Beautiful: Bringing the War Home*. Intended to be handed out at demonstrations and inserted into anti-war pamphlets and broadsheets,[51] the photo-collages comprised photojournalistic images of the ongoing conflict in Vietnam inserted into advertising scenes of domestic luxury. Most of the photographs for the series were gathered from *Life*, a magazine that embodied the paradox of Cold War America – its pages filled on the one hand with celebratory images of the bourgeois trappings of suburban American family homes, and on the other with investigative reports of battles being fought well beyond the borders of this comfort zone.[52] In *Life* magazine, as Laura Cottingham remarks evocatively in the catalogue accompanying an exhibition of Rosler's series in 1991, "documentary accounts of blown bodies, dead babies, and anguished faces flow seamlessly into mattress ads and photo features of sophisticated kitchens, fastidiously fertilized lawns and art-hung living rooms."[53] In response, Rosler's aesthetic strategy was to reveal that these two seemingly irreconcilable pictures of America were actually negative imprints of each other. For Rosler, the photo-collages represented "a felt need to insist that the separation of the here and the elsewhere ... were not simply illusory but dangerous."[54] Thus a perfectly appointed modern kitchen is invaded by two soldiers on the prowl; a Vietnamese woman cradling a wounded child climbs the stairs of a spacious house in search of aid; and the picture windows of a luxury vacation home overlook a fiery battle scene.

A complex matrix of nationalistic priorities would come to link developments in American postwar domestic architecture with an ongoing culture of war. In her 2007 book *Domesticity at War*, architectural historian Beatriz Colomina reveals and examines these sometimes surprising links – from Buckminster Fuller's militarization of the house as a defensive shelter, to suburbia's transformation of the lawn into a "makeshift battlefield" against pest invasions.[55] From the 1950s on, Colomina observes, American-style domesticity was furthermore dispatched quite blatantly as a weapon of the Cold War, with "expertly designed images of domestic bliss ... launched throughout the entire world as part of a carefully orchestrated campaign."[56] This collective facade of peaceful domesticity was also, importantly, deployed as a shield: first to conceal (and protect American's peaceful image against) the disquieting Cold War escalation and then to blunt the corollary execution of war in Vietnam during the 1960s and '70s. As Colomina puts it, "cold-war anxieties about global threats were masked by endlessly multiplied images of the absolute control of domestic details and permanent smiles."[57] The uncanny after-image, however, is of an almost aggressively idyllic vision of domesticity that is deeply traumatized by a militarized culture into whose service it has been covertly enlisted.[58] In this context, *House Beautiful* is best understood as an exposé of that repressed relationship. Consider, for instance, perhaps the most recognizable image from the series, *Cleaning the Drapes*, in which an advertisement pictures a "typical" American housewife with perfectly coiffed hair and a calm, demure facial expression gracefully staging a demonstration of a vacuum cleaner on her damask curtains. Immediately

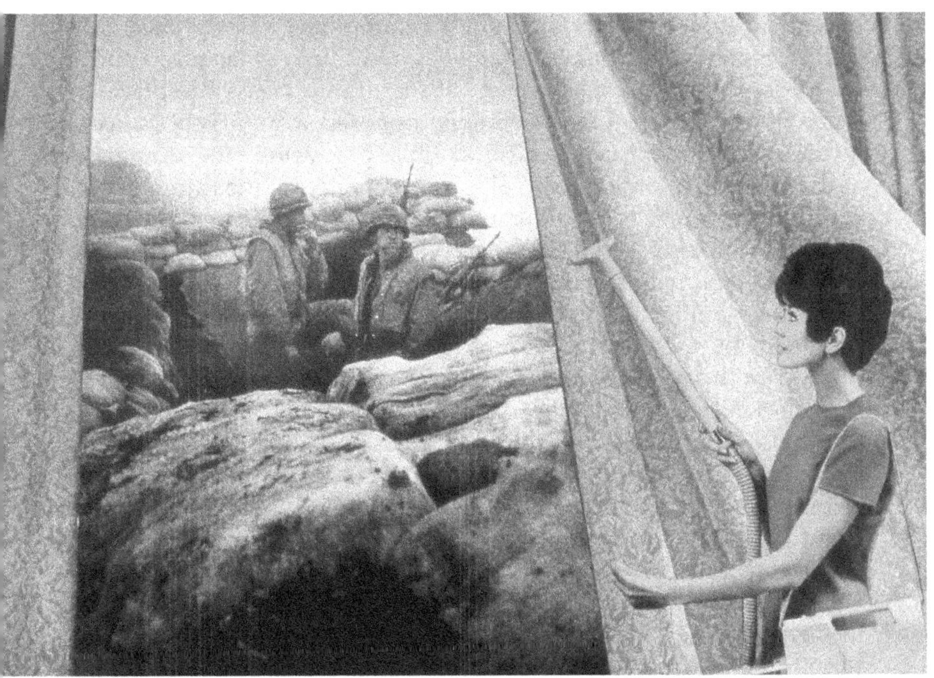

1.4 Martha Rosler, *Cleaning the Drapes*, from *House Beautiful: Bringing the War Home*, photomontage, ca 1967–72. Courtesy of the artist.

beyond the large picture window of her modern suburban home, we are abruptly transported to a rocky terrain in Vietnam, where American soldiers in combat gear appear to be waiting for orders. The woman seems blissfully oblivious to this scene as she concentrates her attention on the task at hand – her insular world is well fortified, and the battleground outside the window is as innocuously distant as if it were broadcasting from the television set. Instead, it is left to the viewer to mark the uncanny proximity of the two stages.

Rosler's technique is informed equally by the early twentieth-century political photomontages of Hannah Höch and John Heartfield and her own photo-conceptualist deconstructions of the medium's discursive functions, such as the photo-text installation *The Bowery in Two Inadequate Descriptive Systems* (1974–5), in which Rosler famously combined Walker Evans–style photographs of New York's infamous "skid row," void of human presence, with lists of synonyms for "drunk," in order to debunk documentary photography's assumption of unmediated objectivity.[59] Significantly, this technique is predicated, as Jacques Rancière has observed, on the deployment of the uncanny as a Brechtian aesthetic device to reveal two seemingly opposed worlds as both deeply imbricated and completely incompatible, producing "the strangeness of the familiar, in order to reveal a different order of measurement that is only uncovered by the violence of a conflict."[60] But while Rancière is correct to suggest that Rosler's collages produce a shock that triggers a transformative moment of political consciousness (what Brian Massumi would call a "shock to thought"),[61] this shock is not simply prompted by the juxtaposition of images. For the fact is that images of peaceful domesticity and protracted war (like those in *Cleaning the Drapes*), while seemingly incapable of coexistence, did indeed appear side by side in visual culture of the 1960s and '70s – on the pages of *Life*, and also on suburban America's increasingly ubiquitous television screens, where nightly broadcasts of death and mayhem in Vietnam led eventually to its common designation as the first "living-room war."[62] For to the limited extent that the Vietnam War was experienced in the US, it was largely mediated as a screened spectacle. In this way, it is useful to consider America's domestic experience of war (and Rosler's equally ubiquitous use of screens in her series) according to Freud's concept of "screen memories" – memories that facilitate the repression of trauma by displacing more painful recollections.[63] Marita Sturken has suggested that Freud's understanding of screen memory is particularly pertinent to the study of contemporary practices of cultural memory production, since "cultural memory is produced through representation – in contemporary culture, often through photographic images, cinema, and television."[64] As Sturken argues, these representations also act as screens, "actively blocking out other memories that are more difficult to represent."[65] And it is precisely in this manner that scenes of domestic order and bliss in the 1960s and '70s, which reflected the American family back to itself in idealized form (for instance, in a host of popular television programs from *Bewitched* to the *Dick Van Dyke Show*), screened those same families from the more disturbing scenes of chaos and brutality being simultaneously broadcast and repressed through their television screens.

With *House Beautiful*, Rosler's intervention was not simply to bring these incongruent but entangled elements together, for they already coexisted in the living rooms of America. Instead, her uncanny move was to render the very familiarity of their coexistence strange, by collapsing or distorting the screen that was their only separation; in Rosler's collages the American home becomes literally invaded by gruesome television scenes. But of course, the screen is not eliminated entirely. Instead, images of war are inserted into more threateningly intimate liminal spaces, such as doorways, staircases, and especially windows. By exposing the American home to the nightmare of war, Rosler also exposes the screen that would otherwise block this nightmare from the collective conscience. In other words, Rosler disturbs conventional understandings of home as a space of comfort and safety in order to mobilize the "return of the repressed," and in this way, her work resonates with (and, as we will see shortly, both predicts and nuances) the unmaking of home in twenty-first-century art. As will become apparent as this chapter, and this book, progresses, Rosler's aesthetic strategy of employing screens to collapse the presumed distance between "the here and the elsewhere" will reappear in contemporary art practices – from Krzysztof Wodiczko's *Ægis: Equipment for a City of Strangers* (1998), which employs video screens as prosthetic speech devices intended to facilitate stranger relations, to Wafaa Bilal's *Domestic Tension/Shoot an Iraqi* (2007), which uses the computer screen to create an interactive war-at-home/home-at-war environment. Here, as in Rosler's work, home figures as a fraught battleground, both materially and ideologically. But in contemporary art, this book argues, the point is no longer to reveal the horrors lurking behind the curtain of domesticity's myth of security and stability, for these curtains have long since become transparent – in America and, much more markedly, in the rest of the world. Instead, contemporary artists are borrowing the aesthetic strategies of Rosler (and, as we will see, Matta-Clark) in order to bear witness to what Judith Butler identifies as the differentially distributed allocation of precariousness and disposability in contemporary global society.[66] I will return to this shift shortly. First, let us turn to Gordon Matta-Clark and his own uncanny renderings of precariously occupied domestic space.

Declaring War on the Home: Gordon Matta-Clark

In 1972, the year Martha Rosler completed her *House Beautiful: Bringing the War Home* series, the US began its protracted withdrawal from Vietnam. That same year, a different sort of war was declared on modernism's project for domestic architecture. On 16 March 1972, the massive Pruitt-Igoe housing complex in St Louis, Missouri, designed by Minoru

Yamasaki (the architect of record for another ill-fated modernist icon, Manhattan's World Trade Center), was demolished in a well-publicized event that marked what has come to be known as the day modern architecture died.[67] A thirty-three-building complex built in 1956 according to the principles of Le Corbusier and the International Congress of Modern Architects (CIAM), Pruitt-Igoe was initially heralded as a breakthrough for urban renewal, and modern architecture's solution to America's low-rent housing shortage crisis. Its demolition only sixteen years later, occasioned by its rapid descent into a crime-ridden ghetto plagued by poor design, mismanagement, disrepair, and unsustainable vacancy rates, represented modern architecture's perceived failure to transform its utopian dream of domestic architecture as a "machine for living" into reality.[68] It also indicated that America's worsening housing situation was reaching an untenable level, and that the architectural profession had limited conceptual resources with which to tackle it.

It was with this housing crisis in mind that, also in 1972, New York–based artist Gordon Matta-Clark began cutting fragments out of the floors of abandoned tenement buildings in the Bronx. The series, entitled *Bronx Floors*, marked some of the artist's earliest interventions into architectural space – interventions that would include massive infrastructural piercings into a suburban home in New Jersey (*Splitting*, 1974), an abandoned pier in lower Manhattan (*Day's End*, 1975), and a pair of townhouses in Paris (*Conical Intersect*, 1975). But as much as the cuts in *Bronx Floors* constituted material incisions into New York City's crumbling domestic infrastructure, they also represented an intervention into both the failing state of urban renewal (as Matta-Clark suggested, "the availability of empty and neglected structures was a prime textual reminder of the ongoing fallacy of renewal through modernization")[69] and the current state of the discipline of architecture, which he believed was itself abandoning the poor in its profitable drive towards urban gentrification.[70] As Matta-Clark explained caustically in 1976, "I don't think most practitioners are solving anything except how to make a living."[71]

One of Matta-Clark's most emphatic responses to the perceived indifference of the architectural elite when confronted with a rapidly decaying urban core came in 1976, when he was invited to participate in the group exhibition *Idea as Model* at the Institute for Architecture and Urban Studies (IAUS) in New York, then a hotbed of current thinking on architectural issues. In an apparently last-minute alteration to his intended contribution, Matta-Clark shot out the windows in the exhibition hall with a pellet gun; in the empty window frames, he installed photographs of the facades of derelict Bronx apartment buildings, whose own broken windows resembled the aftermath of an earthquake or bombing. In this way, as Pamela M. Lee writes, Matta-Clark constructed a visceral link between "the abstract tendencies of modern architecture – the very notion of 'idea as model'" – and "the degeneracy these models wrought in the urban environment."[72] The circumstances surrounding the event (later titled *Window Blow-Out*) are vague, and no photographic documentation exists; what *is* documented is that hours before the exhibition opened, the installation had been dismantled and the windows replaced – a disappearing act that seemed to confirm Matta-Clark's suspicion of the architectural profession's wilful indifference towards, as he puts it, "those condemned to live in social housing projects designed by architects that never set foot in their neighbourhoods."[73]

Several of Matta-Clark's lesser-known projects – from *Garbage Wall* (1970), a shelter prototype built with tar, plaster, chicken wire, and rubbish, to *Open House* (1972), an impromptu dwelling constructed from a dumpster and salvaged doors – were designed, on the contrary, to explore the improvised practices of those city dwellers described by the artist as living "beyond, between and without walls, putting to waste the most presumptuous building plans."[74] In this way, it is not difficult to align his practice with those of Haacke, Wodiczko, Rosler, and other artists in the 1970s who were concerned with drawing attention to the rapidly widening gulf between the haves and have-nots in American cities. But while Haacke's *Shapolsky et al.* dug into city archives to uncover the economic engines of New York's uneven development, Rosler's *If You Lived Here* mobilized communities of art activism around issues of homelessness, and Wodiczko's *Homeless Vehicle*, finally, sought to give voice and space to the city's dispossessed, Matta-Clark's own strategy was to bring to light the conditions and effects of New York's housing crisis by etching them into the very material fabric of the city. In this process of rendering domestic spaces dangerously "unhomely," one can also identify a debt to the "uncanny" architectural musings of Roberto Matta, who likewise sought to transform homes into sites of strangely familiar disorientation. Anthony Vidler, for instance, identifies a direct lineage from Matta, whose uneasy spaces "held out the potential of an architecture that would lend a truly psychological depth to life," to Matta-Clark, who, according to Vidler, "accomplished his father's vision."[75] But to limit analysis of Matta-Clark's iconoclastic

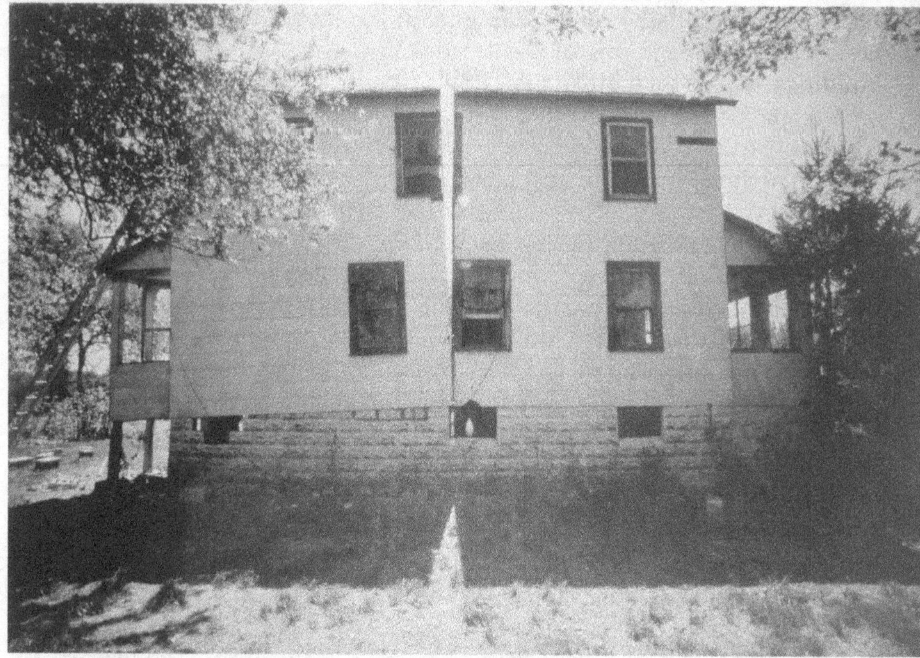

1.5 Gordon Matta-Clark, Documentation of *Splitting* (1974) in Englewood, New Jersey. Courtesy of The Estate of Gordon Matta-Clark and David Zwirner, New York/London.

prototypes and building cuts to questions of "psychological depth" is to neglect the decidedly "unhomely" aspects of his practice. In his pursuit of aesthetic strategies that would chronicle the conditions of alienation and dislocation that increasingly characterized urban living in the 1970s, Matta-Clark's interventions recall Homi Bhabha's formulation of the unhomely as that interstitial space in which "intimate recesses of the domestic space become sites for history's most intricate invasions."[76] And it is this commitment to registering history's "intricate invasions" into the domestic realm that mark Matta-Clark as a significant precedent to the unhomely aesthetics of contemporary art.

The unhomely nature of Matta-Clark's practice is especially evident in his most famous work, *Splitting* (1974), which saw an entire house bisected in Englewood, New Jersey. Already scheduled for demolition, the suburban two-storey house was split in half using chainsaws, and the foundation at one end was gradually chiselled away so that one half of the structure was tilted down and away from the other half. At a formal level, of course, the project illustrates a central tenet of the Freudian uncanny by literally bringing to light the *unheimlich* (repressed) dimensions of the *heimlich* (intimate, concealed) domestic sphere. (With the four corners of the roof removed, the vacated interior space was fully exposed to the exterior world.) And, to the extent that the work was intended as an intervention into the politics of suburban domesticity, *Splitting* illustrates the often elided political nature of Matta-Clark's cuts, thus aligning them not only with the practice of Martha Rosler, but also Dan Graham (and even *Womanhouse*, which likewise uncovered the hidden and repressed aspects of the typical suburban home). But before we consider the implications of an unhomely aesthetic at work in the Englewood cut, it bears noting that interpretations of Matta-Clark's work are surprisingly diverse, even contradictory, suggesting that any one reading will likely be inadequate; indeed Matta-Clark's own shifting perceptions of *Splitting* reveal these same contradictions. In a 1974 interview, he insisted that the work was "anything but illusionistic ... It's all about a direct physical activity, and not about making associations with anything outside it." In the same interview, Matta-Clark refers to *Splitting* as an "exhilarating" process of introducing "motion in a static structure."[77] A year later, the artist would radically revise this stance, arguing that he perceived buildings "neither as objects nor as an art material but as indications of cultural complexity and specific social conditions."[78] The following year, Matta-Clark further clarified that his cuts were a response to the ubiquity of "suburban and urban boxes as a context for insuring a passive, isolated consumer" and "a reaction to an ever less viable state of privacy, private property and isolation."[79] But notwithstanding the artist's own seeming ambiguity regarding the project, critical responses to his cuts do tend to emphasize their thrillingly dangerous nature, especially for the few friends and critics who had the opportunity to visit these sites before their inevitable (usually imminent) demolition. Describing the experience of crossing the widening crack as she made her way up the house's divided staircase, for instance, sculptor Alice Aycock recalls: "You really had to jump. You sensed the abyss in a kinesthetic and psychological way"[80] – a sensation that is elaborated by Thomas Crow in a description of *Splitting* that evokes an aesthetic of the sublime: "As the light stabbed into the previously cramped and dim interior, the visitor's vision ... arced upward toward the sky ... That passage of vision set the course for a disorienting physical journey with sufficient intimation of danger to wrench the experience out of art's normal realm of consoling spectacle."[81]

In her own analysis, Pamela Lee draws on these visceral experiences of Matta-Clark's cuts to explore what she terms a "phenomenology of the sublime" in works such as *Splitting*. For Lee, foregrounding the sublime as an aesthetic strategy is a useful way to avoid more nihilistic accounts that ascribe to Matta-Clark's practice a kind of decadent violence.[82] Instead, Lee suggests that Matta-Clark's actions, while "unquestionably aggressive," provoke a "destabilizing experience of place" that "throws into relief the perspectivism of the building as it sees, and is seen, by the viewer coursing throughout it; and that implicates the communicative and sensorial function of the body in that body's destabilization, vertigo, and even ascension."[83] Lee's analysis relies for the most part on site-specific reception of Matta-Clark's cuts from invited visitors to the sites who might be assumed predisposed to positive response, but she does acknowledge that reactions to his work could also be troubled, even hostile. Perhaps most vitriolic (and also perhaps most apocryphal) is the response of Peter Eisenman, then director of the IAUS, to Matta-Clark's *Window Blow-Out* at the Institute, which Eisenman apparently compared angrily to *Kristallnacht* (the "Night of the Broken Glass") – a 1938 pogrom that saw 30,000 Jewish-German residents deported to concentration camps, and thousands of synagogues, shops, and homes destroyed overnight.[84] Eisenman's response was not unique; instead, it was representative of a sense of anxiety and apprehension that often attended the artist's work. In 1975, for instance, a New York developer to whom Matta-Clark had appealed for a site seemed to equate the artist's practice with a misguided death drive, replying: "I believe in the great demise but I believe in life more and I resent the infringement of death processes prolonged as a devitalization of the living."[85] Matta-Clark also admits, in a 1978 interview, to receiving other angry letters, which ranged from claims that he was "violating the sanctity and dignity of abandoned buildings" to the accusation that he was engaging in a sort of architectural rape.[86] This last criticism is elaborated by critic Maud Lavin in a 1984 review of his work. Responding specifically to Matta-Clark's cuts into domestic spaces, Lavin suggests that they reveal a "modernist macho-individualism," charging specifically that "Matta-Clark's wounding of a house can be seen as a male violation of a domestic realm with female associations."[87]

The danger, though, of reading Matta-Clark's cuts as misogynist (even sexually violent) cleaves into the space of the home is that of unintentionally reinscribing a myth of the domestic sphere as one of (feminine) security and stability – a myth that had already been deconstructed in feminist projects such as *Womanhouse*. If anything, works like *Splitting* serve to unmask what Pamela Lee correctly identifies as "the deep-seated *insecurity* of [middle-class America's] most treasured icon, the suburban home."[88] Lee eventually concludes that *Splitting*, far from an act of destruction, might instead be understood as a "'liberating' gesture, a freeing up of the box-like form of a common frame house."[89] But while this analysis – to which I will return shortly – is persuasive, it also glosses over the cleave itself, which, whether malevolent or liberating, nihilistic or critical, is in any case a gesture that seems to enact or recall a trauma (remembering that a "trauma" is literally a wound to the body). The question then to be asked is whether it is possible (or useful) to read Matta-Clark's building cuts as traumatic re-enactments of the fragility of human inhabitation in modern society. Certain biographical details would seem to support such a reading: in 1973, the artist's only cousin was killed in a freak accident in midtown Manhattan when his apartment ceiling collapsed;[90] then, a few months before the *Window Blow-Out* performance-installation in 1976, Batan Matta (the artist's twin brother) fell or jumped to his death from Matta-Clark's studio window – an event that triggered Matta-Clark's 1977 work *Descending Steps for Batan* (a two-week performance during which he excavated a progressively deeper hole in the ground below the Yvon Lambert Gallery in Paris).[91] Thus, while it must be noted that Batan Matta's death occurred after many of the major building cuts were performed, it is nevertheless tempting to read the IAUS event, at least, as a visceral acting-out of Matta-Clark's grief.

Even without these details, though, Matta-Clark's disorienting interventions into domestic spaces (other examples include *A W-Hole House* of 1973, which saw a square section cut from the pyramidal roof of a building in Genoa, Italy, and *Bingo* of 1974, in which an exterior wall of a house in Niagara Falls, NY, was removed in nine pieces) imbue the uncanny with a criticality that, as Dan Graham has suggested, insistently exposes society's repressed remainders. Matta-Clark, argues Graham, takes on the task that Walter Benjamin assigns to the historian: to "reconstitute memory, not conventional memory as in the traditional monument, but that subversive memory which has been hidden by social and architectural façades and their false sense of 'wholeness.'" Graham's Benjaminian reading of Matta-Clark's cuts as negative monuments that "'open up' history and historical memory … to a critical view of present oppression"[92] usefully aligns Matta-Clark with the contemporary memory sculptures that, as Huyssen notes, likewise work "against the erasure of the past itself."[93]

Huyssen's framework can also be productively applied to one of Matta-Clark's most ambitious projects, *Conical Intersect* of 1975, a cone-shaped hole that bore through two condemned seventeenth-century row houses in Paris's rue Beaubourg to generate a street-level telescopic view of the Centre Georges Pompidou, then being constructed as part of a massive overhaul of the district.[94] *Conical Intersect* was intended from the start to function as a "non-monumental counterpart"[95] to the Pompidou, which was at the time a source of controversy within the complex debates surrounding the Beaubourg district's modernization (Jean Baudrillard, for instance, famously referred to the Pompidou Centre as a "huge black hole" that "openly declares that our age will no longer be one of duration, that our only temporal mode is that of accelerated cycle").[96] In the context of such heated debate regarding the disposability of the past in an age of acceleration, *Conical Intersect*, like the memory sculptures theorized by Huyssen, contemplates "memory at the edge of an abyss."[97] An intervention into two obsolete, even abject relics of an urban context that was being rapidly dismantled to make way for a modernizing Paris, Matta-Clark's massive hole brought to light these concealed (and soon to be destroyed) traces, revealing home's inherent uncanniness as a vehicle for simultaneously evoking human inhabitation, the precariousness of this inhabitation, and furthermore home's precarious role as a memorial to absent human presence. In this way, Matta-Clark's work reveals an analogously uncanny resonance with the unhomely aesthetics of art in the twenty-first century.

But if there is a Matta-Clark image that speaks most evocatively to the figure of home as a witness to precarity in contemporary art, it is a photo-collage that he produced in 1975 as a corollary to the Englewood project. In *Splitting 32* (1974), five photographs of the house's fractured interior are arranged so as to reconstitute the space into a dissected architectural Frankenstein of sorts. Here, the destroyed Englewood home rises from the grave, but it does so as a shattered memory whose reconstitution reveals the past as a series of irrecoverable traces or Benjaminian flashes, melancholic rem(a)inders of home's precarious status as shelter from the world and archive of erstwhile belonging. It is also here that affinities with Martha Rosler become pronounced. Both artists employ the formal properties of collage to "deconstruct"[98] the myths

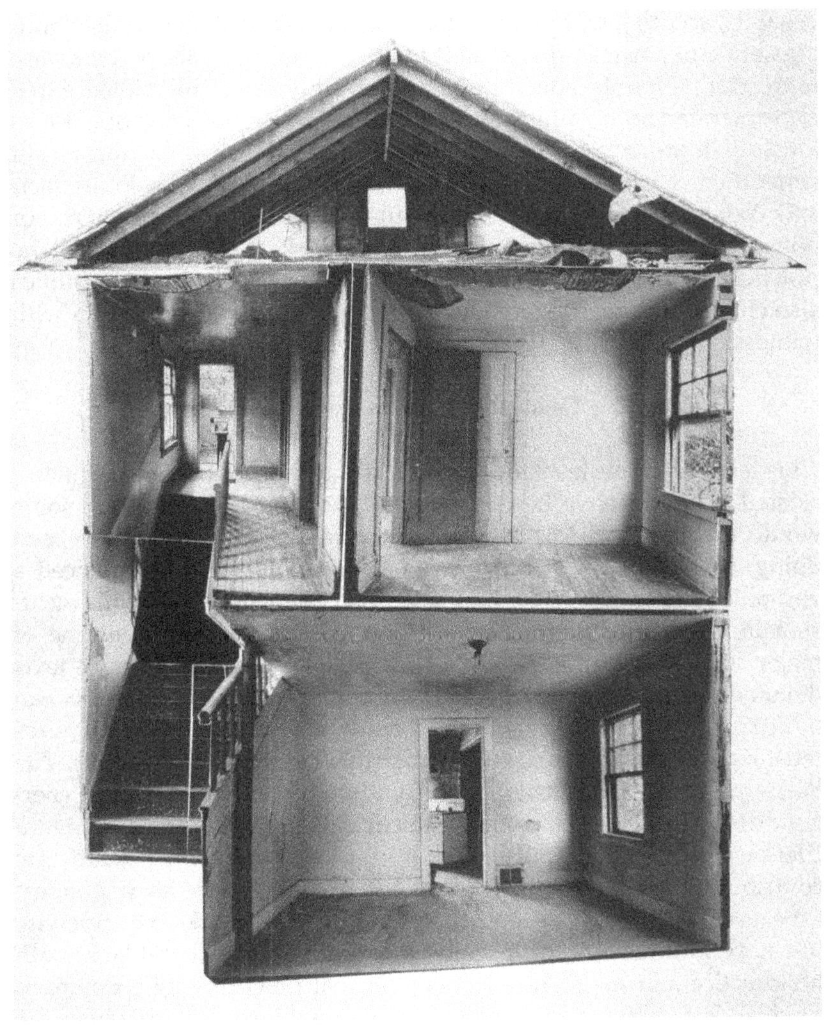

1.6 Gordon Matta-Clark, *Splitting 32*, 1975. Collaged gelatin silver prints, 32 × 22¾ in. (81.3 × 57.8 cm). Courtesy of The Estate of Gordon Matta-Clark and David Zwirner, New York/London.

of safety, security, and privacy that attach to conventional understandings of home, instead revealing it to be a wounded space of *unheimlich* repression whose facade of unity and stability masks the violence that is perpetrated both within suburban homes and in the name of Western ideals of domesticity. These concerns are also shared with a more recent generation of contemporary artists, from Doris Salcedo to Emily Jacir and Wafaa Bilal, to whom we will return in the following chapters. For now, let us turn to a few contemporary artworks that strongly recall the practices of Rosler and Matta-Clark, but whose divergent sensibilities also chart the changing territories of contemporary art's concern with witnessing precarity in global society.

Domestic Tension Revisited

"It is tempting," writes James Attlee, "to say that if Matta-Clark hadn't existed it would have been necessary to invent him – indeed, some would maintain that this is exactly what writers and critics have been doing, ever since his death."[99] In fact Matta-Clark has experienced a veritable renaissance in the past several years, witnessed by his inclusion in a string of international group exhibitions, the mounting of major solo shows, and the publication of several comprehensive texts devoted to his art and writing.[100] In part, this newfound popularity can be attributed to the cyclical nature of cultural nostalgia (as the '60s were fetishized in the 1990s, so too do the '70s fascinate the present). The Western world, in particular, seems enthralled with the scrappy, energetic do-it-yourself politics and aesthetics of the early 1970s, and Matta-Clark embodies that impulse, with the aura of a tragic early death only contributing to his allure.[101] The ongoing relevance of the socio-political aspects of his practice, the ephemeral nature of his works, a compelling life story, and his own propensity to be rather chameleon-like in both his practice and his own reflections on that practice – all conspire to render Matta-Clark a convenient cipher, a palimpsest onto whom the social, ideological, and aesthetic impulses of contemporary art can and have been projected. Indeed, so prevalent has his unique (but easily reproduced) aesthetic signature become that one might furthermore be tempted to say that the ghost of Matta-Clark has taken to haunting the houses of contemporary art. Take, for instance, *Odd Lots*, a 2005 project that saw artists propose works for the unusable gutter spaces of Manhattan property that Matta-Clark had purchased in 1973 as part of an unfinished performance-installation work called *Fake Estates*.[102]

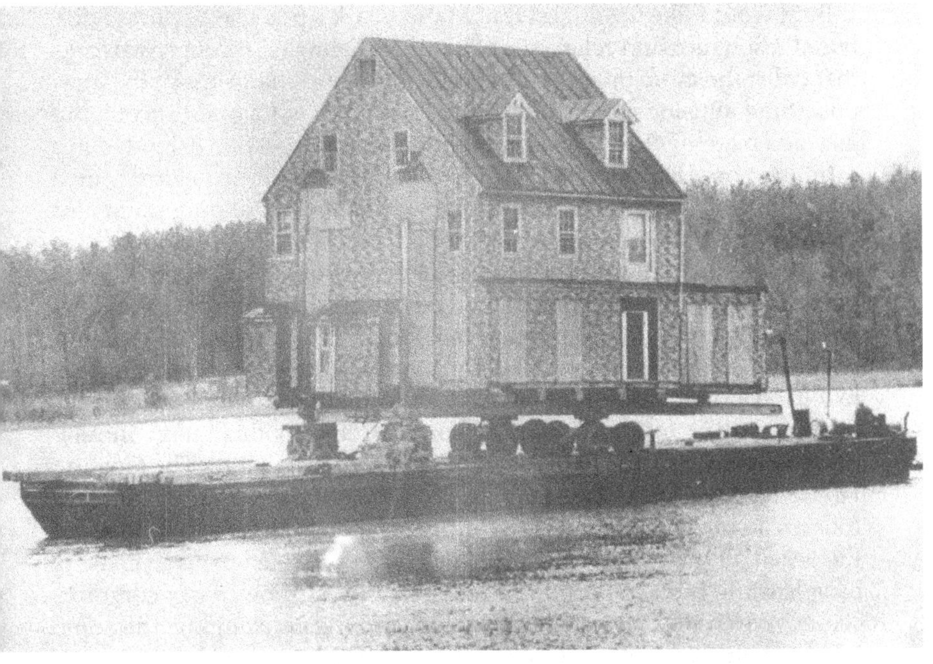

1.7 Gordon Matta-Clark, *Untitled (Anarchitecture – House on Barge)*, 1974. Gelatin silver print, 40.5 × 50.8 cm. Estate of Gordon Matta-Clark on deposit at the Canadian Centre for Architecture, Montreal. © Estate of Gordon Matta-Clark / Sodrac (2015).

Also exemplary is *Airs de Paris*, a group exhibition in 2007 that saw artists updating or "remixing" artworks from the past, with a special emphasis on Matta-Clark. The exhibition included Pierre Huyghe's *Light Conical Intersect* (1996), which projected Matta-Clark's video of the Beaubourg cut onto the building that now occupies that space; Carsten Höller's large hole cut through an interior wall of the exhibition space; and a video of Huyghe and Rirkrit Tiravanija's performance piece *In the Belly of Anarchitect* in which the artists build and eat a *Splitting*-inspired cake.[103] More oblique (and often likely unintentional) references to Matta-Clark have also proliferated, as in Urs Fischer's excavations of gallery spaces (such as *You* at the Gavin Brown Enterprise in 2007) and Richard Wilson's massive, rotating cutout section of a warehouse facade in Liverpool (*Turning the Place Over*, 2008–11).

But I would like to suggest that Matta-Clark's practice acquires additional resonance and relevance when it is channeled through artworks that enlist the more unhomely aspects of his work. Take one of the most unsettling allusions to his work, which invokes not a building cut, but instead an archival photograph collected by the artist and exhibited in a exhibition organized in 1974 by the Anarchitecture group (a term coined by Matta-Clark to refer to an alternative attitude to buildings, and also the name of a short-lived collective of artists who met periodically to explore these alternatives).[104] Part of a display of found and composed photographs depicting, for instance, a train crash, a collapsed building, and Manhattan's newly constructed World Trade Center, this found black-and-white photograph pictures a two-storey house floating serenely on a river barge. No contextual information is provided, save for the enigmatic caption, "Home Moving." Consider this image in relation to Canadian artist Paulette Phillips' video installation The Floating House (2002), a large-scale looping projection of a five-minute film that follows an uncannily similar two-storey clapboard house as it floats on the ocean off the coast of Nova Scotia.[105] Accompanied by five speakers broadcasting both the sounds of the sea and a dinner party complete with children playing, adults laughing, and dishes clanging, the scene becomes ominous as waves begin to pitch the house, which loses balance and descends into the sea. As it does, the volume increases, and the sound of waves crashing into the house overtakes the sounds of the party, which in the din and roar of the ocean come to resemble cries for help. Furniture begins to escape from the windows, and the last trace of the sinking house is an upended kitchen chair drifting in the rough waters.

The two images – Matta-Clark's and Phillips's – share, of course, an iconography that unmoors the home from its terrestrial foundations, setting it adrift at sea and therefore upsetting its putative role as a site of anchoring and stability. But the differences between the two images are equally, if not more, revealing and point to some of the significant concerns that I see circulating in art practices that trope the figure of home in order to convey experiences of loss and suffering. For whereas the Matta-Clark image is loaded with ambivalence (the still photograph might evoke a sense of terror, or instead one of freedom and new beginnings), the ambiguity in Phillips's film is predicated on the unlocalizability of an otherwise unmistakable terror. Indeed, the work is intended, according to the artist, to evoke several scenes of radical dispossession, including the continual displacement of Atlantic Canada's

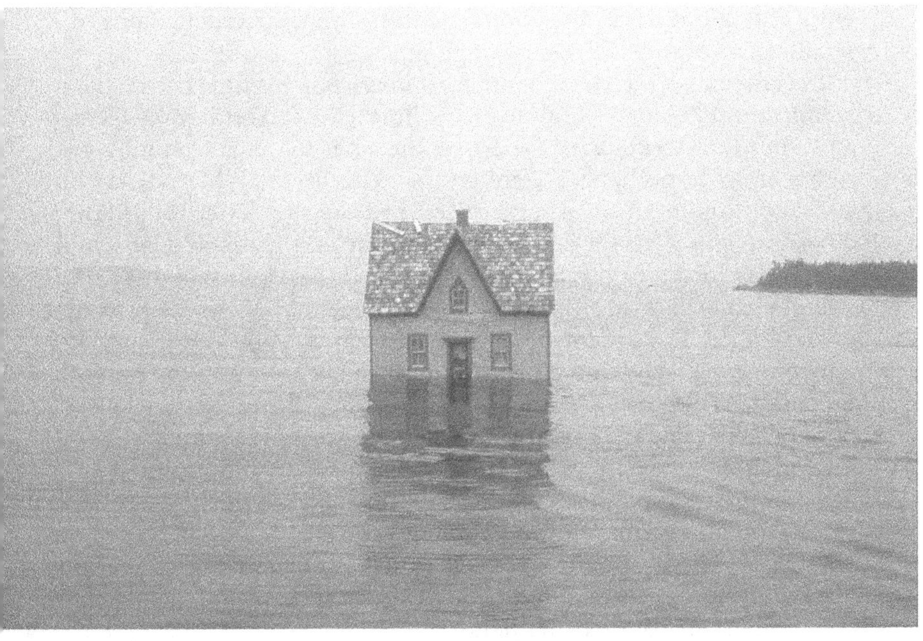

1.8 Paulette Phillips, *The Floating House*, 2002. 16 mm, colour, sound. Courtesy of the artist.

fishing communities in the 1950s and '60s (which often entailed moving entire villages on giant barges), the city-ordinanced destruction of Halifax's Africville community in the late 1960s, and the artist's own haunting memory of the death of a young woman whose naked body was found in a field in small-town Nova Scotia, also in the 1960s.[106] Phillips's *Floating House*, seemingly solid and impermeable but fragilized by myriad forces of destruction, performs its own vulnerability in an almost spectacular scene of elemental ferocity. At the same time, the floating/sinking house points also to the fragility of its erstwhile inhabitants. Phillips's work thus conveys one of the central claims of this book: that the early twenty-first century, which has witnessed what can only be described as a global pandemic of precarity precipitated by war (in Afghanistan and Iraq especially), civil war (in Sudan, Colombia, and more recently Syria), ongoing territorial disputes (in Israel/Palestine and Ukraine), and the radically uneven redistribution of wealth in the West and beyond, has compelled contemporary artists to respond with artworks that register home's increasingly uncertain status as a secure locus of stability and belonging.

To elaborate, let us draw another comparison, this time between two architectural "plans" – both for New York City's World Trade Center, and both tongue-in-cheek proposals, or what the architectural world refers to as hypothetical architecture. The first, by Matta-Clark in 1973, appears in an often-reproduced handwritten letter to his Anarchitecture study group that is for the most part composed of whimsical ideas for grant proposals and group projects. In this three-page letter, Matta-Clark has drawn a crude rendering of the twin towers of the World Trade Center, which had been recently completed and which had radically altered the Manhattan skyline from the perspective of the artist's SoHo studio. In the drawing, the towers are crossed out and separated by a setting sun, a scene accompanied with the following text: "The Perfect Structure. Erase all the buildings on a clear horizon. Return to an infinite horizon off man." Blithely destructive in its utopian yearning for an "infinite horizon," the drawing reflects both Matta-Clark's political critique of the dehumanizing dimensions of modern architecture and his playful attitude towards architectural protocol. But it is difficult, if not impossible, to view this drawing today without ascribing to it the ominous power of prediction. Here, we see how Matta-Clark's practice manifests a troubling resonance today, when such a proposal would be unthinkable (or at least unsayable). This tension becomes clearer when we compare Matta-Clark's drawing to Vito Acconci's 2002 proposal for reconstruction on the site of the World Trade Center. Acconci is best known for video and performance works of the 1970s, but his architectural practice since the late 1980s has proven as incisively critical of architectural convention as Matta-Clark's anarchitectural provocations in the 1970s, and indeed, Acconci's WTC proposal reveals a strong affinity with Matta-Clark's building cuts. The plan calls for a hyperbolically massive structure, encompassing the entire sixteen-acre site and rising to 110 storeys – a promise, Acconci suggests, of "more private office space than anybody could possibly need."[107] Thus exaggerating the fulfilment of excessive corporate indulgence, the proposal then proceeds to carve elliptical holes into the space, such that the building resembles an enormous block of Swiss cheese soaring above the skyline. The allusions to Matta-Clark's building cuts are clear here: consider the giant hole sliced through the Paris apartments, or, more persuasively still, the complex series of incisions into Chicago's Museum of Contemporary Art in 1978 (*Circus*,

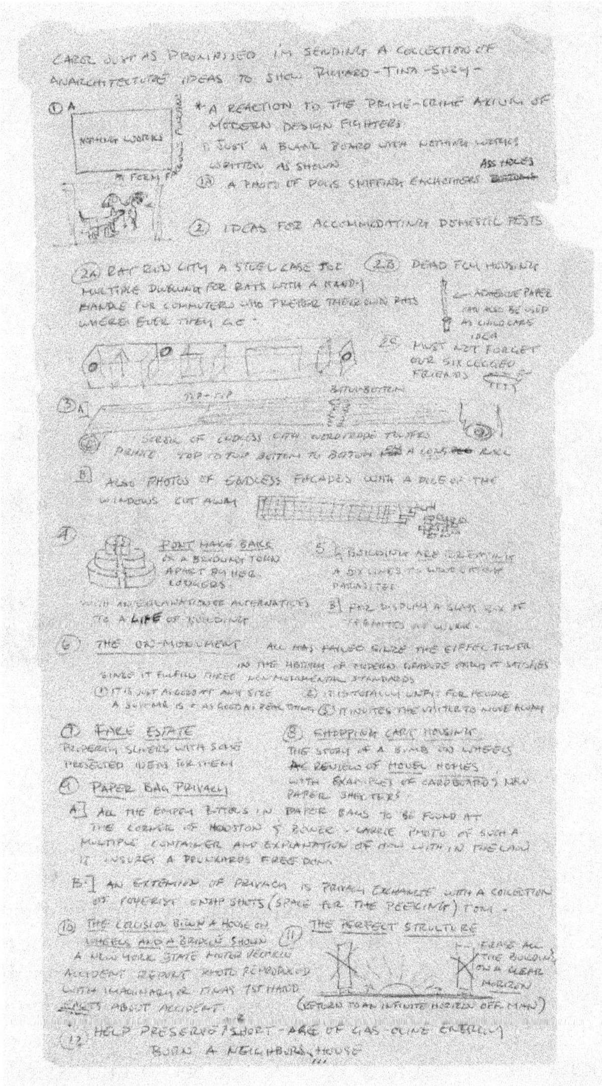

CAROL JUST AS PROMISED I'M SENDING A COLLECTION OF ANARCHITECTURE IDEAS TO SHOW RICHARD - TINA - SUZY -

① A

NOTHING WORKS

* A REACTION TO THE PRIME-CRIME AXIOM OF MODERN DESIGN FIGHTERS

JUST A BLANK BOARD WITH NOTHING WORKS WRITTEN AS SHOWN

1B A PHOTO OF DOGS SNIFFING EACHOTHERS ASS HOLES

② IDEAS FOR ACCOMMODATING DOMESTIC PESTS

2A RAT RUN CITY A STEEL CASE FOR MULTIPLE DWELLING FOR RATS WITH A HANDY HANDLE FOR COMMUTERS WHO PREFER THEIR OWN RATS WHERE EVER THEY GO -

2B DEAD FLY HOUSING

2C MUST ART FORGET OUR SIX LEGGED FRIENDS

TOP-TOP

BOTTOM-BOTTOM

③ A

PRINT TOP TO TOP BOTTOM TO BOTTOM

B ALSO PHOTOS OF ENDLESS FACADES WITH A PIECE OF THE WINDOWS CUT AWAY

4

5

TO A LIFE OF BUILDING

⑥ THE ON-MONUMENT

SINCE IT FULFILLS THREE NON MONUMENTAL STANDARDS

① IT IS JUST AS GOOD AT ANY SIZE

② IT IS TOTALLY UNFIT FOR PEOPLE

③ IT INVITES THE VISITOR TO MOVE AWAY

⑦ FAKE ESTATE

⑧ SHOPPING CART HOUSING

THE STORY OF A BUMB ON WHEELS

WITH EXAMPLES OF CARDBOARD & NEW PAPER SHELTERS

⑨ PAPER BAG PRIVACY

A] ALL THE EMPTY BOTTLES IN PAPER BAGS TO BE FOUND AT THE CORNER OF HOUSTON & BOWERY

B] AN EXTENSION OF PRIVACY IS PRIVACY EXCHANGE WITH A COLLECTION OF

⑩ THE COLLISION BETWEEN A HOUSE ON WHEELS AND A BRIDGE SHOWN

A NEW YORK STATE MOTOR VEHICLE ACCIDENT REPORT PHOTO

⑪ THE PERFECT STRUCTURE

ERASE ALL THE BUILDINGS ON A CLEAR HORIZON

(RETURN TO AN INFINITE HORIZON OFF MAN)

⑫ HELP PRESERVE SHORT-AGE OF GAS-OLINE ENERGY

BURN A NEIGHBORS HOUSE

1.9 Gordon Matta-Clark, letter addressed to *"The Meeting,"* care of Carol Goodden, 10 December 1973. Ink on blue airmail paper with ink stamps, postage stamp, and printed label 29.4 × 16.6 cm. Collection Centre Canadien d'Architecture/Canadian Centre for Architecture, Montreal. Gift of Estate of Gordon Matta-Clark. © Estate of Gordon Matta-Clark / Sodrac (2015).

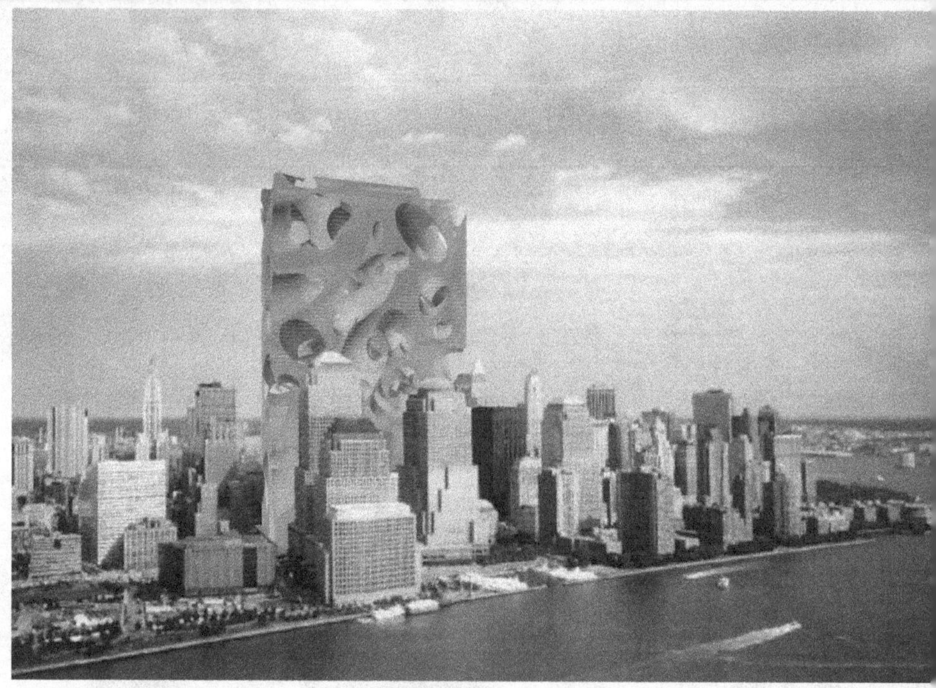

1.10 Acconci Studio (Vito Acconci, Dario Nunez, Peter Dorsey, Stephen Roe, Sergio Prego, Gia Wolff), *New World Trade Center*. New York, 2002. Courtesy of Acconci Studio.

or *The Caribbean Orange*), also once compared to Swiss cheese.[108] But consider also Acconci's intention, which was to create what he calls a "pre-exploded" building. Acconci explains: "A terrorist flying above might look down and say, 'Oh, we don't have to bother about this one, it's already been dealt with.'"[109] Besides exposing a playfully iconoclastic streak that certainly further aligns Acconci's practice with that of Matta-Clark, the implications of Acconci's proposal also reveal the radically transformed nature of Western society's traumatized relationship with architecture – a transformation that Acconci registers with a melancholic reminder of our collective precarity. As he suggests, "It's not that we want to make a space that falls apart. But we want people to realize, well, let's not feel as sure of ourselves as all that."[110] Here, the screen that projects the illusion of domestic security is revealed to be permanently pierced – a revelation that is traced in art practices that, like Acconci's, likewise mobilize an unhomely aesthetics to bear witness to human precarity in all its devastating materiality.

But the incongruence that marks off Matta-Clark's early articulation of an unhomely aesthetics also marks the moment at which his art practice can be productively pulled into the twenty-first century to nuance what might be considered the more nihilistically melancholic inclinations of contemporary art. For while Matta-Clark surely figures home as a troubled space whose facade of stability screens the contradictions and contestations hidden within, then his mode of shedding light on these repressed aspects of home is as productively ambivalent as the photograph of a house floating down a river or a playful proposal to "erase all the buildings for a clear horizon." This becomes particularly clear if we reconsider the wounded domestic space of *Splitting* in the context of Jean-Paul Sartre's observation, which opened this chapter, that the house and the body are deeply imbricated modalities of inhabitation.[111] According to this logic, it becomes useful to read the wound that slices through the Englewood house in line with art historian Petra Kuppers's idea that the wound, the scar, and the cut are "not simply tragic sites of loss, but also … sites of fleshy (and skinly) productivity, if productivity at a price."[112] In her analysis of visual representations of medicalized bodies, Kuppers argues provocatively that the wound represents "the knitting together of life and disruption, as not only a spatial site but also a temporal journey that highlights survival"[113] – an argument that can be productively applied to the cuts made by Matta-Clark into the spaces of home. Uncanny incisions into the domestic realm that brutally reveal its hidden dimensions, Matta-Clark's cuts nevertheless operate, like the cracks in Leonard Cohen's famous tune, to "let the light in." In this way, Matta-Clark reformulates a relationship with loss that abjures the catastrophic, tearing into the past in ways that also seem to acknowledge the needs of the future. Matta-Clark's practice is thus well positioned to motivate the generative and intersubjective potential of artists' contemporary engagements with traumatic experience, while also signalling the ways in which the figure of home can be productively employed to this end.

Not unlike the resurgence of interest in Matta-Clark since the 1990s, Martha Rosler's practice has begun to attain new resonance in the context of contemporary art's investigations of the unsettled nature of home, particularly in the context of late modern war culture. And once again, attention to both similarities and divergences between her works in the 1970s and more contemporary art practices reveals the changing stakes of these investigations. A salient example is photojournalist Melanie Friend's *Homes and Gardens: Documenting the Invisible*, a 1996 exhibition that paired sixteen colour photographs of pristine, seemingly peaceful houses in Kosovo with audio testimonies revealing these homes as unlikely (but very real) sites of government-sponsored terror and atrocity during the Milošević regime leading to the war of 1998–9.[114] Thus, for instance, an innocuous shot of a typical Kosovar living room with couches, rugs, potted plants, and framed portraits on the wall is juxtaposed with unsettling oral testimony that marks this home as a site of violent incursion:

> They met me in the field outside the house. Right away, one of them grabbed me around the neck, and the other one kicked me, so I fell. About six or seven policemen kicked me continuously. They stopped when they thought it was enough and took me to the garden. There, another ten to fifteen of them beat me up ... When I got to the house, everything was broken, and my sixty-seven-year-old father was beaten almost to death.[115]

The affinity here with Rosler's project is quite apparent: photography is employed to construct a juxtaposition of war and domesticity, with the project's title (*Homes and Gardens*, also invoking a popular American design magazine) again pointing to the unsettling incongruousness of this juxtaposition. In Friend's series, this incongruousness is produced not through competing visual markers, but instead by a competition of word and image – in this way, Friend's aesthetic strategy also hearkens back to Rosler's *The Bowery in Two Inadequate Descriptive Systems*, using word and image to demonstrate the limited representational capacities of both.

But two significant features of Melanie Friend's photo series distance her project from Rosler's *House Beautiful: Bringing the War Home* project. First, the domestic scenes recorded in *Homes and Gardens* admit no human presence, which is instead indexed by the traces of lived experience – in family portraits, in the worn condition of the furniture, and in subtle markers like fresh-cut flowers and empty coffee cups. Unlike Rosler, who inserts images of Vietnamese victims of the US aggression into the pristine spaces of the American home in order to shock viewers into new modes of witnessing the havoc of war, Friend's objective is instead to avoid what she terms the "photojournalistic convention that visualizes violence through the body of the 'victim.'"[116] In opting for this aesthetic strategy of non-representation, Friend renders human presence a gaping absence, performing what Chilean artist Alfredo Jaar refers to as a "lament of the images"[117] in a way that seems to preclude, or at least pre-empt, visual culture's tendency to spectacularize the suffering Other (although Rosler's *Bowery* project is also renowned as an early disavowal of documentary culture's visual spectacularization of the Other). But Friend's series diverges from Rosler's in another significant way. In Rosler's work, recall, scenes of war abroad are superimposed onto domestic spaces in America with the dual aim of exposing the hidden connections between these two paradigms and, as the title suggests, "bringing the war home" – that is, exposing the American home, relatively untouched by the violence of war, to the devastation wrought in its name. Friend's series, instead, is a blunt reminder that in many parts of the world, the presumed (and admittedly superficial) border between the safety of domestic spaces and the destructive spaces of armed conflict is dangerously fluid. And if these renderings of home as a space that is always already in danger of being infiltrated by aggression are especially resonant to Western audiences today, it is perhaps because, as Homi K. Bhabha maintains, "our current [post-9/11] situation is much more problematic – or liminal, in a word."[118] In a conversation with Beatriz Colomina regarding "domesticity at war" in the twenty-first century, Bhabha suggests that Martha Rosler's 1967–72 series does not resonate with the current global situation of fear and uncertainty, where perceived threats from "outside" national boundaries have become "as ubiquitous as the air we breathe"[119] – not only omnipresent, but dangerously viral spores that attack suddenly and stealthily. In Rosler's collages, Bhabha argues, "the outside is brought as close as possible, but there is still an inside and an outside ... There is a curtain that can be opened or closed, and there is the plate-glass window that allows you to see outside but also protects you."[120] Now, on the contrary, the curtain is no longer capable of screening out the world, and instead we are compelled to recognize the fluidity of national borders and the vulnerabilities of home(land) security.

In a published response to Bhabha, Martha Rosler challenges his observations regarding cultural assumptions of safe borders and boundaries in the 1960s and '70s. First, Rosler points out that of twenty photo-collages in the *House Beautiful* series, only four employ windows as aesthetic devices of distantiation – although she does not add that other screens (including picture frames, mirrors, and threshold spaces) proliferate. More saliently, Rosler furthermore observes that fear of the "other" in the Cold War and Vietnam era was, much like today, the fear of a spreading virus, and indeed, as Rosler remarks, "the spore as an invader vehicle from inside/outside" was one of the central motifs of the era.[121] The Cold War inspired an entire culture of insecurity, generating rampant fear of foreigners, communists, Black militants, and marijuana. In countless B-movies of the period, Martians, killer tomatoes, and body snatchers also filled in as ciphers for the threat of alien invasion. But the essence of Bhabha's comments remains incontrovertible: as terrified as Western citizens might have been in the 1960s by various threats of invasion, that threat (whether real or collectively imagined) was inevitably a mediated (and often fictional, or fictionalized) experience. Today, it would seem, that threat has become a lived condition in the Western world, where the perception (often exaggerated for political purposes) is that borders and guards are no longer capable of rendering us safe in our homes – a collective perception of perpetual threat that has been the grounds for a bevy of unprecedented fear-based initiatives that operationalize what Joseph Masco refers to as "national security affect,"[122] ranging from the colour-coded threat level system operated by the US Department of Homeland Security to the "If you see something, say something" advertisements that entreat New Yorkers to spy on each other in public places.

At the same time, those very agents tasked with keeping citizens safe seem increasingly likely to "bring war home" in the form of the excessive militarization of domestic police forces, particularly in the US – a condition that became especially apparent in the summer of 2014, when a police shooting of an unarmed black teen in Ferguson, Missouri, prompted public demonstrations that were met almost immediately with a quasi-military police response that included tear gas, armoured vehicles, and the imposition of martial law.[123] But the Ferguson police department is not alone in its amassing (and, perhaps inevitably, deployment) of military-grade weaponry. As journalist Radley Balko has documented, the Department of Homeland Security has funded the purchase of billions of dollars worth of military gear for domestic use; in 2011 alone, according to Balko, a Pentagon program donated $5.1 billion worth of equipment to local law enforcement agencies. The consequence, he concludes, has been the emergence of what he calls the "warrior cop" mentality: "Driven by martial rhetoric and the availability of military-style equipment ... American police forces have often adopted a mind-set previously reserved for the battlefield."[124] These conditions – the collective perception of terrorist threat combined with the actual threat of increasingly militarized police forces – lead to the perhaps inescapable conclusion that if home has always been a fictional realm of safety and sanctuary in the Western world, it is becoming increasingly difficult to maintain that fiction. This emerging set of conditions, along with the so-called "militarization of culture"[125] (or what we might also term the domestication of military culture), has been addressed in several photo series projects, including Lisa Barnard's *Blue Star Moms* (2007), which documents the mundane consumer goods sent in care packages to troops in Iraq and Afghanistan,[126] Nina Berman's *Homeland* (2008), which depicts what she describes as America's "love affair with war and violence,"[127] and Christopher Sims's *Theater of War: The Pretend Villages of Iraq and Afghanistan* (2008), which brings viewers into the US military training camps in Louisiana, Michigan, and elsewhere staged as uncannily accurate warzone villages.

Melanie Friend's most recent project, *The Home Front* (2009–12), likewise registers the uneasy domestication of war culture in the post-9/11 Western world. Like her earlier *Homes and Gardens* series, *The Home Front* is presented as a photo essay, in this case documenting seafront air shows for civilians across Britain over a four-year period. Unlike *Homes and Gardens*, however, the text that accompanies each photograph does not illuminate that which is otherwise invisible. Here, instead, the text drily records the mundane details regarding place, date, and the type of military aircraft on display (for instance: "Hawk T1 military trainer, Dawlish Air Show, Devon, 19 August 2010"). And yet the seeming incongruence of text and image is equally fraught in this work, for what is foregrounded in the photographs is not the display of aerial virtuosity, but rather families – mostly children – picnicking on beaches. In some cases it is easy to miss the planes altogether and to mistake the photos themselves for vacation snapshots. Only when we have sought out and located the silhouetted Hawk T1 far up in the clouds do we register the uneasy but apparently naturalized (and thus neutralized) propinquity of the spaces of leisure (the "home" of Friend's series title) and spaces of war (or the "front"). It is at this moment of registration, I suggest, that the condition described by Berland and Fitzpatrick as an emergent "military-cultural complex"[128] is revealed via the unhomely aesthetics of Friend's photographic practice. It is similarly registered in Martha Rosler's updated *House Beautiful* series, which responds to the Iraq War launched by the US in 2003. I conclude this chapter with a brief analysis of this series, which reflects both the ongoing relevance of her early project and the changing circumstances that call for a revised set of aesthetic strategies with which to respond to the contemporary global condition of unhomeliness.

Bringing the War Home Again

At the height of the second Iraq War in 2004, Martha Rosler revisited her *House Beautiful* series, exhibiting a set of photo-collages that again conveyed the radical disconnect between the affluence of middle-class America and the devastation being wrought abroad in its name. Juxtaposing markers of Western excess (high-end fashion, high-tech consumerism, stylish domestic interiors) with scenes of chaos, violence, and torture (bombed houses, legless soldiers, Abu Ghraib prison abuse), Rosler once again tropes Western conceptions of home in ways that expose its flawed status as a refuge from the world, and collapses the perceived distances between inside and out in order to remind us, as Heather Diack suggests, that "'home' can be a very uncomfortable place."[129] A continuum is therefore established between the conflicts in Vietnam and Iraq, both of which are screened in American society by projections of (mythical) comfort and safety (and, in the latter instance, rampant consumerism),[130] and both of which, when they do enter American homes, do so in highly mediated ways that clearly delineate the "here" and the "there" (as Rosler notes, the war in Iraq was even less visible than that in Vietnam).[131] But Rosler's Iraq series also speaks eloquently to the viral nature of unhomeliness in the twenty-first century and to the fact that "home," for the most part, is no longer able to accommodate the myths of refuge and security that it once signified. Indeed, subtle differences can be observed in the new series: whereas war tends to occur mainly (but with some exceptions) outside the principal spaces of Rosler's Vietnam-era homes, the Iraq collages blur any distinction between inside and out, with the bodies of war victims splayed on living room furniture and scantily clad models occupying the same pictorial space as hooded prisoners of war.

This is not to suggest that the Iraq series abandons the screen; if anything, it multiplies and mutates wildly here, with large-screen televisions, computer screens, cellphones, and picture windows all competing to divert our attention. Take, for instance, a work entitled *Point and Shoot*, in which a glamorous female model in a full-length gown, carrying a professional fashion camera and gazing out coquettishly at the viewer, has been collaged onto a busy street in an undisclosed location in the Middle East. The model is characteristically oblivious to the scene unfolding behind her: a British soldier, carrying a rifle and flanked by a tank and other armed soldiers, appears to accost a clearly frightened woman and child (who are, however, also inserted into the

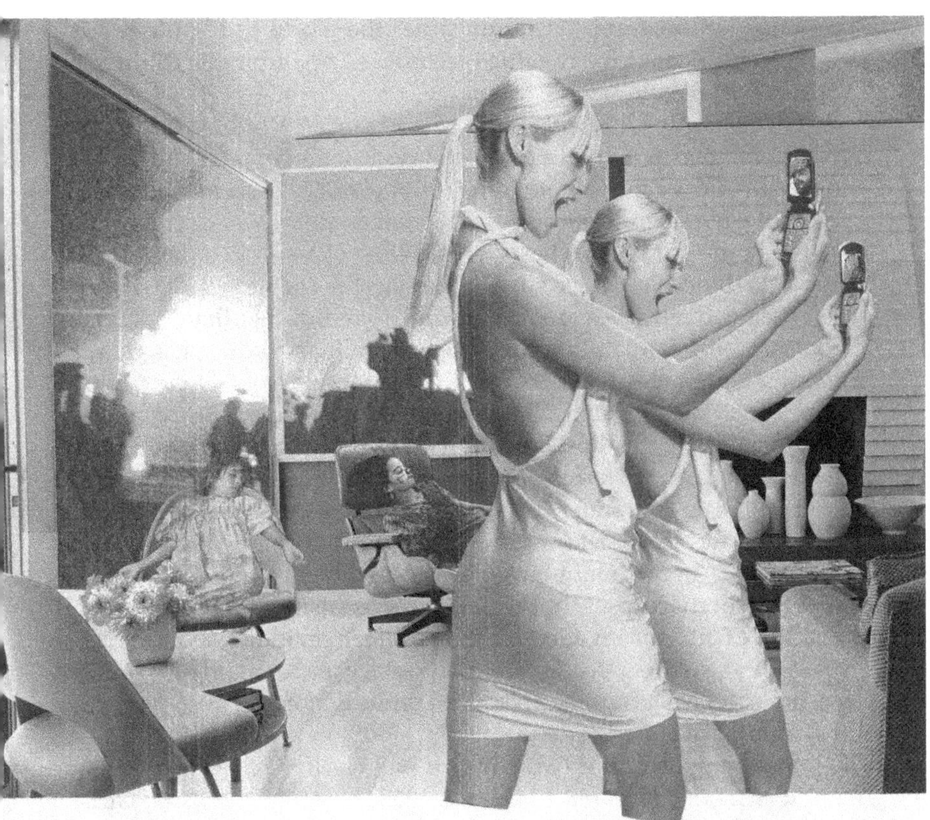

1.11 Martha Rosler, *Photo-Op*, from *House Beautiful: Bringing the War Home, New Series*, photomontage, 2004. Courtesy of the artist.

scene). Another image, *Photo Op*, pictures a modern living room with minimalist decor and (in an obvious nod to the earlier series) two picture windows, outside of which is a dark battlefield, with soldiers in American combat gear gazing out at a landscape of smoke and fire. Inside the room, two children in bloodied nightdresses are both slumped in chairs, apparently lifeless. In the foreground are two identical models (actually one figure, in duplicate) wearing slinky white dresses and striking a pose in front of their cellphone cameras – again oblivious to the scenes of senseless violence both outside and inside their interior space. In both cases, the use of screens subtly conveys that it is no longer the suburban enclave, but rather the world of high-tech communications technology, to which we now escape from the frightening world outside.

Thus a sharply different story emerges from Rosler's Iraq series. First, no longer do images of war and destruction appear suddenly as violent incursions into an otherwise spotless, idyllic scene of domestic bliss. Instead, the infiltrations seem more infectious. War does not burst into the home – it encroaches slowly, calmly, like a virus. In part, this can be attributed to Rosler's use of new technology in the 2004 series. The collages themselves are produced by hand (rather than, say, using Photoshop software) but they are then digitally reproduced, giving the images a flattened-out effect.[132] But the smoothing out of twenty-first century technology can also be understood as a metaphor for contemporary geopolitics: as Rosler acknowledges, "'the here' and 'the there' are now one place in terms of representation."[133] Second, and perhaps most significant, the Iraq series destabilizes conventional understandings of "home" as somehow an inherently American paradigm. In the 2004 collages, home might be a wealthy American split-level contaminated by bloody corpses, but it might just as easily be a busy Baghdad street full of citizens invaded by Western fashion ideals and terrorized by American soldiers. As if turning the tables on her earlier *If You Lived Here* project, Rosler implies in the Iraq series that if you lived *here*, your life would be in constant danger.

A close comparison of two collages will clarify the distinction I am making. *Cleaning the Drapes* from the 1968–74 series, discussed earlier, and *Gray Drape* from the 2004 series, are uncannily similar images; in both, a suburban housewife poses in front of a picture window, seemingly unperturbed by the scene of war raging on her lawn. Indeed, the later image seems clearly intended to recall the first: besides the allusive title, both domestic scenes have been clipped from a 1960s-era *Life* magazine spread extolling suburban femininity. But the differences between the two images are even more revealing. First, while the Vietnam-era collage doubtless intends to juxtapose a familiar (if already nostalgic) image of peaceful domesticity with the horrors of war, the Iraq version is surely not likewise intended to jar its viewers out of a comforting sense of identification with this scene of domestic bliss. As contemporary viewers presumably savvy to the fact that this is an archival advertisement, we are implicitly interpellated to recognize this glamorous scene as a nostalgic invocation of postwar suburban comfort, which we now understand to have been an untenable

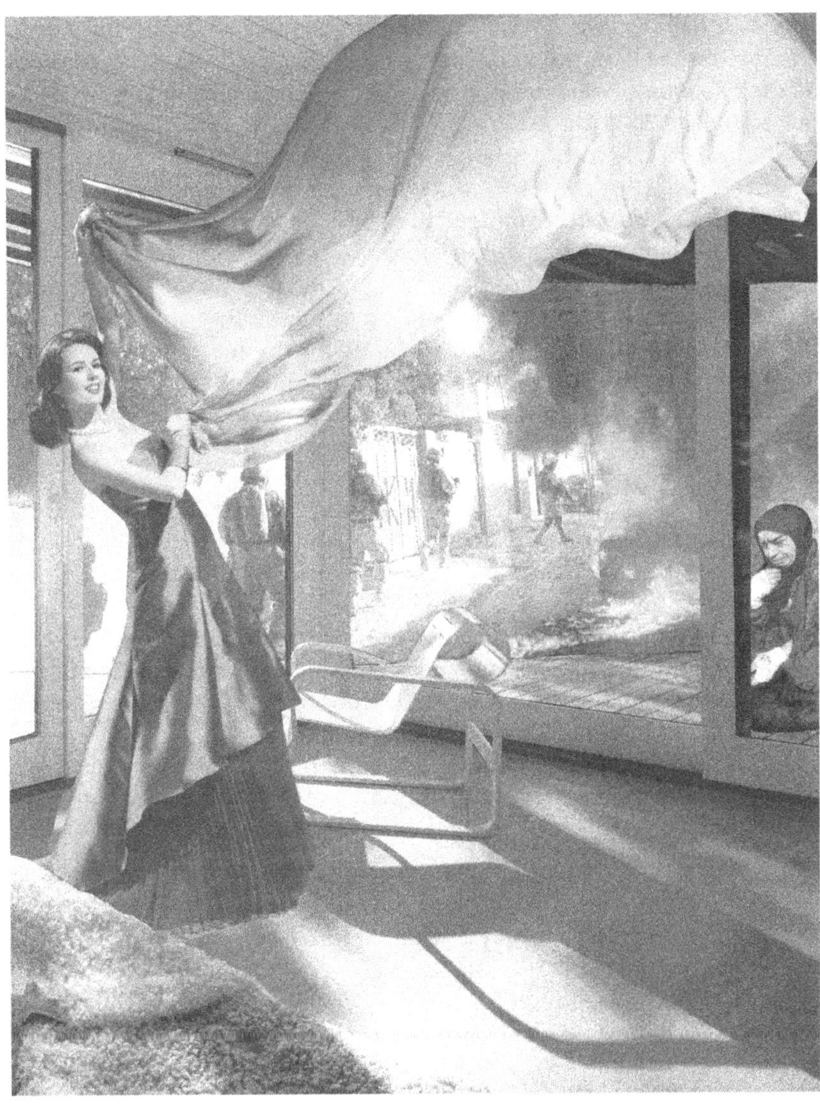

1.12 Martha Rosler, *The Gray Drape*, from *House Beautiful: Bringing the War Home, New Series*, photomontage, 2004. Courtesy of the artist.

myth. Somehow, we identify less with the woman inside the house than with the chaos outside. Today, as Bhabha reminds us, we are not so easily screened from the threat of displacement and loss. Even more jarring in the 2004 image, however, is the presence of an Iraqi woman and child, clearly in distress, positioned precisely in the liminal area of the picture window – the border between here and elsewhere. This detail triggers us to recall that the conditions of war require us to remain vigilantly aware of the price of our own domestic comforts, but furthermore that these comforts are not afforded to those who live in the midst of war, those who occupy domestic spaces with the provisionality and precariousness that comes with conflict, poverty, and/or territorial occupation. What Rosler's Iraq series articulates so clearly is contemporary art's unique capacity to mobilize the precariousness with which home is occupied as a vehicle for ethical witnessing practices.

In their own practices of the 1970s, Gordon Matta-Clark and Martha Rosler remind us, with Homi Bhabha, that "the anxiety of belonging encourages us to choose to live in a house whose shifting walls require that stranger and neighbor recognize their side-by-sideness."[134] And it is this emerging understanding of home as a concept that both reflects our anxieties of belonging and encourages new models of intersubjective encounter that animates the unhomely aesthetics of contemporary art. Indebted to the aesthetic strategies laid out by Gordon Matta-Clark and Martha Rosler in the 1970s, contemporary practices propose revised strategies for emerging paradigms of the unhomely in contemporary global society.

2
The Art of Longing and Belonging

Crossing borders, in all senses of the word, is traumatic. Consider the aftermath, with all of the legal issues, hostility, euphoria, and disappointment. The stages of transformation of identity for the immigrant, the internal dialogues and disagreements, create a very stressful complexity. In the process of becoming a new person, an immigrant must imagine, examine, and question all identities – the past, present, and future. Those who are ready to negotiate these psycho-political roles need this equipment, an artifice or prosthesis, to begin this demanding process of fearless speech. I do not propose how all of this should be resolved. I only suggest that artists, who are situated between technology, discourses of democracy, and the lives of people, have unique opportunities to create practical artifacts that assist others in this migratory and transitory world.

Krzysztof Wodiczko

You want to stick your finger in the wound and say that the work is definitely torture, that it is indeed a punishment of biblical proportions. And when you put your name on the work it seems that you're held responsible for the capitalist system itself. Many of the people who make these criticisms have never worked in their lives; if they think it's a horror to sit hidden in a cardboard box for four hours, they don't know what work is ... I do things because I think they should be included in the art world, but I don't have grandiose dreams that I'll actually achieve anyone's redemption ... When you sell a photograph for $11,000, you can't possibly redeem anyone except yourself.

Santiago Sierra

In New York in 2003, Polish-American artist Krzysztof Wodiczko exhibited *Dis-Armor*, a high-tech wearable communications instrument equipped with video camera, microphone, speakers, and LCD screens broadcasting stories of alienation and cultural displacement, designed to facilitate public testimony and eventual (re)integration into the social body. The same year, Mexico City–based Spanish artist Santiago Sierra represented Spain at the 50th Venice Biennale with *Wall Enclosing a Space* and *Covered Word*, an installation that saw the national pavilion bricked in and accessible only through the back entrance, and only to those who presented a Spanish passport. In their diverse art practices, both Wodiczko and Sierra have engaged with dislocation, displacement, and the vicissitudes of belonging and unbelonging that are attendant to the precarious occupation of space in contemporary global society, and have sought to convey the difficulties associated with attempting to situate oneself psychically, culturally, and geographically, when "home" becomes a floating signifier of belonging, loss, return, and new beginnings. Treating this experience as one of profound alienation, even traumatization, both artists employ an unhomely aesthetics to express the socio-political implications of "strangeness." In their practices, unhomely becomes both metonym and metaphor for the traumatic aspects of radical cultural and geographical displacement; in the process, this chapter argues, both Wodiczko and Sierra intervene productively in theorizations of art's capacity to facilitate ethical practices of witnessing traumatic experience.

Not simply a literal translation of the psycho-aesthetic category of the *unheimlich* as theorized by Freud, the unhomely also conveys a sense of geopolitical displacement that is mobilized by postcolonial theorists like Homi Bhabha, who asks us to understand the unhomely as an experience of liminality that unsettles national borders by highlighting the existence of "the minority, the exilic, the marginal and emergent," who gather "on the edge of 'foreign' cultures."[1] But while one of this book's objectives is to shift the psychoanalytic category of the uncanny into the geopolitical realm of the unhomely, psychoanalytic understandings of traumatic experience do play a central role here. Indeed, Krzysztof Wodiczko's art practice marshals psychoanalytic discourses associated with trauma theory as a key component of his aesthetic interventions. Combining D.W. Winnicott's notion of the therapist as "good enough mother," psychotherapist Judith Herman's assertion of the critical role that public testimony plays in healing traumatic wounds, and Julia Kristeva's theorization of the uncanny as an intrusion of the foreign into the presumed cohesion of the national body,[2] Wodiczko's unhomely aesthetics are emphatically therapeutic. Then, Santiago Sierra is equally invested, if not in the discourses surrounding trauma, then in seeking ways to convey the traumatizing experience of radical dislocation. My

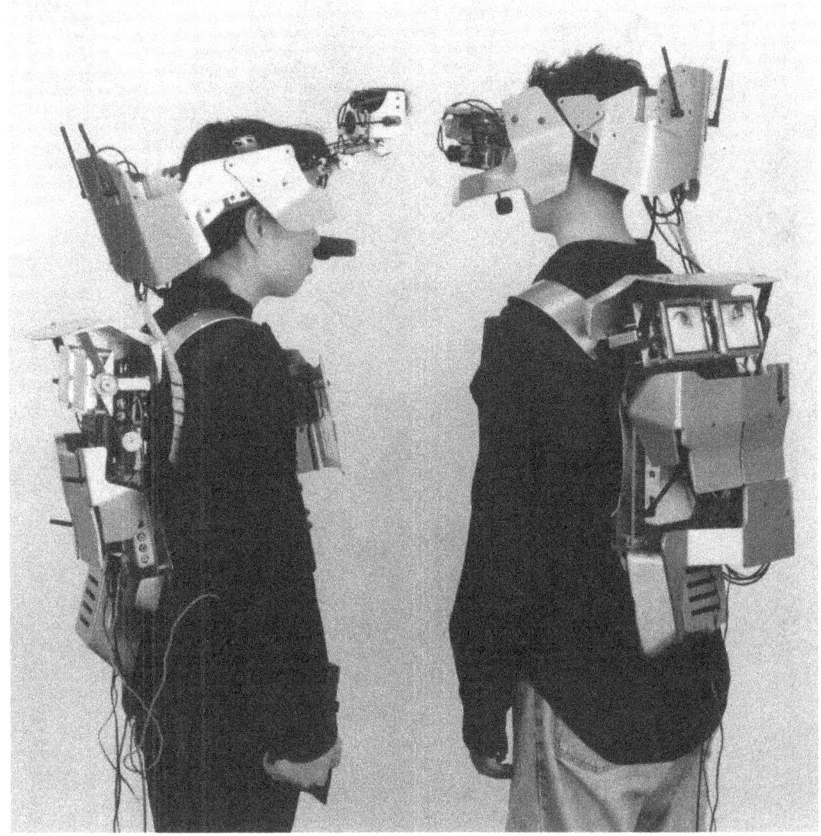

2.1 Krzysztof Wodiczko, *Dis-Armor*, 1999–2001. One laptop computer, three LCD screens, speaker with amplifier, microphone, augmented speech recognition software, three video cameras, electric engine, batteries and internal and external aluminum components. © Krzysztof Wodiczko. Courtesy of Galerie Lelong, New York.

own intention here is neither to apply nor further develop an orthodox psychoanalytic position, but to chart how salient concepts from psychoanalytic trauma theory are articulated in certain art practices. I propose that those strands of trauma studies that question and deconstruct art's presumed role as a mediating party prove to be a useful lens through which to examine the risks and promises of socially engaged art that seeks to register or represent traumatic experience.

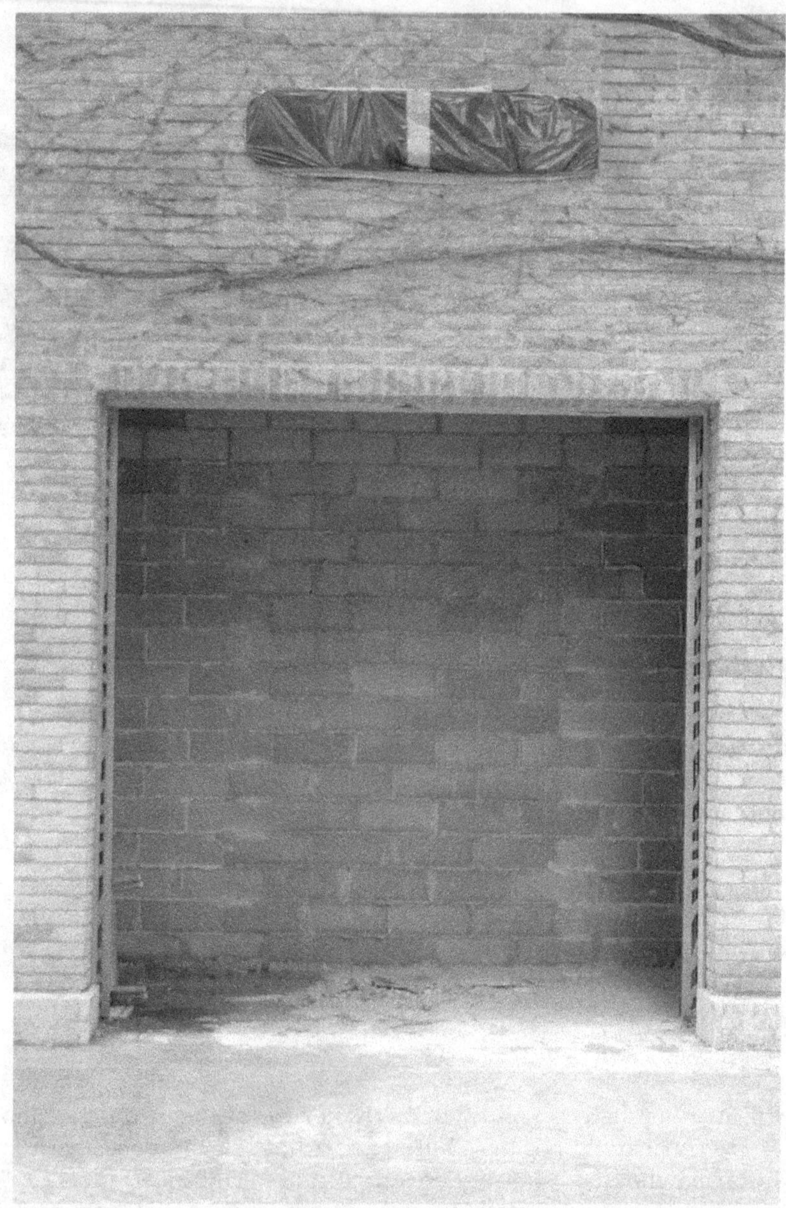

2.2 Santiago Sierra, *Covered Word*, 2003. Installation view, Venice Biennale. © Santiago Sierra. Courtesy of Lisson Gallery.

Significantly, while Wodiczko and Sierra both evoke the uncanny in their investigations of the suffering associated with exile and estrangement, the ways these artists negotiate conditions of alienation and strategies of "unhomely" intervention differ substantially. Wodiczko calls forth the uncanny in order to defuse it through primary testimony, secondary witnessing, and collective healing; his work seeks to work through traumatic memory, with the eventual aim of reconciling self–other relations. Employing Winnicott's notion of the "transitional object" (intermediary devices that assist the patient's transition towards psychic independence), Wodiczko's intention with instruments like *Dis-Armor* is, he suggests, to "aid the stranger in making the transition to nonstrangeness while assisting the local in recognizing his or her own strangeness."[3] Santiago Sierra, on the contrary, creates antagonistic situations haunted by melancholic restagings of the traumas wrought by the tensions and conflicts produced by the unhomely experience. In Sierra's actions and installations, the "repressed" returns repetitively, compulsively even, and "home" is exposed as a heavily policed borderline of self–other tension.

The Art and Science of Strangers: Krzysztof Wodiczko's "Xenology"

Since the early 1980s, artist and professor Krzysztof Wodiczko has been designing both artefacts and more ephemeral projects intended to draw attention to and empower immigrants and otherwise disenfranchised individuals, such as the urban homeless. Wodiczko has created over seventy public projections of still and video images, and he has also developed a series of vehicles and instruments designed for urban intervention, including the *Homeless Vehicle* (1988–9) and *Poliscar* (1991). Wodiczko began to attend specifically to the migrant experience in 1992, when he launched his ongoing Xenology project with *Alien Staff*, the first of several instruments meant to open channels of communication between immigrants and non-immigrants. Coining "xenology" (from the Greek *xenos*, or alien) as both "the art and science of the stranger" and "the immigrant's art of survival,"[4] Wodiczko designed the *Alien Staff* to resemble a high-tech biblical shepherd's rod, with a small video monitor, loudspeaker, and Plexiglas cylindrical containers for the display of "immigration relics" such as visa applications, photographs, and personal letters.[5] Participants in cities around the world were invited to use the staff as a conduit for telling stories (both pre-recorded and live) of their immigration experience to passers-by on the street. This project was followed in 1993 with *Mouthpiece (Porte-Parole)*, a piece of equipment that attached to the wearer's head with a small screen and loudspeakers covering the mouth. The work was inspired by cybernetics founder Norbert Weiner's advocacy of prosthetics for the improvement of society,[6] and was also, like the *Alien Staff*, intended as a vehicle of Brechtian distantiation – or *Verfremdungseffekt* – a technique for preventing audiences from abandoning themselves to the spectacle of narrative content and character identification, in order to reveal underlying social relations and political messages.[7] A bizarrely prosthetic artificial mouth that would both underline and undermine the apparent strangeness of the speaking subject, *Mouthpiece* would ideally "help create new links and affinities between immigrants and nonimmigrants on the basis of the recognition of their common strangeness."[8]

Both *Alien Staff* and *Mouthpiece* exemplify a methodological framework deeply informed by Julia Kristeva's reading of the Freudian uncanny, likewise premised on building affinities on the basis of shared strangeness. Whether he is designing artifices that "double" for the speaking subject (such as the 1998 *Ægis*) or projecting images of the poor onto civic monuments in order to bring to light that which "ought" to have remained hidden (as in the *Homeless Projection: Place des Arts* of 2014), Wodiczko's practice has, like Kristeva's, sought to acknowledge that we are all "strangers to ourselves." In her 1991 book of the same title, Kristeva takes her own theory of abjection – briefly, the maternal body against which the child must revolt as s/he enters the realm of the (patriarchal) symbolic, extended to describe all that which threatens the subject's corporeal borders[9] – and exends it even further to the condition of the migrant, who is under constant threat of expulsion by the social body that seeks to maintain its *cordon sanitaire*, and whose ongoing presence is considered a threat to the homogeneity of that body. Drawing an explicit parallel between the uncanny in the psychic realm and xenophobia in the socio-political sphere, Kristeva hypothesizes that non-violent political stability can only be achieved upon recognition (and acceptance) of our irreconcilable *interior* alterity – that is, via recourse to psychoanalysis. Freud, argues Kristeva, "brings us the courage to call ourselves disintegrated not in order to integrate foreigners and even less to hunt them down, but rather to welcome them to that uncanny strangeness, which is as much theirs as it is ours."[10]

In his own writing on the subject, Wodiczko conceptualizes the uncanny as both a socio-psychic condition to be overcome ("Our strangeness is a strangely familiar secret, an uncanny condition which … can explode against the presence of the actual stranger … Between the speechless pain and despair of the actual stranger and the repressed fear of one's one strangeness … lies the real frontier to be challenged")[11] and an aesthetic tool for overcoming that very challenge: "If, however, there was some kind of strange object between this person and them, they would focus on the strangeness of the object first, somehow putting aside for a moment the presence of the stranger. Perhaps in this intermediate moment, through this intermediate object, they might more easily come to terms with some kind of story or story-telling, some kind of performative experience, some kind of artifice."[12]

Not necessarily a paradoxical position, the uncanny as an aesthetic practice for reconciling with the uncanny can be understood as a homeopathic remedy for the fear of strangers, again reminiscent of Brecht's distantiation effect (often translated in English to the "alienation effect") as an antidote to social alienation. But while the Freudian uncanny and Brechtian distantiation share a motivation to make the familiar strange, Brecht's project was to mobilize the revolutionary dimensions of this effect, while Freud's intention was to heal.[13] Freud himself posited that the frightening nature of the uncanny could be neutralized by cultural products such as fairy tales, which exaggerate and thus contain strangeness, rendering it unthreatening – a process likewise advocated by Wodiczko. As art historian Rosalyn Deutsche observes, the Xenology project's Freudian effort to neutralize the fear of strangers reaches its apogee with *Ægis: Equipment for a City of Strangers* (1998),[14] and it was with *Ægis* that Wodiczko's projects began to be conceived less as vehicles for drawing attention to the unhomely condition of societal alienation, and more as instruments that might provide actual therapeutic benefits for both wearer and viewer. With a closer look at *Ægis*, we can begin to map out some of the questions that Wodiczko's practice raises in relation to trauma, testimony, and the art of social relations.

Ægis, like its precursors *Alien Staff* and *Mouthpiece*, is a wearable communications apparatus that facilitates speech via audio-visual proxy. Named after the cloak of Athena, which bore a Gorgon's head and was used by the goddess to shield herself and others,[15] the instrument is composed of a backpack equipped with two screens that unfold on command and play sequences pre-recorded by the wearer. The wearer's identity (as signified by the face) is thus *doubly* doubled, as if to reflect the "disintegrated" self to whom Kristeva refers. But as Wodiczko notes,

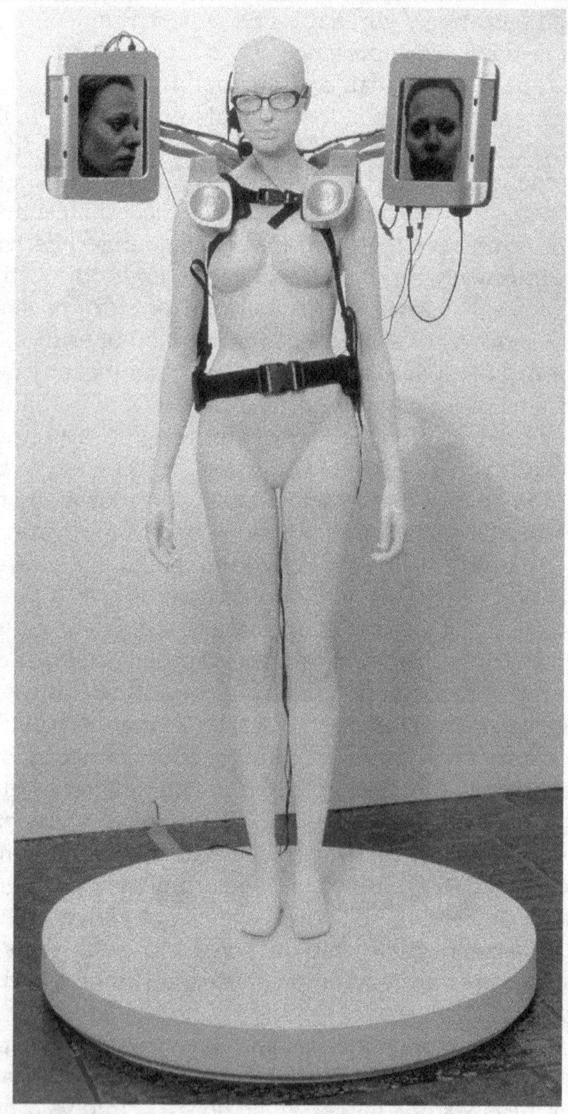

2.3. Krzysztof Wodiczko, *Ægis: Equipment for a City of Strangers*, 1999–2000. Two augmented laptop computers, two LCD screens, two loud speakers, augmented speech recognition software, aluminium structure, electric engine, batteries and plastic parts, and mannequin/base. © Krzysztof Wodiczko. Courtesy of Galerie Lelong, New York.

the screens are also intended to resemble the wings of an angel, linking their design to the artist's vision of immigrants as "messengers of a better world to come as well as critics of the unacceptable world in which they live. They announce and denounce the world."[16] To expedite this reading, Wodiczko created a script for a preliminary video recording that rehearses one of the more alienating conversations an immigrant might be expected to endure, while layering it with multiple, sometimes conflicting and even multiply confrontational responses to the largely benign but often demoralizing question, "Where are you from?":

Left screen	**Right screen**
Where are you from?	Is that any way to start a
Where are you from?	conversation?
Where are you from?	Where are you from?
	I'm from here!
Enough!	I'm me.
I don't want to hear that anymore!	Just like you.
Fi-gu-red out!	You're yourself.
I don't want to be figured out	With your own first and last name...[17]

In this passage, Wodiczko produces a dialogue with the questioning subject that aligns with what political philosophers Ernesto Laclau and Chantal Mouffe term agonistic pluralism: a principle of radical democracy that hinges on the recognition that whereas consensus entails the silencing of dissent, adversarial socio-political relations must be acknowledged – even cultivated – in order to create the conditions for actual democracy.[18] In this respect, *Ægis* appears to be aligned less with the preceding Xenology instruments than with Wodiczko's even earlier, arguably more provocative, projects such as the 1986 *Homeless Projection Proposal* (which drew damning attention to the burgeoning housing crisis in New York as a result of gentrification) or even the 1988–9 *Homeless Vehicle* (intended to operate like a bandage that "covers and treats a wound while at the same time exposing its presence").[19] If the *Homeless Projections* proposed to haunt city streets with the return of the dispossessed, the *Alien Staff* sought ways to resolve or reduce the conflicts borne of dispossession. If the *Homeless Vehicle* offered, as Dick Hebdige has suggested, a Swiftian "modest proposal" for the housing crisis in America,[20] the Xenology instruments were instead proffered as "therapeutic devices" that "allow [users] to develop their speech – to help them with this final stage of healing."[21]

Wodiczko reintroduces conflict and dissent in his conceptualization of *Ægis*, but it is a carefully scripted conflict premised on an assumption of eventual, if not imminent, resolution. The scenario prepared by Wodiczko, excerpted above, concludes on a note of (albeit cautious) reconciliation and empowerment:

Left screen:
Independent, independent.
And again, independent.
Reconstructed.
Remodeled,
Strong.
With faith in oneself
Because she proved herself in a
foreign country.
Is that me?
But there's that tiny nose-tweak.
"Where are you from?"
Is the building already
tottering?

Right screen:
Because that question creates an
abyss between us.
And it makes me feel
As tiny
As a dwarf
Next to you.

And I thought
I was grown-up.
Do you really
Want to be
A giant
Next to me? [22]

Like the Xenology project, then, *Ægis* exposes conflict in order to defuse it. Being adversarial, Wodiczko proposes, is not about "escalating hostilities, but is a way to develop the dynamic conditions from which people learn to respect each other."[23] These conditions, his art production further suggests, can be fostered in relation to the concepts of truth, testimony, and reconciliation, and it is therefore neither surprising nor inappropriate that Wodiczko has sought to merge his unhomely aesthetic with the discourses that comprise trauma theory. Thus while cultural theorist Ben Highmore has likened Wodiczko's role to that of "artist as uncanny ethnographer" whose instruments challenge "the uncanny strangeness of geographical displacement,"[24] I propose that Wodiczko is better understood in the role of "artist as uncanny therapist," taking on the uncanny as both symptom and cure for the experience of unhomedness or unwelcomeness.

Trauma and the Art of Testimony

Let us return to *Dis-Armor* (2003), a helmet equipped with a microphone and video camera, attached to a backpack with screens that display live images of the wearer's eyes and speakers that amplify her or his voice. A camera attached to the backpack conversely feeds video to a screen at the wearer's eye level. First produced for and used by adolescents in Hiroshima, Japan, *Dis-Armor* was the first of Wodiczko's instruments intended to address purely psychic estrangement – specifically, the psychological difficulties and stressful lives of socially alienated youth "who have survived overwhelming life events (violence, neglect, and abuse) and who now wish to overcome their false sense of shame, to break their silence, and to communicate their experience in public space."[25] A second incarnation of *Dis-Armor*, at the Massachusetts Museum of Contemporary Art in 2004, follows an Arab American woman testifying to the abuse and ostracization she has suffered since 9/11, thereby mapping an overtly geopolitical theme onto the investigation of psychological stress. But what connects the two versions, and what connects *Dis-Armor* more broadly to the Xenology project, is its insistence on the healing properties of public testimony – or what Wodiczko refers to, after Michel Foucault, as "fearless speech."[26] As Wodiczko explains, the prosthetics constitute "a way of giving them a possibility of developing their capacity to speak. And also for [those] who are strangers to them to become close and to open their ears."[27]

Integral to Wodiczko's overall project is the notion that recovery from traumatic experience requires both the opportunity to testify to one's experience and the presence of an empathetic listener – an idea he credits to psychoanalyst Judith Lewis Herman. Herman, a key thinker in the field of trauma theory, is the author of the influential 1992 book *Trauma and Recovery*, which posits that "private" traumas (particularly those caused by the deliberate infliction of pain, such as rape and incest) demand public airing, and that trauma recovery depends upon socio-political intervention. For Herman, attention to psychological trauma is an "inherently political enterprise"; situations and agents that are able to offer "voice to the disempowered," she suggests, create the conditions for victims to become fully aware of their traumatization and to begin the process of recovery.[28] Herman's analysis is essentially an extension of now-classic trauma theory (founded on the Freudian notion that the traumatized subject is unable to integrate the experience into memory without an active interlocutor willing to bear witness to that experience) from its focus on calamitous events, such as the Holocaust, to domestic, everyday traumatic experiences. In keeping with trauma theory's insistence that an ethics of witness must acknowledge the incommensurability of experience, Wodiczko concurs that, "To say 'I understand what you went through' is the most unacceptable response. The opposite may be more appropriate. 'I will never understand what you went through.'"[29] But in creating therapeutic testimonial situations, Wodiczko also positions himself as a conduit through which the patient/user can narrativize and reconcile her traumatic experience, insisting, "Before they can add their voice to the democratic agon, these actors must again develop their shattered abilities to communicate." Relating this to his own efforts to facilitate public communications, Wodiczko adds, "The process of unlocking their post-traumatic silence requires not only critical, but also clinical, approaches and attention."[30] Interestingly, in the interview from which this passage originates, Wodiczko dissociates his current attention to testimony and healing in the public sphere from his earlier affinity with the agonistic theories of democracy as proposed by Mouffe and Laclau, insisting that Mouffe's theory must be "injected" with "a call for psychotherapeutic recovery through 'reconnection' that emphasizes the role of public truth-telling and testimony."[31]

In this way, the prosthetic devices that Wodiczko produces and deploys undergo a subtle but significant transformation. As his work becomes less invested in the political visibility of social actors and more in their psychic capacity to speak publically, so do his uncanny devices go from being objects of distantiation designed to communicate that we are all "strangers to ourselves" to therapeutic devices designed to heal the subject traumatized by the experience of social, geographical, or psychological alienation. More precisely, they become what Freudian psychoanalyst D.W. Winnicott called "transitional objects." For Winnicott, the process of "working through" traumatic loss requires an empathetic interlocutor through whom the suffering person can detach from his or her melancholic attachment to loss. Observing that children often rely on objects (blankets, teddy bears, and the like) to cope with the dissolution of the mother–child dyad, Winnicott postulated that certain objects might also be required as intermediaries to move the patient from attachment to self-sufficiency, from melancholia to mourning.[32] Wodiczko's wearable instruments are designed specifically to act as transitional objects, and interviews with participant-users confirm that the instruments may play an empowering intermediary part in the testimonial act. Nathalie, a participant in the *Mouthpiece* project in France, for instance, relates her transformative experience: "When you wear the object in the street, people can easily think that it is not your mouth that is on the screen. It's reassuring, and that feeling takes away some of the responsibility."[33] *Dis-Armor* was likewise designed to empower young Japanese participants unaccustomed to public speaking, its backside screens allowing the user to face away from their intended audience and therefore take shelter in the partial anonymity afforded by the device. A videotaped segment of one such encounter demonstrates the effective, and strangely affective, dimensions of such a design. The video, two minutes long, begins with an adolescent girl in a school uniform donning the apparatus in a small room. She appears to make herself comfortable, then joins a group of girls – friends or classmates, presumably – who erupt into peals of laughter at the sight of her. The stage is thus set for a light-hearted performance of cyborg playfulness, but as the girl approaches two men seated in the cafeteria of an office building, a sense of discomfort quickly begins to pervade. The men seem bemused, and even as the girl turns her back to them and recounts how her family and world have collapsed since her father left suddenly, they try to cheer her up with good-natured assurances. The girl begins to cry, and the camera filming the scene zooms in for a close-up on her distraught face.

It is impossible, of course, to surmise whether this young woman's testimony to strangers had any transformative effect. No available documentation exists as to whether she, like Nathalie in France, felt reassured or empowered by the instrument, and we are not informed as to whether her life has improved since the encounter. But then, as Wodiczko admits candidly, he is "[neither] a therapist [nor] a healer."[34] At best, his instruments are "interrogative designs"[35] – efforts to imagine how public speech might facilitate psychic healing and repair social relations. As a therapeutic project, then, *Dis-Armor*'s efficacy cannot, and perhaps should not, be gauged. But as an art project proposing a methodology for mediating the experience of trauma, questions can and should be raised. To begin, to what extent can a project like *Dis-Armor* escape the spectacle of trauma that reduces its representation to a cathartic, even exploitative, exercise in viewer titillation? And, if the wearable instrument is a "transitional object," what role does the unacknowledged third-person video camera play? Does it further enable the transitional moment or encounter? Intrude upon it? Aestheticize it? Then, does *Dis-Armor* mobilize an empathetic response in the viewer, and if so, does this response carry any social, political, or even aesthetic valence? And what of viewers who fail to sympathize with, or are even antipathetic to, the young woman's plight? Does the project assume a pre-constituted audience, and if so, might this preclude the possibility of sustained (agonistic) dialogue on human rights and public speech? *Dis-Armor*, like most of Wodiczko's projects, raises more questions than it presumes to answer, and this is perhaps its most constructive intervention into the politics and aesthetics of trauma representation. To further probe these questions, let us consider a work whose situation both on and in relation to national, cultural, and corporeal borders allows us to better comprehend Wodiczko's uncanny practice through the lens of unhomely aesthetics.

The Therapeutic Uncanny

In a 2014 interview, Wodiczko explains the psychotherapeutic dimensions of his practice for participants: "By publicly telling the truth of their unacceptable experience they may inspire, develop, or reinforce their wish and will to contribute to new public consciousness toward the large change – perhaps toward the future world … Perhaps this is the aim of the kind of art I do? Not art therapy, but art that has a social, critical, and therapeutic effect and a psychoanalytic dimension."[36] Wodiczko is referring here to his *Tijuana Projection* of 2001 – a work that gestures towards filling all three roles. A synthesis of the artist's projections and instruments, the project is also one of the most uncanny of his projections, and it epitomizes Wodiczko's careful attendance to both the therapeutic and ethical dimensions of public art. In the context of inSITE2000, a binational and biennial contemporary art exhibition held in San Diego and neighbouring Tijuana, live video footage was projected onto the sixty-foot-diameter spherical facade of the Omnimax Theater at the Cultural Center of Tijuana (CECUT) for two nights running. The footage was fed by a specially designed headset with camera and microphone worn by local women who gave stirring testimony about domestic violence, sexism, and misogyny in their community, and the harsh, often dangerous working conditions in the multinational-owned *maquiladora* factories where most young women in northern Mexico's poverty-ridden border towns eke out a living.[37] The participants were members of Factor X, an association of female *maquiladora* workers formed to promote education and workers' rights, and with whom Wodiczko spent one year preparing for the intervention.

Employing a monumental facade not simply as a site, but also as a subject, of his intervention, the *Tijuana Projection* recalled the artist's more politically oriented projections of the 1980s and '90s, such as the 1985 action that saw the image of a swastika projected stealthily onto

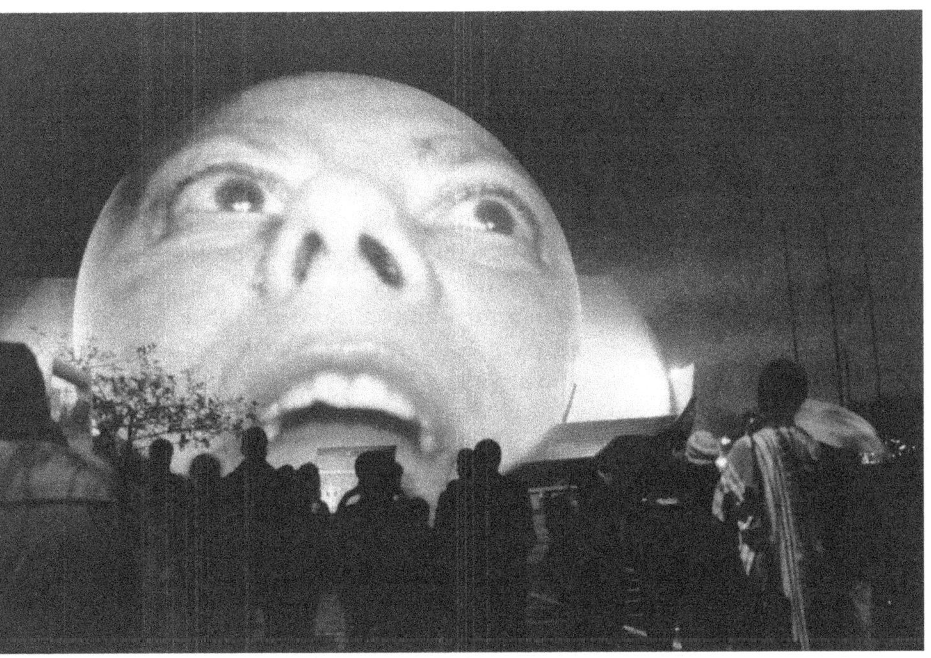

2.4 Krzysztof Wodiczko, *Tijuana Projection*, 2001. Public video projection at the Centro Cultural Tijuana, Mexico. Organized as part of the event InSite 2000. © Krzysztof Wodiczko. Courtesy of Galerie Lelong, New York.

the facade of the South African embassy in London's Trafalgar Square to protest that country's racist apartheid regime. Recognizing, with contemporary theorists of monumental art and architecture, that they tend to promulgate narratives of sacrifice, glory, and progress that erase discord and naturalize exclusion,[38] Wodiczko's interventions have, as Rosalyn Deutsche puts it, functioned as "projections upon projections," uncanny exposés of that which is repressed from monumental – usually nationalist and patriotic – history. As Deutsche further observes, "if dominant representations imprint their messages on receivers by inviting immediate identification with images so 'natural' they seem uncoded, Wodiczko's transformed images have the opposite effect [of] impeding both the monuments' messages and the viewer's identification with authoritative images."[39] One salient example is the *Border Projection* of 1988, a two-site projection on San Diego's Museum of Man and, again, the Cultural Center of Tijuana. The still image in this case depicted the back of a man's head, hands clasped behind him as though being held under arrest and framed by two large question marks. An unflinching comment on the tense relationship between Tijuana and San Diego and the border that divides them, the doubled image exposes the consequences of that tension in a way that accords with Jacques Rancière's notion of dissensus: inclusive adversarial discourse that acknowledges and exposes the social exclusions in normative discourse.[40] In the *Border Projection*, Tijuana's CECUT – a celebratory monument to progress, modernity, and cultural wealth in Mexico – becomes a blank screen onto which are projected the very citizens these discourses erase: those who are compelled, by often abject poverty, to flee the country.

Notwithstanding Wodiczko's increasing mistrust of Rancière's dissensus model for critical inquiry,[41] in many respects the *Tijuana Projection* of 2001 evokes similar concerns using analogous aesthetic strategies. First, public projection itself seems an uncannily disturbing medium, more conducive to Brechtian distantiation than to therapeutic mediation. The women's disembodied faces, distorted almost comically onto the curved structure of the CECUT's Omnimax theatre, render the testimony emanating from the speakers even more affectively unsettling. And indeed, it is an unsettling performance. The women's words, ringing out across the border, speak also *about* the border, about how largely and humiliatingly it looms in their lives. One participant, for instance, delivers the following prepared monologue:

> When you tried to cross the border, you were so dignified with your new American girlfriend. Better life, without children. A better job, more money. But, when you arrived at the border the roles were reversed. They handcuffed your wrists, as if you'd committed some kind of crime. All your fingerprints were taken. You were put on a bus. Your feet handcuffed. You were locked up for three days ... You were stomped on. And that's how you made me feel, each time you yelled at me, with each slight, that I wasn't worth anything, that I was a stupid person, a dummy.[42]

Like the *Homeless Projection Proposal*, then, which used monumental sculpture against itself in a jujitsu-like move that denaturalized the inequalities and exclusions upon which myths of progress and achievement are built, the *Tijuana Projection* treats the CECUT as both a signifier of Mexico's failure to reconcile its modernizing economy with its explosion of poverty and emigration and as a mass medium through which to broadcast the devastating results of this failure (as Luiza Nader suggests evocatively, the facade was "'attacked' by the artist" in a way that revealed "the unspeakability of what is hidden behind").[43] Whereas, however, the *Tijuana Projection* arguably revived Wodiczko's interest in using projection to achieve uncanny effects aimed at promoting agonistic public speech, this concern is now folded into the language of therapy, which, he suggests after Herman, will itself produce socio-political resonance and relevance. Wodiczko notes that "the clinical can be critical in the sense that it detects and investigates symptoms," adding: "In the case of my work, the analogy might go even further, from the diagnosis to the actual healing."[44] As already indicated, this is not to suggest that Wodiczko considers himself a "healer" – instead he regards his work as catalytic, although his choice of language sometimes seems to reveal slippage between analogizing and conflating art and clinic. Reflecting on the *Tijuana Projection*, for instance, Wodiczko suggests that "the participants ... use the project for themselves: they are both doctors and patients, which is the nature of the clinic. It is a kind of public clinic, all of this."[45]

This clinical aspect of the project extends cheekily to Wodiczko's monumental critique. If the architectural spaces in earlier works were commandeered as palimpsests for the uncanny emergence of repressed histories and counter-narratives, they are now more likely to be conceptualized by the artist as equally in need of therapeutic treatment: "In fact, the monuments are not in very healthy condition. They suffer in a state that is similar in many ways to post-traumatic stress, mostly because they are isolated from the events and life of people who very often live on their steps ... They are, in fact, dumb and numb. They suffer through this traumatic speechlessness, and any possibility to be of any use to the living would be a great relief for them."[46]

Wodiczko's "diagnosis" of public monuments reveals, on one hand, the playfulness with which he often approaches his methodology. The anthropomorphization of monumental architecture, combined with a satirical concern for its psychic well-being, hints that Wodiczko's primary project is not *literally* to heal, but to probe the ways in which artists can respond creatively to both psychological and collective trauma while closely examining the often-occluded linkages between them. Thus operating within a self-imposed aporia, wherein art is imbued with the power to heal but cannot presume to be accountable to this promise, Wodiczko's practice raises important questions about art's capacity to productively mediate or otherwise intervene in the representational regimes that circumscribe the experience of trauma.

Testimony and the Aesthetics of Social Relations

One of the key questions that have emerged in respect to the application of trauma theory to an increasingly broad range of contexts is the extent to which a discourse rooted in personal therapy can or should be mapped onto structurally inflicted and societally inflected suffering. For cultural theorist Andreas Huyssen, to favour narratives of personal suffering, recovery, and redemption is to risk minimizing the political dimensions of historical violence and thus the more pressing questions of human rights and restitution. Huyssen's argument, that "the transnational discourse of human rights may give us a better handle on such matters than the transfer of psychoanalysis into the world of politics and history,"[47] must also inform any reading of Wodiczko's Xenology project and its increasingly assertive doctrine of truth, testimony, and reconciliation. Take, for instance, the assumption that the receiver of traumatic testimony is an always already (or at least an always *ready*) empathetic witness. For psychoanalyst and trauma theorist Dori Laub, the transmission of traumatic memories (specifically Holocaust experiences) requires an interlocutor who acts as a "blank screen on which the event comes to be inscribed."[48] The task of the listener, then, is to participate in, even co-own, the event: "through his very listening he comes to partially experience trauma in himself."[49] But can such a transmissive relationship be presumed in the context of a public art event attended by a diverse group of (often accidental) listeners? As noted by Ewa Lajer-Burcharth, Wodiczko's projects take considerable pains to draw attention to the multifaceted, even fragmented identity of the user-speaker (consider, for instance, the multiple faces of *Ægis*). His equipment, she observes, "aims at generating an image of the self as a kind of fiction – a story of masks, disguises, personae."[50] At the same time, however, the prevailing sense is of a stable, coherent receiver-listener willing and capable of accepting the communication without conflict. Hence, whereas Wodiczko has sought to distance his work from a Habermasian model of public communication that privileges what the artist correctly refers to as a "blind drive for consensus,"[51] his methodology for facilitating a relational sphere aligns better with Habermas than, say, with Chantal Mouffe or Jacques Rancière, both of whom advocate agonistic dissensus over blind or coerced consensus in the public sphere.

To better comprehend the complexity of Wodiczko's aesthetic-political gesture towards suturing both psychic and social wounds by creating opportunities for audiences to acknowledge the "foreignness in ourselves," it is useful to align his work with the relational art practices that emerged in the 1990s to "elude alienation" and "fill in the cracks in the social bond"[52] by operating in the interstices of "these new interactive technologies that are threatening to commodify human relations within 'spaces of encounter.'"[53] Likewise, Wodiczko's interventions into the interstitial realm of communication technology disrupt its somewhat paradoxical tendency to impede, rather than facilitate, communication. *Dis-Armor*, for instance, is designed according to the artist "to meet the communicative needs of the alienated, traumatized, and silenced residents of today's cities" and to counter "the dichotomy of the present explosion in communication technology and rampant cultural miscommunication."[54] But to what extent are Wodiczko's vehicles, projections and prostheses capable of avoiding an appeal to a counter-model of communication that only reifies the presumed collapse of communication in the public sphere, a question that has also been raised regarding the so-called social or participatory turn in contemporary art? As Jacques Rancière argues, "The loss of the 'social bond,' and the duty incumbent on artists to work to repair it, are the words on the agenda. But an acknowledgment of this loss can be more ambitious."[55] It is this premise that motivates recent reconsiderations of the politics and ethics of participatory art, and one of the voices at the forefront of these reconsiderations has been that of art historian Claire Bishop, for whom participatory practices in general – and the "micro-utopian"[56] gesture of relational art in particular – demonstrate "a compromise, rather than an articulation of a problem."[57] Advocating instead a "disruptive" version of social relations, which she terms "relational antagonism,"[58] Bishop looks to Santiago Sierra, best known for actions that involve paying the poor and disenfranchised "as little as possible"[59] to perform mundane, repetitive, meaningless, and often humiliating tasks, as exemplary. Sierra's "delegated performances,"[60] as she calls them, produce relations "marked by sensations of unease and discomfort rather than belonging, because the work acknowledges the impossibility of a 'microtopia' and instead *sustains* a tension among viewers, participants, and context."[61]

This idea – that art can or should sustain, rather than neutralize, tension – is key to understanding Sierra's own unique contribution to the unhomely aesthetics of contemporary art. Sierra's confrontational set of practices, which range from shocking but relatively straightforward institutional critiques such as *Gallery Burned with Gasoline* (1997) to "remunerated actions" like *Line of 30 cm Tattooed on a Remunerated Person* (1998), are typically subject to criticism that concentrates on his efforts to draw attention to the hypocrisies of the art world and the economic exploitation of underclass workers. Some, if not most, collapse Sierra's theme to a core issue of capitalist exploitation – a Marxist metanarrative of post-Fordist labour alienation re-enacted to provoke the discomfort of the bourgeoisie.[62] But this genre of analysis, while not inaccurate, has tended to underplay the significance of the geopolitical particularities that frame and nuance each of Sierra's actions. Indeed, one of Sierra's most significant objectives has been to draw attention to, indeed activate, specific forms of alienation that are almost invariably products of largely arbitrary but nevertheless strictly policed borders – whether national, cultural, or economic. Indeed Sierra can be understood to conduct his own xenological experiments, although his "objects" of experimentation, as will become evident, are less transitional than obstructive in both form and function. Situated uncomfortably on the boundary between the strangely familiar and the all-too-familiarly inhumane, Sierra refuses, as Bishop observes, to "offer an experience of human empathy that smoothes over the awkward situation before us,"[63] instead presenting scenes of radical non-identification that privilege friction, awkwardness, and discomfort. In this way, Sierra's projects can be understood to correspond to Butler's conception of "melancholic agency"[64] – a politicization of loss that contests psychoanalysis's emphasis on "working through" in favour of practices that resist "narrative closure."[65]

Antagonizing Social Relations: Santiago Sierra's Dystopian Aesthetics

A Spanish artist based, since 1995, in Mexico City, Santiago Sierra stages actions that employ sometimes architecture, sometimes humans, and often both, as what he calls "performative readymades."[66] While Sierra has become notorious for projects that re-enact oppressive economic relationships, many of his works have also challenged the naturalization of national borders, thus illuminating the geopolitical implications of his wider project. More specifically, projects that most evocatively reveal Sierra's critical commitment to laying bare the traumatizing consequences of border policing in contemporary global society are

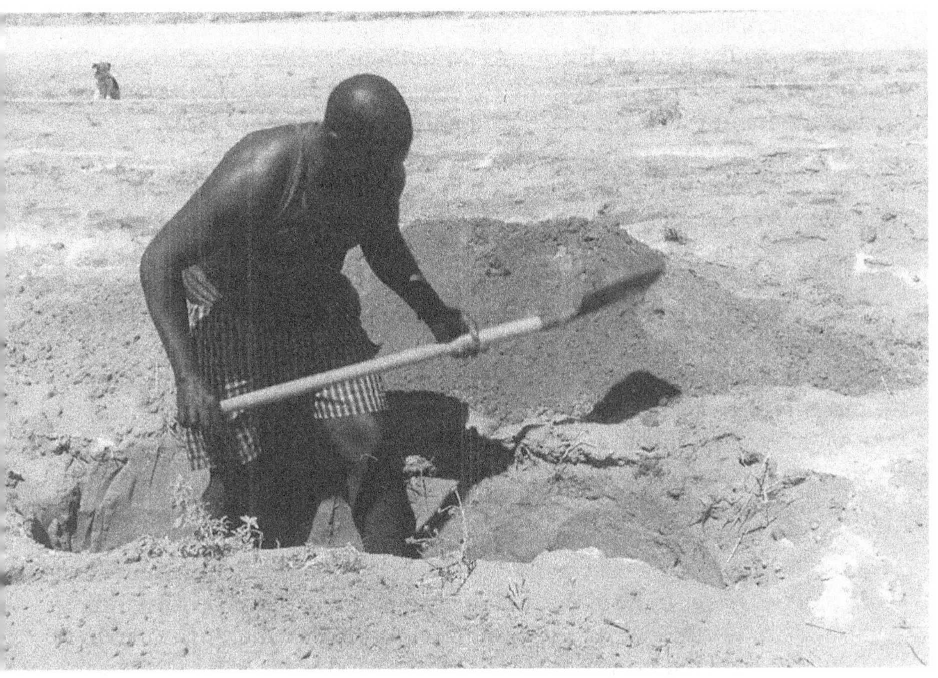

2.5 Santiago Sierra, *3000 Holes of 180 × 50 × 50 cm Each*, 2002.
© Santiago Sierra. Courtesy of Lisson Gallery.

those that combine subversive border roving with his better-known investigations of economic exploitation, all of which, it must be added, are themselves implicit critiques of the cruel limits and excesses of globalization.

Take *3000 Holes of 180 × 50 × 50 cm Each*, a work produced in 2002 on the Spanish coast facing Morocco. Formally, the project resembles a well-known performance by fellow Mexico City–based artist Francis Alÿs of the same year, *When Faith Moves Mountains*. For that work, carried out on a sand dune near Lima, Peru, Alÿs directed 500 volunteers to stand in a row and move the sand at their feet four inches as an "epic response, a 'beau geste' at once futile and heroic, absurd and urgent,"[67] to the dire situation on the Ventanilla dunes of Peru, where thousands of internally displaced settlers from the countryside live in shanty towns without electricity or running water.[68] Alÿs's project was staged as a social allegory to demonstrate the utopian ideal that "sometimes to make nothing is to make something";[69] Sierra's action, on the contrary, acted out a dystopian sense of despair and hopelessness. For the month-long project, Sierra paid undocumented North African workers fifty-four Euros per day (Spain's mandated salary for foreign day labourers) to dig rectangular holes – each three by six feet, approximately the size of a human grave – into a sandy lot facing the Strait of Gibraltar. The site, besides being a fraught zone on the border between Spain and Morocco, was furthermore replete with symbolic tension – a beach where the corpses of African men and women, who make the treacherous crossing daily in search of work or asylum, wash to shore with alarming frequency.[70] Almost as if mocking Alÿs's ephemeral testament to the collective resilience of the human spirit, Sierra's project – which transforms the landscape into a mass graveyard (dug, at least figuratively, by its eventual inhabitants) – bears witness to the agonizing nature of the migrant worker experience. And it is this compulsion to enact or re-enact the traumatic experience of the unwelcome stranger that sets Sierra's project in sharp relief to Wodiczko's, which is to ameliorate, even heal, the unhomely condition. But notwithstanding Sierra's anti-redemptory positioning vis-à-vis the migrant experience (and vis-à-vis the power of the artist to intervene in that experience – recall, in this chapter's epigraph, Sierra's insistence that "When you sell a photograph for $11,000, you can't possibly redeem anyone except yourself"),[71] it is worth attending briefly to the fact that, to the extent that both artists are concerned with drawing attention to the traumatic deprivations endemic to the unhomely condition, Sierra and Wodiczko share a methodological framework that sheds significant light on art's unique capacity to register trauma.

"That which ought to have remained hidden ..."

Drawing on Schelling's definition of the *unheimlich* as "everything that ought to have remained ... secret and hidden but has come to light,"[72] Freud theorized the uncanny as "something which is familiar and old-established in the mind and which has become alienated from it only through the process of repression."[73] This conceptual lever has proven useful for analysis of Krzysztof Wodiczko's art practice, particularly his projections of homeless and destitute men and women onto the statues of civic leaders in the *Homeless Projection* proposal, which effected what I have already described as a return of the *dispossessed* in the rapidly gentrifying context of New York City.

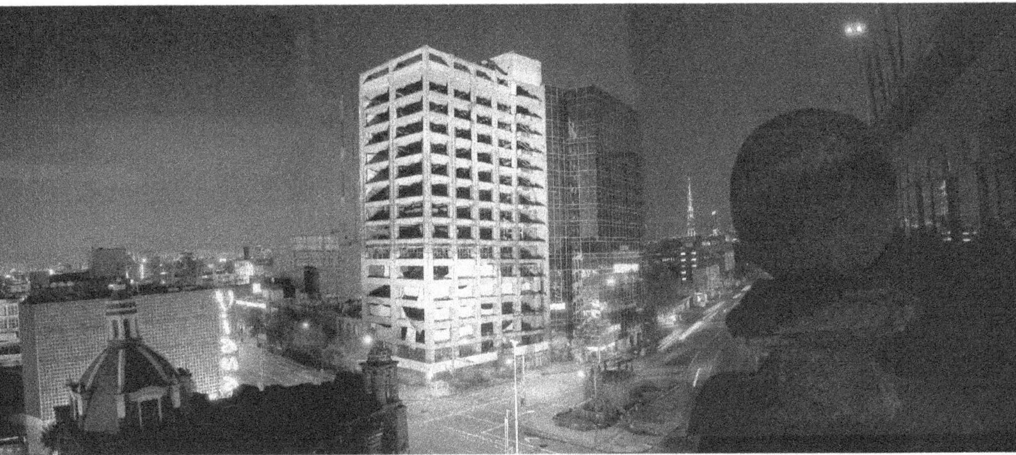

2.6 Santiago Sierra, *Lighted Building*, Mexico City, 2003. © Santiago Sierra. Courtesy of Lisson Gallery.

I'm also interested in how the concept of the uncanny bridges Wodiczko's practice with that of Sierra, and one project in particular should clarify the connections (as well as distinctions) I am drawing between the two artists.

In 2003, Sierra produced *Lighted Building, Mexico City*, using reflectors to light up an earthquake-damaged and abandoned sixteen-storey warehouse in downtown Mexico City now occupied by homeless residents as a makeshift shelter. Like Wodiczko's *Homeless Projection* proposal, Sierra's action *literally* brings to light that which "ought" to have remained hidden – a swelling population of inner-city homeless whose very existence must be repressed in order to maintain the neoliberal façade of progress and wealth in the late-capitalist urban environment. But whereas Wodiczko's project, as Rosalyn Deutsche observes insightfully, transformed "an evicting architecture" into "an architecture of the evicted,"[74] Sierra instead took advantage of an already existing "architecture of the evicted," turning it into a lighthouse in distress that broadcast its indictment of societal indifference across the skyline. In this respect, it is useful to compare Sierra's action with Chilean artist Alfredo Jaar's *Lights in the City*, which saw the installation of dozens of thousand-watt red light bulbs in the cupola of Montreal's Bonsecours Market in 1999. The lights were connected to switches at the doorways of three nearby homeless shelters, causing

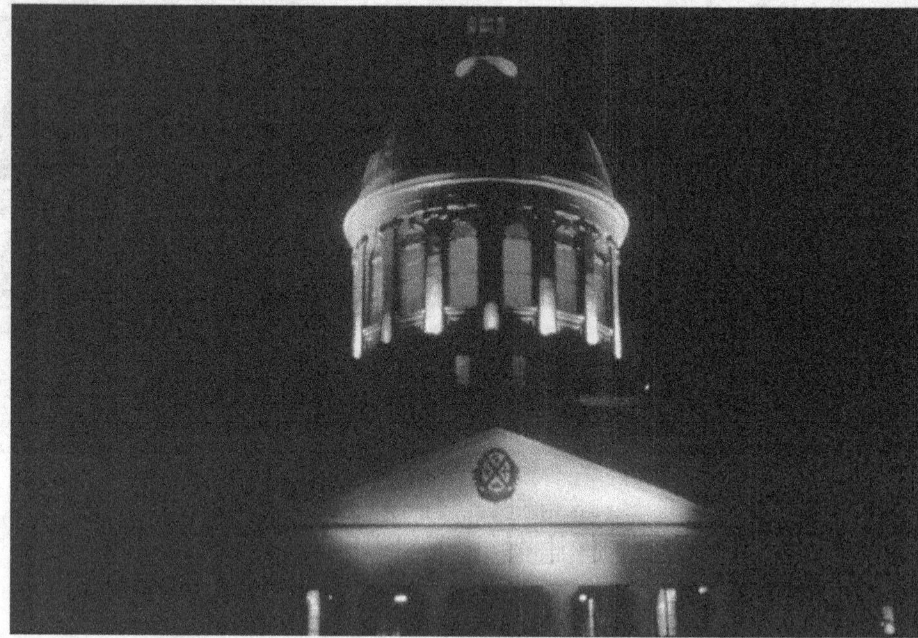

2.7 Alfredo Jaar, *Lights in the City*, 1999. Public intervention, Marché Bonsecours, Montreal, on the occasion of Le Mois de la Photo, Montréal. © Alfredo Jaar. Courtesy of Galerie Lelong, New York.

the cupola to light up each time a person entering a shelter chose to activate the switch.[75] Jaar reports that shelter residents he interviewed in preparation for the piece "wanted people to acknowledge their presence, through a smile, a hello, but they were over-looked, as a garbage can or a lamppost is ignored."[76] His response, a cupola that flickered continually for the six weeks of the installation, was conceived as a "distress signal to the city"[77] – an effort to draw attention to a social condition that often goes neglected, indeed wilfully ignored, in gentrifying urban contexts.

What Wodiczko, Sierra, and Jaar share – and what they inherit from Gordon Matta-Clark's conceptual legacy of (an)architectural intervention – is a profound appreciation for the ways in which architectural spaces can be employed (almost inevitably against their discursive intentions) as sites of silent witness to difficult knowledge. But this imperative to bear witness to the traumatic impact of social, economic,

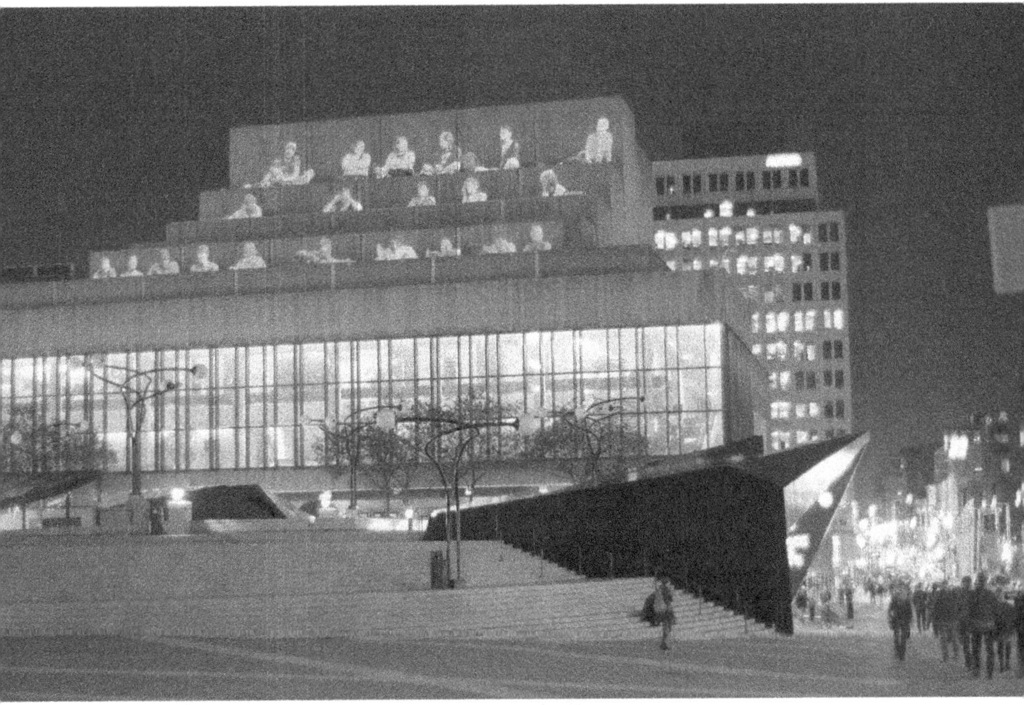

2.8 Krzysztof Wodiczko, *Homeless Projection: Place des Arts*, 2014. Photo: Kes Tagney. Courtesy of the artist and Galerie Lelong, New York.

and political alienation intersects with, and is both complicated and nuanced by, what has now become a common injunction against the spectacularization of suffering in visual culture. The call to develop an ethics of looking at difficult images is a primary motivating factor particularly in the work of Alfredo Jaar, who refers evocatively to his ongoing project as a "lament of the images."[78] When offered the Bonsecours Market cupola's windows for an installation of photographs, for instance, Jaar instead chose a representational strategy of "making the homeless visible without pointing at them directly."[79] Jaar's complex approach to visual representations of human suffering is perhaps best exemplified by his *Real Pictures* installation in 1995, which saw hundreds of photographs, taken by the artist in the aftermath of the 2004 Rwandan genocide, sealed in black linen archival boxes, each with a written description of the image inside. This project, like *Lights in the*

City, was propelled by Jaar's belief that "we have lost the ability to see and be moved by images."[80]

Krzysztof Wodiczko's methodology for keeping the witness at a safe distance from the spectacle is perhaps best revealed in a recent work, commissioned in 2014 for the Montreal Biennale of Contemporary Art. For *Homeless Projection: Place des Arts*, the artist collaborated for several months with the St Michaels Mission in downtown Montreal to produce a series of interviews with twenty-five members of the city's urban homeless population. The result is a large-scale fifteen-minute audio-video installation, projecting their thoughts, insights, and stories onto the stepped upper facade of Place des Arts – a concert hall in Montreal's Quartier des Spectacles (Entertainment District) that hosts ballet, opera, and music concerts. The location for the projection was, characteristically, not a coincidence. First, the neighbourhood is also home to a high percentage of the city's homeless, whose presence is normally marginalized, even actively discouraged, but who here reappropriate that space in a way that seeks legitimation of both physical presence and the collective right to shape and make meaning of it. In this way, their presence (and their stories of abuse, neglect, fortitude, and resignation) deconstructs the spectacle of urban gentrification (which Place des Arts so clearly symbolizes) while at the same time constructing a counter-spectacle of sorts – a reading endorsed by the shape of the facade itself, which resembles a theatrical setting, a proscenium on which this group of actors both watch us from above and at the same time demand our attention. We are indeed called upon to look, but the presumed authority of our spectatorship is inevitably and immediately compromised by our encounter with the return of the dispossessed: from the street, we are required to look up at bodies we would normally look down upon, and to listen to voices that are customarily silenced in these spaces where poverty and homelessness are not only concealed but indeed actively criminalized.[81] As the artist explains, "Usually, we are tall and they are sitting or laying on the ground. They see the city from the bottom, from want and poverty. This time, they'll be above us, so we will feel smaller. The issue is not so much to make them bigger, but to make us smaller."[82]

Notwithstanding his own protestations regarding the futility of art's engagement as political intervention ("An artist is a producer of luxury goods and from this point of view the notion of political commitment is quite unconvincing"),[83] Santiago Sierra likewise employs the uncanny to unequivocally political ends, deliberately conflating the return of the repressed with the return of the dispossessed while consistently

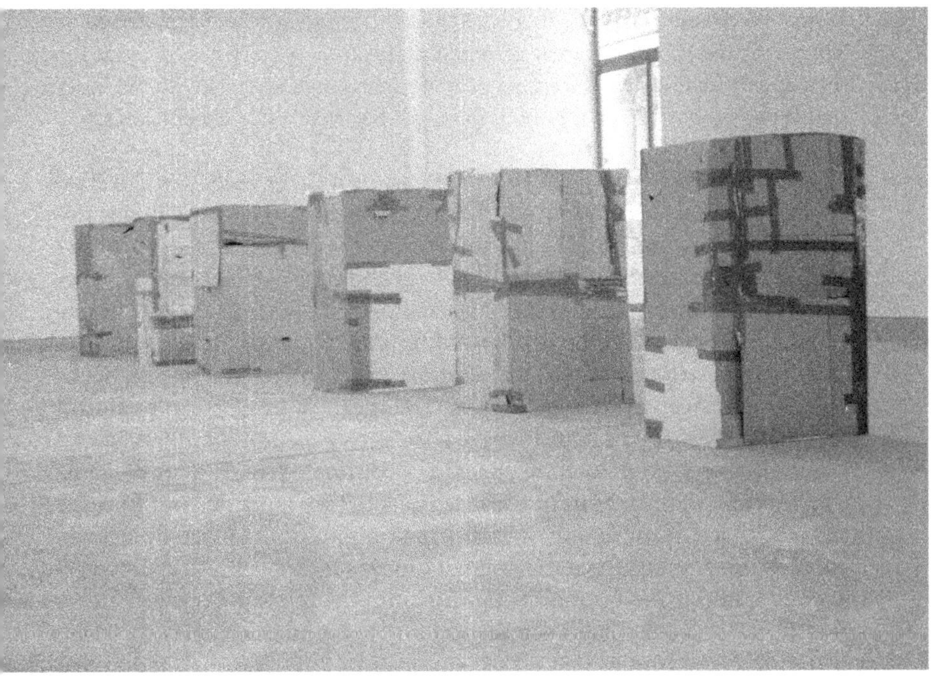

2.9 Santiago Sierra, *Workers Who Cannot Be Paid, Remunerated to Remain inside Cardboard Boxes*, Berlin, 2000. © Santiago Sierra. Courtesy of Lisson Gallery.

foreclosing on the potential for visual spectacle, catharsis, or mastery. Consider two actions – *Workers Who Cannot Be Paid, Remunerated to Remain inside Cardboard Boxes* and *3 People Paid to Lay Still inside 3 Boxes during a Party* – both of which involved hiring disenfranchised and socially alienated individuals to conceal themselves in crudely constructed boxes. For *Workers Who Cannot Be Paid, Remunerated to Remain inside Cardboard Boxes* at the Kunst Werke in Berlin in 2000, Sierra hired six undocumented Chechen asylum seekers to spend four hours per day for six weeks inside boxes installed in the gallery. He describes the work as a comment on Germany's treatment of immigrants, while also implying a variation on institutional critique that required the gallery to implicate itself in a wider social critique:

> In the summer of 2000, there was much heated discussion about German policy with respect to political refugees, a debate that reached its climax when neo-Nazis from nearby Leipzig killed an African asylum seeker. At

> Kunst Werke our project ... involved Chechen refugees who were not permitted to work, under threat of repatriation ... Consequently, we could not openly state that we were paying the refugees, and in a sense the institution had become an ally, both to me as the artist and to the refugees.[84]

In *3 People Paid to Lay Still inside 3 Boxes during a Party*, staged at the 2000 Havana Biennial and sometimes referred to as *Santiago Sierra Invites You for a Drink*, three Havana-based sex workers were concealed, in prone position, in horizontally placed boxes for the duration of a vernissage-cocktail party. International Biennial visitors, unaware of the sex workers' presence, used the boxes as seating benches, unwitting actors in Sierra's staged re-enactment of what art critic Julian Stallabrass accurately describes as the *already existing* "relations of power and exploitation between art-tourists and natives."[85]

Sierra has referred to himself as a "Minimalist with a guilt complex,"[86] and certainly both of these actions betray a propensity to push the vocabulary of minimalism to its breaking point. As Coco Fusco has observed, Sierra "recasts a minimalist inquiry into the relation between the viewer and mass as an investigation into the relation between viewers and 'the masses.'"[87] Claire Bishop also weighs in on Sierra's intervention into the minimalist ethos, suggesting that his inhabited cubes *literalize* the silent human presence identified by Michael Fried in his excoriation of minimalist sculpture.[88] Bishop's observation reveals not only Sierra's formal indebtedness to minimalism, but also, more importantly, his effective use of concealment as a strategy of anti-redemptive representation. In both Berlin and Havana, Sierra draws attention to the already-existing conditions of social invisibility while imposing, in place of visual access, an arrangement that implicates his audience as participants in the very context of exploitation. Thus we might suggest that where Wodiczko tends to implicate his audience as always already sympathetic witness, Sierra draws us continually into the position of perpetrator at worst and uncomfortably complicit bystander at best. Sharing with Wodiczko and Jaar a scepticism regarding the power of images to effect social change and a commitment to mobiilizing an affective register for ethical investment in the lives of others, Sierra's aesthetic strategy for engaging with difficult knowledge renders his project singular. For Sierra's art practice obstructs visual access not to create therapeutic contexts for healing and reconciliation, nor, necessarily, to foreclose the risk of spectacular indifference, but rather in order to retrace and reiterate the borders, exclusions, and injustices that render traumatic the condition of unhomeliness. The artist explains:

"There are determined forces that, in order to create order, generate borders, and this has to do with visuality. Society administers images, and it marks the path of what is visible and what is not. Therefore, the obstructions that I create delimit things that can be done and things that cannot be done. The art spectator can access any site … It's very strange to be denied entrance to an image, and I insert these wedges that put him on the other side."[89]

It is Sierra's seeming compulsion to repeat, rather than ameliorate, experiences of unbelonging and alienation that can be understood as a counter-argument to Wodiczko's therapeutic approach to trauma – a counter-argument based on the premise that melancholic attachment to suffering and loss can create a more effective, and affective, context for political agency than the reconciliatory approach favoured by Wodiczko.

Consider *Submission* (2007), a project carried out near the Mexican border town of Juárez. Infamous worldwide as a destination for poverty-stricken southern Mexicans seeking employment in the dozens of foreign-owned *maquiladora* factories that dot the landscape and hoping eventually to cross the Rio Grande into America, Juárez is also notorious for its unparalleled rates of poverty and violent crime. Ciudad Juárez is, for thousands, the place where the American dream goes to die. For the project, Sierra hired a group of local unemployed men to carve the word *SUMISION* (submission) into the land with letters each fifteen metres long, several metres away from the site where a controversial border wall was at the time scheduled to be constructed[90] and currently where dozens of homeless prospective immigrants live. Local authorities scuttled Sierra's original plan, which was to fill the hollowed letters with gasoline and set fire to them, but nevertheless the intervention – which scarred the landscape with a message of defeated (but also somehow defiant) acquiescence reminiscent of the grave-like holes dug on the coast of Spain – articulated the artist's insistence on registering the border as a gaping wound. Compare this to Wodiczko's *Tijuana Projection* of 2000, which, recall, saw local *maquiladora* workers in that border city project their stories of poverty and domestic violence onto a public monument. Both projects speak to, from, and about the Mexico–US border as a site of deprivation, humiliation, and alienation. Both call upon residents of two of Mexico's most disquieted border towns – Tijuana and Juárez – to testify to these conditions, and both imply the presence of a "Northern" audience to bear witness to the suffering endured on the Mexican side of the border. For Wodiczko, the audience's positionality of witness is contingent upon our capacity and

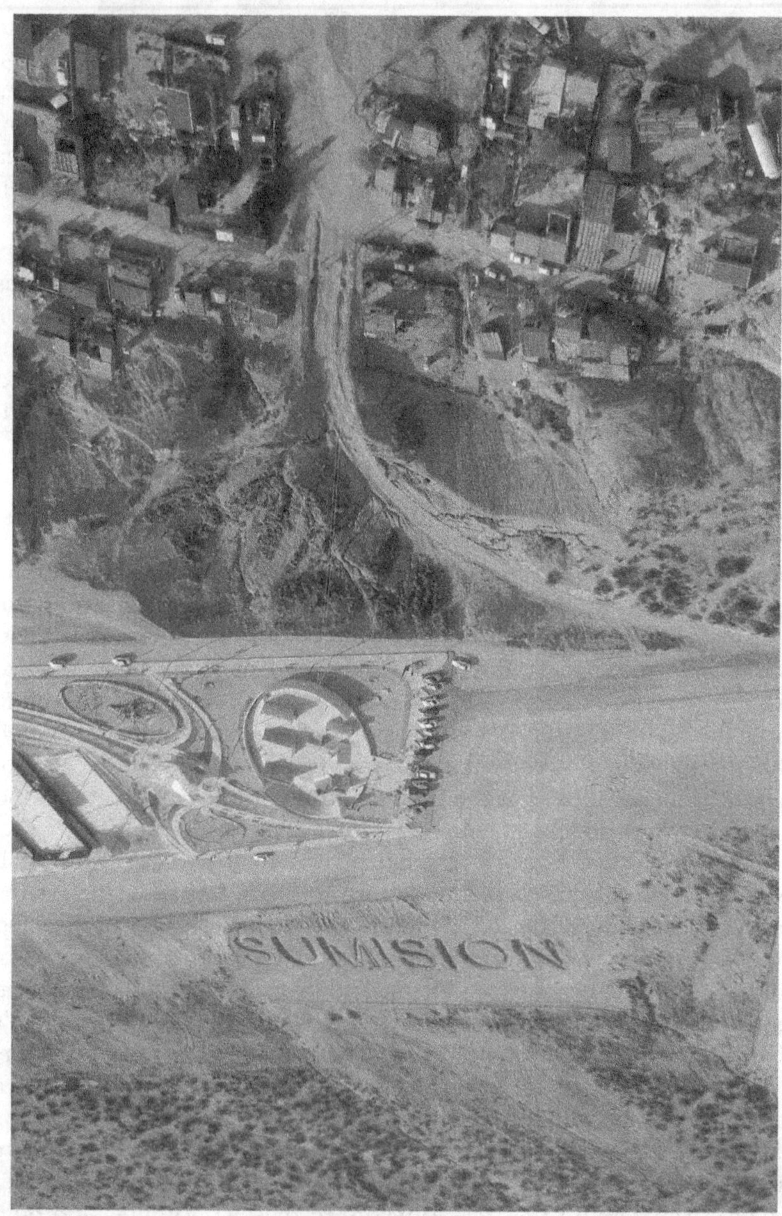

2.10 Santiago Sierra, *Submission*, Ciudad Juárez, Mexico, 2007. © Santiago Sierra; Courtesy of Lisson Gallery.

willingness to be moved by the women's testimony and reliant on our adherence to the ancient Quaker dictum that to bear witness to injustice is to bear the responsibility that comes with knowledge. Sierra, on the contrary, demonstrates an acute suspicion regarding both the efficacy of testimony as a means of generating empathy and the efficacy of art as a vehicle for galvanizing change. So whereas Wodiczko conceptualizes his art practice as a bandage that "covers and treats a wound while at the same time exposing its presence,"[91] Sierra's aesthetic strategy of engagement with traumatic experience and circumstance is, as he puts it, "to press my finger on the sore places."[92]

According to this logic, borders and boundaries, along with other markers and manifestations of socio-economic oppression and alienation, are treated as wounds that must be constantly aggravated – if only to confirm and remind us of their existence. But while this strategy does open itself to the critique of being at best a reflection of callous indifference and at worst the exploitation of what Mark Selzer refers to as "wound culture" and Eric Cazdyn calls the "new chronic,[93] Sierra's intervention must rather be understood instead as an enactment of exploitation, alienation, and submission whose motive is critique from within. From this claustrophobic space of complicity, the viewer is offered no opportunity for solace, catharsis, or false empathy based on what Kaja Silverman terms "idiopathic identification" with the suffering other. Indeed, Sierra's "blatant disregard for the niceties that most of us create in order to camouflage our unavoidable participation in a system we may find a little more than distasteful"[94] aligns his work with a contemporary trend towards reconsidering trauma theory's insistence on the merits of "working through" traumatic memory, to which we now turn.

Mapping Melancholia: Acting Out on the Border

"Spain means nothing to me – like any other country, it's an ideological construction with political effects," declared Sierra on the eve of the inauguration of the 2003 Venice Biennale, where he was representing his native country.[95] It is this contempt for national allegiance that permeates and gives meaning to the artist's installation *Wall Enclosing a Space*, which saw the Spanish pavilion transformed into a guarded fortress. A brick wall was erected just inside the entrance to the pavilion (thus facilitating entry only to the side washrooms), and the pavilion's "España" crest, affixed to the facade, was crudely covered in black plastic.

The interior was accessible through the back door, but only to those who could present a Spanish passport to a hired security guard; those permitted entry were, however, treated to nothing but the remnants of the previous year's exhibition. The action was a complex critique of both the arguably outdated national pavilion model of the Venice exhibition *and* Spain's emerging role as "border guard for Europe, in the face of migratory pressure from North Africa and Latin America."[96] As such, it captures Sierra's ongoing concern for the geopolitical conditions of exclusion, and the art world's often inadvertent (or wilfully oblivious) mirroring of these very conditions.

Sierra, of course, is not the first artist to intervene physically in a pavilion in order to critique the Venice Biennale's arguably anachronistic system of national representation as reflective of the politics of arbitrary borders and the often seedy underbelly of nationalistic patriotism. In 1976, Venetian architect Carlo Scarpa built a rubble wall to conceal the Fascist facade of the Italian pavilion, and in 1993, German-American artist Hans Haacke won the Golden Lion (shared with Nam June Paik) for *Germania*, an installation that saw a temporary wall in the building's entrance adorned with a 1934 photograph of Adolf Hitler, and the interior marble floors smashed to pieces. In fact, Santiago Sierra's intervention at Venice was itself criticized as anachronistic. As some art critics observed, since the inception of the European Union in 1993, a Spanish passport is no longer the sole privileged arbiter of access to the country.[97] But this critique largely misses Sierra's point. Certainly, holders of an EU passport (not to mention US, Canadian, and Australian citizens) would rarely (if ever) be barred entry into Spain, and many of these same privileged passport holders would have been surprised and chagrined by their seemingly random exclusion from the Spanish pavilion in 2003. It is exactly the randomness and illogicality of such moments of exclusion (rarely experienced by Western travellers, but a matter of daily humiliation for the underclasses of the global stage) that Sierra recreated for his Venice audience. And it is this persistent resolve to retrace Spain's mostly invisible but still operational lines of exclusion that renders his work as aesthetically and politically relevant in 2003 as Scarpa's condemnation of lingering Fascist tendencies was in 1976. In this way, the work also resonates strongly with another analogous work by Haacke, the 1990 installation *Freedom Is Now Simply Going to Be Sponsored – Out of Petty Cash*. While the world celebrated the fall of the Berlin Wall, Haacke erected a huge Mercedes-Benz logo atop a former East German guard tower, prompting Irit Rogoff to note: "In the middle of all the euphoria of unification, Haacke has animated the evacuated border and spatialized it as a heterotopia of internal contradictions." And, in an observation that applies equally to Sierra's 2003 Venice intervention, Rogoff continues: "This work manifests a kind of physical stamping of the terrain, an insistence on a border where everyone else is denying its existence."[98]

This emphasis on invisible borders – whether geographic, social, or economic – is indeed a recurring motif in Sierra's practice, and, as in *Wall Enclosing a Space*, Sierra's articulation of this motif often involves the literal construction of a barrier. Other instances include *68 People Paid to Block a Museum Entrance* (2000) at the Museum Contemporary Art in Pusan, Korea, and *Space Closed Off by Corrugated Metal* (2002) at London's Lisson Gallery, both of which manifest the artist's conviction that "there are immaterial walls that render unnecessary the other, brick, walls, or those of which the bricks are only the visual materialization, and redundantly so."[99] In 2001, Sierra produced *430 People Remunerated with 30 Soles per Hour* at Galería Pancho Fierro in Lima, Peru, an action during which hundreds of underprivileged local women were paid to occupy the gallery space for four hours, leaving an uncomfortably narrow corridor through which visitors were compelled to pass. Creating what art critic Katya García-Antón describes as a "sheer mass of alien presence,"[100] this work – like all of Sierra's obstructions – is perhaps best described as a macabre combination of Richard Serra's iron constructions (the controversial *Tilted Arc* of 1981, for example), Marina Abramovic and Ulay's *Imponderabilia* of 1977, and Vanessa Beecroft's *VB* performances, with Beecroft in particular providing a compelling subject of comparison. Like Sierra, Beecroft hires "models" to stage melancholic scenes of boredom verging on the painful; in both cases, the intenion is to discomfort the audience's privileged gaze. Beecroft's performances, in which groups of nude or semi-clad women stand near-motionless in public gallery spaces for hours at a time, operate, as art historian Christine Ross suggests, as "laboratories of depressed subjectivity" whose criticality lies in the failed effort of the models to perform femininity in a context that exploits the "to-be-looked-at-ness" of the gendered spectacles she creates.[101] Sierra's performances are more like laboratories of disavowed subjectivity, compelling his audience to acknowledge not its naturalized scopophilia, but rather its blindness to subjects who already publicly inhabit institutional spaces – as cleaners, guards, and in other invisible roles. As Sierra reflects, "At the Kunst Werke in Berlin they criticized me because I had people sitting for four hours a day, but they didn't realize that a little further up the hallway the guard spends eight hours a day on his feet."[102]

Such performances of disavowed subjectivity dovetail in important ways with theorizations of melancholia's agential capacity, a key example being theorist Leigh Gilmore's mobilization of Freud's distinction between mourning and melancholia to propose a politics of loss that embraces, rather than seeking to transcend, melancholic attachment to a lost object or ideal. Acknowledging that Freud considered melancholia (or "profound mourning") a pathological inability to resolve grief that he opposed to "normal mourning," she nevertheless observes Freud's eventual admission that melancholia and mourning tend to unfold simultaneously (rather than consecutively). Indeed, Freud himself demonstrates a marked uncertainty towards his own theory of melancholia, observing: "It is really only because we know so well how to explain [normal mourning] that this attitude does not seem to us pathological" and, further, that "melancholics" have a "keener eye for the truth than other people who are not melancholic."[103] For Gilmore, Freud's own ambivalence opens a space for reconceptualizing the persistence of melancholic attachment as a useful lever for politicizing and, importantly, depathologizing, responses to trauma:

> How can melancholia end when the effects that produce it cannot themselves be said to be sufficiently past? … For melancholia to end, the forces and processes that structure the melancholic's narcissism … must, too, in some way, cease to operate. In the absence of that transformation (which might include reparations or other forms of justice), I would want to speak of a *will to melancholia*, of an embrace and extension of melancholia in which melancholia becomes a technique for knowing the relation of the present to the past [and] becomes a kind of testimony.[104]

Gilmore's evocative proposal for a "will to melancholia" as its own kind of testimony, which quite accurately describes Santiago Sierra's aesthetic strategy for bearing witness to traumatic experience, also captures what has become a prevalent impetus to undo trauma theory's insistence on "working through" loss and suffering, which arguably traffics in facile harmonization and premature closure. According to this line of reasoning, working through is understood as "a kind of extreme redemptive mode"[105] of response that can best be avoided through the deliberate acting out of melancholia's sense of loss. If, in other words, "acting out" constitutes a refusal to let go, then this refusal becomes understood as a powerful agent for social and political activism; as David Eng and David Kazanjian suggest, "melancholic attachments to loss might depathologize those attachments, making visible not only their social bases but also their creative, unpredictable, political aspects."[106]

What renders Santiago Sierra's art practice a critical catalyst for reconceptualizing the role of art in conveying traumatic experience is precisely this attachment to representing borders as sites of xenophobic exclusion and forced containment. Sierra's ongoing, even compulsive, effort to irritate already existing wounds, to situate audiences as complicit in processes of oppression and disenfranchisement, and to refuse to offer avenues of harmonization and closure, therefore constitutes his practice as a powerful counter-argument to Krzysztof Wodiczko's privileging of testimony and recovery. This is not to suggest, however, that Sierra's melancholic aesthetic somehow trumps Wodiczko's, or (ironically) resolves the myriad questions surrounding art's capacity to respond to difficult knowledge. Indeed, both Wodiczko and Sierra offer ways for engaging what Kristeva calls a "paradoxical community," constituted by "foreigners who are reconciled with themselves to the extent they recognize themselves as foreigners."[107] In other words, both artists ask us to reconcile to the *impossibility* of complete reconciliation in the formation of ethical self–other relations, and it is this paradox that gives ethical purchase to the unmaking of home in contemporary art.

3
Unhomely Archives

> What does it mean to be at home in the world? Home may not be where the heart is, nor even the hearth. Home may be a place of estrangement that becomes the necessary space of engagement; it may represent a desire for accommodation marked by an attitude of deep ambivalence toward one's location. Home may be a mode of living made into a metaphor of survival ... It is as if home is territory of both disorientation and relocation, with all the fragility and fecundity implied by such a double take.
>
> Homi K. Bhabha, "Halfway House"

Lida Abdul's video *Housewheel* (2003) follows the Afghani artist as she walks and runs through the streets of inner-city Los Angeles, dragging a doll-sized white plaster house behind her with a rope. As it is jolted along, the house becomes dented, chipped, and battered; within minutes, it is reduced to scattered, abandoned pieces. Created during the Taliban regime while Abdul was living in exile, the work is a poignant performance of Gaston Bachelard's observation that homes "are in us as much as we are in them."[1] As much as we consider (or long for) home as a space that we occupy, "home" is also an entity – whether material or phantasmatic; whether ancestral land, childhood residence, or dream house – that occupies *us*, taking up residence in our identifications, our memories, our imaginations, our dreams, and sometimes our nightmares. But, as Abdul's performance demonstrates, this reciprocal occupation can also be a dangerously unstable one, particularly for those vulnerable to contingency – the exile, the migrant, the asylum seeker, the homeless – for whom home exists simultaneously as a site of provisionality, a lost territory of belonging, and a tenuously sustained but tenaciously held memory. And it is the precariousness of this reciprocal occupation – performed by Abdul and theorized by Bhabha ("home is territory of both disorientation and relocation, with all the fragility and fecundity implied by such a double take") – that itself occupies the present chapter.

The unhomely aesthetics of contemporary art have emerged as a strong catalyst for ethically grounded intersubjective relations based on what Kaja Silverman theorizes as the heteropathic acknowledgment of our capacity to be "wounded by others' wounds."[2] Neither nostalgic nor fatalistic, the articulation of the unhomely in contemporary art visualizes home as a site of what, in this chapter, I will call melancholic archivization – a site, in other words, of contingent, dynamic, and tenacious dwelling. Drawing from contemporary theorizations of the archive as a tenuous repository for traces of (often suppressed) histories, we can begin to see how the archive can be constructed in such a way as to give loss a material home. Concentrating primarily on a large-scale installation produced by the Colombian artist Doris Salcedo for the Istanbul Biennial in 2003, I suggest in what follows that this work – and Salcedo's practice broadly conceived – radically reconsiders the archive's putative status as a "home" for memory, at the same time figuring home as an (impossible) archive for memories of loss, terror, and displacement.

Salcedo is a Bogotá-based sculptor whose career (spanning 1985 to the present) has primarily involved transforming testimonies of political violence in her home country into abstracted sculptural assemblages that bear witness to suffering and loss. Engaging with both first-hand and archival interviews with torture victims and relatives of the dead and "disappeared" of Colombia's so-called "Dirty War" as direct sources of inspiration for her work, the artist nevertheless insists, "I do not illustrate testimonies"[3] – and it is indeed the oblique nature of her practice that charges the work with richly associative affective dimensions. Salcedo works mainly with domestic furniture – sometimes worn and discarded, and sometimes manufactured to the artist's specifications – that is fused awkwardly but painstakingly with materials as fragile as lace, silk thread, and human hair, and as rigid (but equally redolent) as nails, concrete, and human bones. The result is a series of installations that capture both the mutilating, dehumanizing nature of political violence and the domestic, deeply intimate consequences of civil strife. Since 2001, Salcedo's work has become increasingly installation-based, employing gallery spaces and site-specific locations to create environments infused with politics and histories that reach beyond the specificity of Colombia to tackle global issues of racism, inequity, suffering, and displacement. But even in these later works, Salcedo continues to contemplate the precariousness of home, the politics of belonging, and the artist's capacity to register the pain of others in ways that will generate empathetically unsettling practices of ethical witnessing.

In ways reminiscent of the strategies of Santiago Sierra, Doris Salcedo draws attention to and emphasizes traumatic sites of pain, suffering, alienation, and injustice, as if to carry (and pass on) the burden of witness that such attention requires. But in her own articulations of radical unsettlement, and specifically in her depictions of the precariousness of human dwelling, Salcedo eschews melancholic re-enactments of suffering in favour of aesthetic interventions that enact a constant transgression of the borders that would otherwise seal person from place and impede comprehension of the suffering of the other. In her practice, Salcedo begins to reconceptualize failure – the failure to communicate, the failure to belong, the failure to heal the wounds of injustice – as a source of agency rather than futility and immobility. Treating empathy itself as a profoundly unsettling entanglement of (mis)understandings, Salcedo conveys the notion that it is precisely our inability to fully comprehend the enormity of the walls separating "self from home"[4] that compels us as viewers into an ethically and affectively charged viewing experience.

An "Anarchival" Impulse

In the summer of 2003, Salcedo participated in the Eighth International Istanbul Biennial with an untitled installation of 1,150 chairs piled into an empty lot in a working-class residential-commercial neighbourhood of the city.[5] This jumbled mass of modest wooden kitchen chairs, of varying shapes, sizes, and degrees of wear and tear, was jammed tightly between two neighbouring buildings, reaching three stories high and somehow achieving a flush vertical surface that belied its seemingly haphazard instability.[6] The intention of the installation was to reproduce what Salcedo calls a "topography of war,"

> so deeply inscribed in everyday life that, in spite of the fact that it represents an extreme experience, the point where normal conditions of life end and war begins can no longer be clearly discerned. An image where the private and the political collide, producing a complete sense of

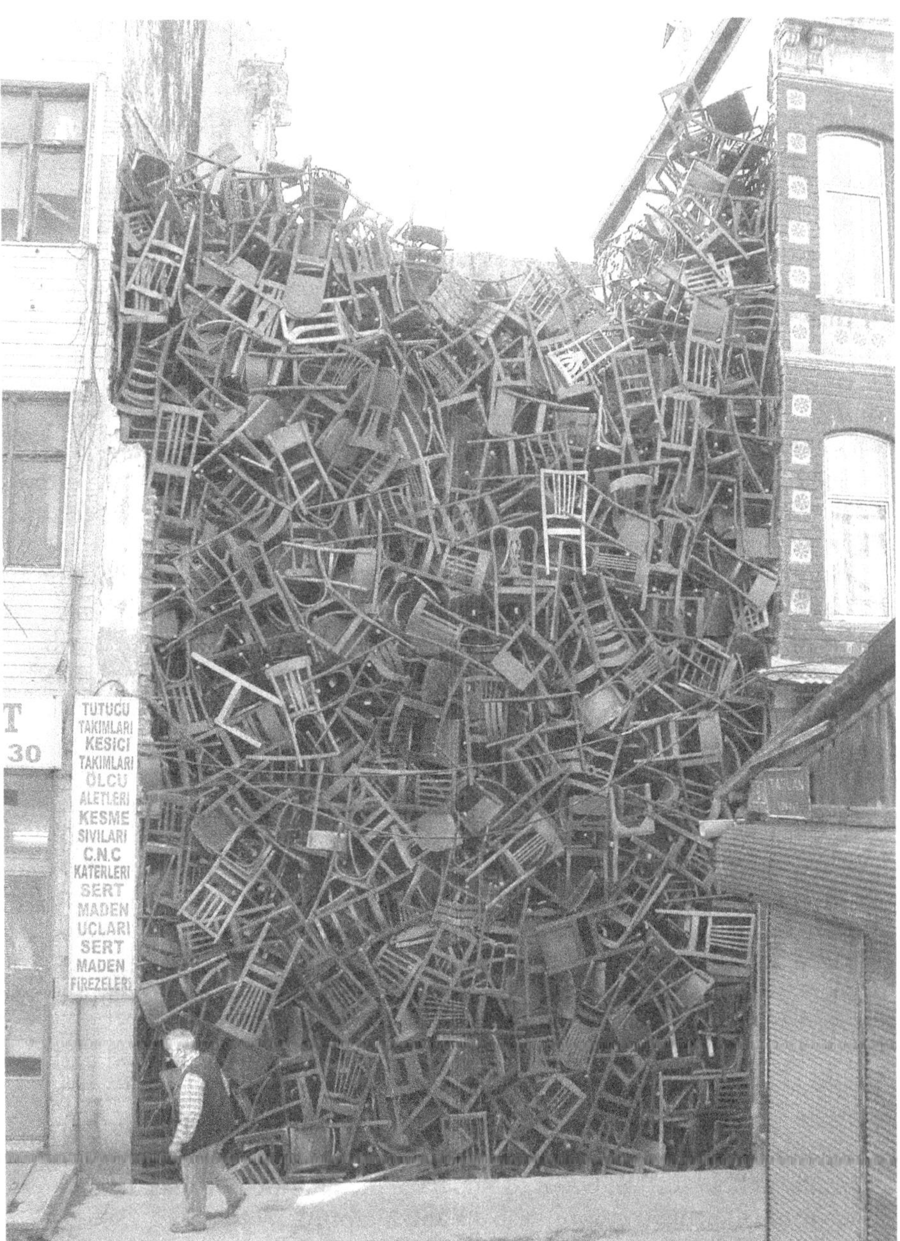

3.1 Doris Salcedo, *Untitled*, 2003. One thousand one hundred and fifty wooden chairs, 8th International Istanbul Biennial, Istanbul, 2003. Photo: Muammar Yanmaz. Courtesy of Alexander and Bonin, New York.

> disorientation [reflecting] the complex and difficult relations that emerge in contested spaces or sites of war.[7]

To reveal the catastrophic consequences of the inevitable collision between the private and the public in times of war and upheaval has been an ongoing imperative in Salcedo's work. Here, the theme is materialized with a profusion of disorienting collisions, both material and metaphorical. The chairs, to begin, appear caught in a frozen state of perpetual collision, producing an effect of sheer vertiginous tension that is only heightened by the unsettling juxtaposition of the orderly, flush, perfectly enclosed installation with the chaotic jumble of objects contained within. Like a meticulously assembled house of cards, the structure appears ready at any moment to collapse. Furthermore, there is a disorientation of our desire to shape meaning from this work. On one hand, it seems to offer a surfeit of detail: the installation, we are clearly informed, laments the chaotic, uncertain inhabitation of contested spaces – a lament that is invested with indexical detail by the chairs, each worn by use, each with a history of belonging that subtly transforms 1,150 unique objects into traces of absent human presence. But this abundance of referentiality clashes with an undeniable dearth of contextual information, leaving questions to hang as awkwardly as the chairs themselves. What (or whom) do these chairs represent? Are they stand-ins for lives lost to violence, or do they represent the domestic spaces left vacant by civilians fleeing war? Are we meant to infer a garbage heap of abandoned furnishings, a pile of personal belongings suggesting a pogrom or massacre, or perhaps an entire house demolished by aerial bombardment? There are no certain answers to these questions; not even a title is supplied to provide context – surprisingly, from an artist whose sculptures and installations frequently bear evocative, multilayered titles that add nuance and complex associations. Here, the indexicality of the chairs is as frustratingly elusive as an untraceable footprint in the sand: each an anonymous relic of lives lived, together they point us towards a past that cannot be reconstituted with any certainty. As such, these chairs both reflect and challenge what Hal Foster calls the "archival impulse" of contemporary art. But in order to better comprehend the significance of this challenge, let us first look briefly at how the last twenty years have seen the archive itself become a site of challenged authority in art and literature.

The archive, Jacques Derrida reminds us, is an inherently unstable repository for traces of the past. Although it clings resolutely to its claim of unmediated objectivity, the archive is inevitably a construction of its makers – "archive" derives from *arkhé*, which denotes "origin" but also "authority."[8] Produced by and within a complex matrix of power relations and structures, the archive is therefore predisposed to privilege certain historical records over others; archivization, in other words, is as much an act of suppression as of preservation. But because the archive is perpetually guilty of omission, it is also perpetually open to contestation. And although the archive aspires to be a direct conduit to the past, the origin to which it is etymologically beholden remains inexorably elusive. The archive reaches for, but never manages to grasp, the totality of knowledge that seems to hover just out of its reach. It is this set of irresolvable internal contradictions that makes the archive, according to Derrida, a "feverish" site of knowledge production.

Reflections on the fallibility of the archive have tended to follow two courses, one of which has been to contest archival authority by proposing alternative sources of collective knowledge. This is the strategy proposed by performance theorist Diana Taylor, who builds a framework for theorizing the unique role played by performance in the transmission of memory. Taylor distinguishes between the archive and what she terms the repertoire (performance, oral storytelling, song, dance, etc.), which enacts the "embodied memory" of "ephemeral, nonreproducible knowledge" and therefore encompasses all that which cannot be contained within the archive.[9] Resisting the imposition of a binary relationship between what might be simplistically understood as the hegemonic power of the archive and the counterhegemonic challenge of the repertoire (the repertoire, she notes for instance, is also a highly mediated form of transmission, and embodied performances are no less likely to contribute to repressive social systems), Taylor posits that the archive and the repertoire "exist in a constant state of interaction" which, however, is occluded by a tendency "to treat all phenomena as textual" – a tendency that necessarily privileges the archive. Taylor's reading of the archive as an over-privileged storehouse of historical understanding is compelling in its insistence on tracing those sources of knowledge that exceed or resist current practices of archivization, but it does not fully address the possibility that the archive itself, whose authority and privilege are based on inherently unstable underpinnings, is equally susceptible to critique and dismantling from within. In other words, the aporetic condition of the archive – as a site of origins and authority structurally unable to achieve its own mandate – makes it particularly vulnerable to transgression and contestation.

For the past twenty years, a diverse and international body of artists – including Walid Raad, Allan Sekula, Christian Boltanski, and Tacita Dean – have been examining the archive's fraught role as a keeper of collective knowledge. Inspired by theoretical reassessments of the archive by philosophers such as Derrida and Foucault (but also Gayatri Spivak, Paul Ricoeur, Giorgio Agamben and Pierre Nora), these artists have themselves become the subject of art-historical analysis for their capacity to dispute archival authority and address the suppression of marginalized histories therein, while reconfiguring the archive as a porous, dynamic, even ephemeral cultural institution. Perhaps the most robust analysis to date of the so-called "archival impulse" in contemporary art comes from art historian and theorist Hal Foster, who argues that contemporary archival practices are marked by a tendency to treat "information" as "a kind of ultimate readymade"[10] (think, for instance, of the altars and kiosks of Thomas Hirschhorn and Sam Durant's critical revisions of mid-century modern design principles.) Not to be confused with Nicolas Bourriaud's category of "postproduction" in contemporary art, which describes current practices of editing, cutting, dubbing, and otherwise manipulating existing cultural artefacts and products,[11] the archival impulse (which Foster also passingly but provocatively refers to as an *an*archival impulse) "is concerned less with absolute origins than with obscure traces [and] drawn to unfulfilled beginnings or incomplete projects."[12] As such, according to Foster, contemporary archival practices both *manipulate* and *produce* archives, underscoring "the nature of all archival materials as found yet constructed, factual yet fictive, public yet private."[13] For Foster, these artists – who challenge both the parameters and the authority of the archive – assume a critical stance towards public archives that emerges from a shared sense of official cultural memory as a failed project. For instance, Thomas Hirschhorn's monuments to philosophers Spinoza, Bataille, and Deleuze are staged in marginalized urban spaces like the red-light district of Amsterdam and the North African quarter of Avignon in order to re-evaluate both *what* is remembered and *who* is charged with the authority of remembering, and therefore temporarily transform the logic of the monument from a "univocal" structure that conceals social and political antagonisms into a "counter-hegemonic archive" where these antagonisms are offered space to unfold.[14]

Foster concludes that the production of alternative archives in the practices of artists like Hirschhorn and Dean is as much a utopian venture as a critical project, manifesting a collective desire "to recoup failed visions in art, literature, philosophy and everyday life into possible scenarios of alternative kinds of social relations."[15] The archival impulse, he suggests, produces "construction sites" instead of "excavation sites," and thus represents a shift away from the melancholic cultural practices of the 1990s, which treat "the historical as little more than traumatic."[16] Here, Foster is intimating a critique, fully elaborated in his 1996 book *The Return of the Real,* of what he regards as the problematic troping of trauma in contemporary art. In that earlier text, Foster argued that trauma has overwhelmed aesthetic practices that obsessively produce and reproduce the abject or obscene body (as in, for example, the anal fixations of the late Mike Kelley), exhibiting little more than an embrace of the Lacanian real as respite from the disembodied discourses of deconstruction.[17] Acknowledging cursorily that the "return of the real" in contemporary art is in large part fuelled by the ravaging effects of war, poverty, AIDS, and other phenomena that have arguably conspired to render the twentieth century (and, thus far, the twenty-first) the age of trauma, Foster nontheless warns that when all experience is filtered through the language of trauma, the "politics of alterity" devolves into the apolitical realm of nihility.[18] However, in his resolve to welcome the "constructive" element of contemporary art's archival impulse as a reprieve from the "excavations" of trauma culture, Foster arguably glosses over the rich and potentially transformative effects of negotiating an archival aesthetics within the context of melancholic agency.[19] For when employed as an aesthetic strategy of engagement with the past, melancholy has the capacity to mobilize what Jean-Luc Nancy might term an "inoperative community" of loss. As Butler suggests: "Loss becomes condition and necessity for a certain sense of community, where community does not overcome the loss, where community *cannot* overcome the loss without losing the very sense of itself as community. And if we say this second truth about the place where belonging is possible, then pathos is not negated, but it turns out to be oddly fecund, paradoxically productive."[20]

It is this mobilization of loss as "condition and necessity for a certain sense of community" that, in contrast to Foster's privileging of "construction sites" over "excavation sites," enables contemporary archival practices to exhibit a uniquely *anarchival* impulse, underwritten by the premise and promise of melancholic agency. Employing the language (and sometimes the practice) of excavation to reimagine Foster's proposal for "alternative kinds of social relations," certain contemporary art practices activate what I am calling unhomely archives.

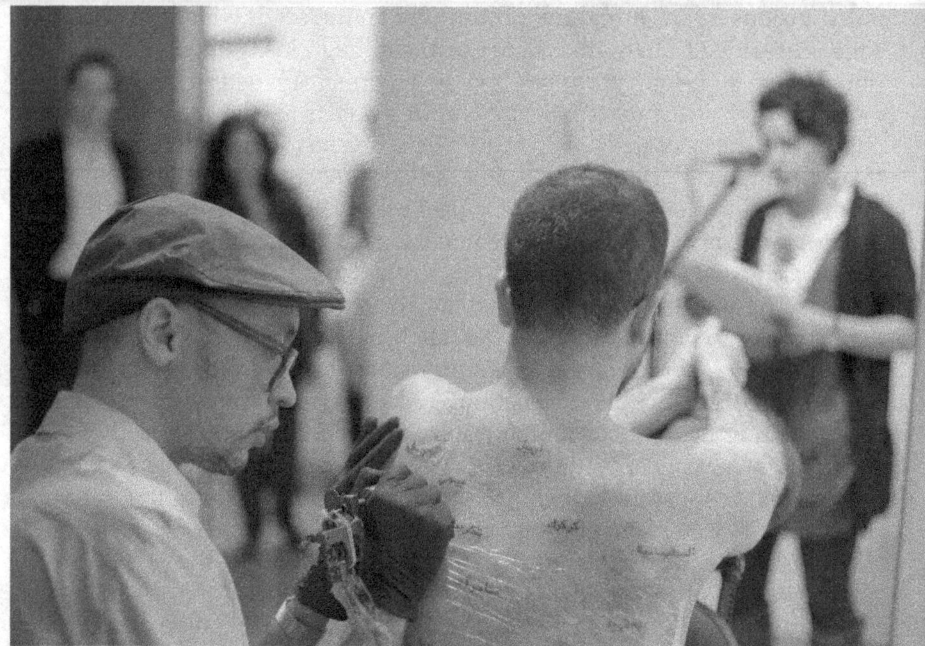

3.2 Wafaa Bilal, detail from *And Counting …*, performance, 2010. Photo: Brad Farwell. Courtesy of the artist, Driscoll Babcock Galleries and Lawrie Shabibi Gallery.

Charged with bearing witness to the injustices of the past and present, these practices reconceive the archive not just as a repository, but as an open wound, in constant need of diligent attention – an archive that challenges its own affirmative mandate, instead recognizing itself to be contingent, fragmented, and ephemeral. In essence, the unhomely archive takes on the task that Michel Foucault assigns to heritage: not "an acquisition, a possession that grows and solidifies," but instead "an unstable assemblage of faults, fissures, and heterogeneous layers that threaten the fragile inheritor from within or from underneath."[21]

The twenty-first century has witnessed numerous works of art that align productively with the concept of melancholic archivisation. Lida Abdul's performance-video *Housewheel*, which opened this chapter, materializes loss through its traces, as does Iraqi artist Wafaa Bilal's *And Counting ...* (2010), a project motivated by the death of the artist's brother during a CIA drone attack at a checkpoint in Kufa, Iraq. During a twenty-four-hour performance at the Elizabeth Foundation for the Arts in New York City intended to address the West's indifference to thousands of civilian deaths during the most recent Iraq war, Bilal had his back tattooed with an unbordered map indicating, in Arabic script, Iraq's major cities. While volunteers took turns reading out the names of American and Iraqi casualties, thousands of dots were then tattooed onto the artist's back – one for each soldier or citizen, in the vicinity of the cities where they died. The five thousand dead American soldiers are represented in permanent red ink, while each of the 100,000 Iraqi casualties is memorialized with green ultraviolent ink, invisible except under black light.[22] In this way, the artist's own body has become a melancholic archive of sorts, a reliquary that not only accommodates but also sheds light on the enormity of violent loss, so much of which tends to go underreported in mainstream Western media. Finally, in the practice of Doris Salcedo, melancholic archivization becomes a process of reassembling the faults and fissures of Foucauldian archaeology in order to bear witness to the material losses they trace. In Salcedo's artworks (as in those of Abdul and Bilal), the archive takes on the role of silent, incomplete, and unstable witness to traumatic loss, whose existence nevertheless signals an insistent desire to house our memories, however imperfectly. For if "archive fever," as Derrida suggests, is a sort of homesickness – an "irrepressible desire to return to the origin"[23] – then Doris Salcedo's unhomely archives remind us that this home we seek cannot be sustained as a stable source of identification and attachment, instead articulating a relationship to home that is as contingent, embodied, and performative as Diana Taylor's repertoire and as utopian in its efforts to reinvigorate social relations as Hal Foster's archival impulse.

Memory, Home, and the Body

The concept of melancholic archiving animates much of Doris Salcedo's practice, from early sculptural assemblages of domestic furniture to large-scale installations such as the Istanbul installation. In her practice, the archive challenges its own ontological certainty while nevertheless acknowledging a cultural desire to continue building storehouses for our precious, and precarious, memories of loss. In Istanbul, this challenge to how we bear witness to loss and trauma is articulated via a crumpled, chaotic, and precarious home space that struggles but inevitably fails to accommodate its own memories. Salcedo's work – driven, as she suggests, "by this need to try and fail, over and over"[24] – reconceptualizes failure as both a ceaseless process of building intersubjective connections and a challenge to the tendency to conflate empathy with identification. In Salcedo's work, the motif of the wooden chair in particular draws palpable links between the precariousness of occupation, the vulnerability of human existence, and the fallibility of memory, facilitating a rich set of associations between memory, home, and the human body as structures of inhabitation and belonging. As a familiar piece of domestic furniture that is so often imbued with an aura of personal belonging (I'm thinking here of my mother's favourite sewing chair, or the seat to which I inevitably gravitate at dinnertime), as furniture that bears the wear of intimate human contact, and as an object whose design (back, seat, legs) seems even to mimic the human form, conforming to the shape of the body at rest and designed to accommodate human dimensions, the chair (and the empty chair especially) is unique in its uncanny capacity to evoke the human body. Indeed, so saturated is the chair with references to the body that it has become a fairly standard motif in memorial projects. In September of 2011, 2,753 chairs were installed on the lawn at New York City's Bryant Park to mark the tenth anniversary of the World Trade Center disaster, while in Oklahoma City, 168 chairs have been permamently installed to remember victims of the 1995 bombing of the A.P. Murray Federal Building.[25] In such spaces of mournful commemoration, as in Salcedo's work, chairs occupy a threefold purpose of rendering the absent body a palpable presence – as metonym, indexical trace,[26] and symbolic reference.[27]

What differentiates Salcedo's practice is that her spaces are not only uncanny, unhomely even, but indeed uninhabitable. Salcedo's chairs materialize a series of *unincorporable* traces that, to quote Walter Benjamin, "seize hold of a memory as it flashes up in a moment of danger."[28] Unlike the Oklahoma City Memorial, which invites survivors and relatives to occupy the empty chairs and to seek solace in this act of occupation and identification, Salcedo's sculptures and installations offer neither consolation nor the opportunity to assume the position of the victim. A pertinent example is an untitled sculptural work from 2008, one in an ongoing series of pieces in which furniture is eerily impaled with rebar and encased in concrete. Here, concrete fills a wooden chair and the space surrounding it in a way that inevitably recalls Rachel Whiteread's furniture casts, particularly *Untitled (One Hundred Spaces)*

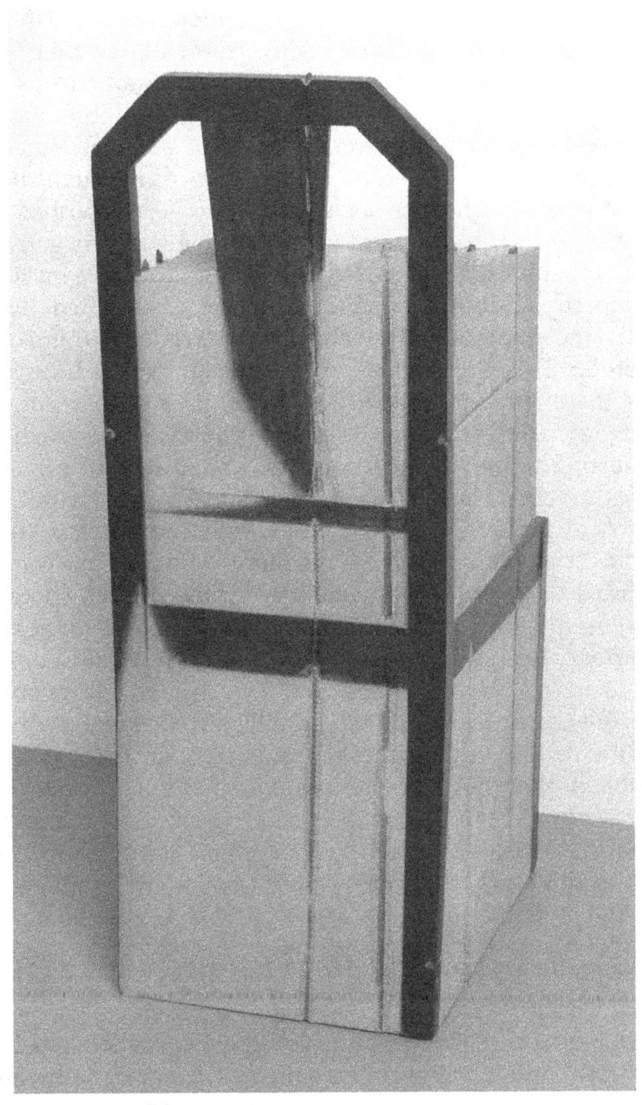

3.3 Doris Salcedo, *Untitled*, 2008. Wood, metal, and concrete, 39⅜ × 16½ × 18½ in. / 100 × 42 × 47 cm. Photo: Todd White Art Photography. Courtesy of Alexander and Bonin, New York.

(1995) – an installation of resin casts of the spaces underneath one hundred school chairs (itself a critical update on Bruce Nauman's influential *A Cast of the Space under My Chair* of 1965).[29] Like Salcedo's concrete-encased chair, Whiteread's installation simultaneously marks and unmarks the memory it conveys, tracing the forgotten detritus that accrues in the constant accumulation of archival material.[30] In Salcedo's work, however, these investigations of negative space take on additional melancholic resonance. With a self-described debt to Gordon Matta-Clark, who likewise drew attention to negative, often uninhabitable spaces,[31] Salcedo treats negative space as a metaphor for the space occupied by subjects whose presence is ignored, denied, or contested – the immigrant, the exile, the displaced, the imprisoned, the disappeared.[32] Salcedo's chair, muted and immobilized, furthermore imagines these subjects trapped in scenes of imprisonment, torture, and interrogation.[33] And here, another comparison is extremely relevant. Referring to the "radical muteness" of Salcedo's untitled furniture pieces, art critic Nancy Princenthal draws a parallel with Krzysztof Wodiczko's *Mouthpiece*, discussed above. Both, she suggests, "force language and silence to occupy the same place"[34] But here the comparison is complicated by Wodiczko's commitment to "fearless speech" – by his undeterred belief in art's capacity to create devices that will give the disenfranchised and traumatized "a possibility of developing their capacity to speak."[35] Doris Salcedo, on the contrary, creates spaces not simply of silence, but of utter unspeakability. To that end, her work resonates with the role of the witness as understood by Giorgio Agamben, who maintains that "whoever assumes the charge of bearing witness … knows that he or she must bear witness in the name of the impossibility of bearing witness."[36] And it is this impossibility of witnessing – precisely, in this work, the impossibility of inhabiting the space of the victim – that renders Salcedo's work an exercise in unsettling processes of (over)identification with the suffering of the other.

In this way, Salcedo's practice also recalls and enriches historian Dominick LaCapra's notion of "empathetic unsettlement" – an idea that bears rehearsing here. In his investigations of the ways in which collective traumatic experiences mark history, historiography, and critical theory, and how these disciplines in turn shape cultural registrations of trauma, LaCapra is especially interested in how historians – particularly in the context of Holocaust studies – record, translate, or otherwise bear witness to catastrophe. Applying Freud's psychoanalytic insights into the processing of traumatic memories to the production of history (and, by extension, to other cultural practices of representation), LaCapra identifies two approaches to historiography that correspond to a subject's propensity to "act out" or "work through" traumatic experience.[37] LaCapra uses "working through" to describe the practice of "objectivist" historicism, which seeks to establish critical distance in order to uncover documented, evidentiary truths. "Acting out," conversely, is a symptom of the radical constructivist approach to history, which eschews objectivity in order to pursue emotional and experiential links to the past. LaCapra is critical of both – the working-through method for delivering totalizing, "spiritually uplifting" accounts of historical experiences that risk premature or facile closure, and the acting-out model for its tendency to "speak in the other's voice" as either "surrogate victim or perpetrator."[38] The challenge is to develop what he terms empathetically unsettling strategies that will respond ethically to histories of suffering by encouraging emotional investment while simultaneously recognizing the spatio-temporal gap separating survivors of trauma and the interlocutors to whom stories of traumatic experience are told.

This concept of empathetic unsettlement aligns usefully with Kaja Silverman's idea of heteropathic recollection, which calls upon the mediating party or secondary witness to "participate in the desires, struggles, and sufferings of the other" while relinquishing the assumption of "psychic access to what does not 'belong' to us."[39] Silverman is especially concerned with visual cultures of memory, and in particular the ways in which art can mediate a relationship between the suffering other and the viewing spectator, who "can be brought to identify at a distance with bodily coordinates which are ... markedly divergent from his or her own."[40] For Silverman, such a relationship can be facilitated by art practices that acknowledge that "it is not possible to 'remember' someone else's memories," and that instead perform a sort of memory work that remembers "imperfectly." Silverman identifies two modes of self–other identification: "idiopathic" identification, which forms an incorporative, assimilative, even annihilatory relationship with the other; and "heteropathic" identification, which exteriorizes, rather than interiorizes, one's position in relation to the other.[41] Acknowledging some congruence with Bertolt Brecht's theatrical model for counteracting "crude empathy" with the "alienation effect," she challenges what she considers his "adversarial relation to identification," instead insisting on the value of identification as "an agency of psychic and social change."[42] Thus for Silverman, certain aesthetic practices have the capacity to facilitate ethical relations that validate otherwise neglected subject positions when these practices foreclose on the tendency to seek idiopathic identification and insist instead on relations based on heteropathic recollection – the introduction of the "'not me' into my memory reserve."[43] The goal of ethical aesthetic enterprises, she insists, must be to facilitate heteropathic forms of identification: to designate "the scene of representation as radically discontinuous with the world of the spectator."[44] Silverman points specifically to Chris Marker's 1982 film *Sans soleil* as a work that conveys the impossibility of accessing authentic memories, while creating the conditions for the past to "reverberate within" the spectator in the present.[45] I'd like to suggest that even more so, Salcedo's empathetically unsettling sculptures, which preclude any desire an audience might have to occupy the position of the traumatized subject idiopathically, facilitate precisely the heteropathic processes of identification and recollection advocated by Silverman. Presenting domestic spaces torn asunder by acts of violence, Salcedo creates the conditions for her audience to inhabit not the traumatized spaces of uninhabitability, but perhaps a more nuanced understanding of home's precarious status as a space of safety and belonging.

The *Casa Viuda (Widowed House)* series of 1992–5 clarifies this point. The series – which features narrow, weathered wooden doors, combined with fragments of other furniture and embedded with cloth, zippers, and bones – invokes the violent invasion of the political into domestic spaces, insisting that in times of war, the spaces of home are perpetually threatened by intrusion (the title, of course, is evocative in this respect). Itself an unhomely archive of the traumatizing domestic consequences of political violence (inscribed into each piece, according to Salcedo, is a specific testimony from a survivor of the Dirty War), *La Casa Viuda* does not narrate stories of loss and upheaval but instead conveys "a place transformed by pain."[46] Thus the first in the series, *La Casa Viuda I*, recalls the testimony of a young boy who, after being warned by his parents not to open the front door to strangers, did so – only to have his home invaded by paramilitary troops and his father assassinated on the doorstep.[47] An oblique reference to this testimony, the sculpture consists of a framed wooden door abutted by a section of a chair partially wrapped in a gauzy lace that appears to cling to, even disappear into, the wood. Here, it is clear that the door, that threshold between home and not-home designed both to open us out to the world and to protect us from it in times of trouble, has been divested

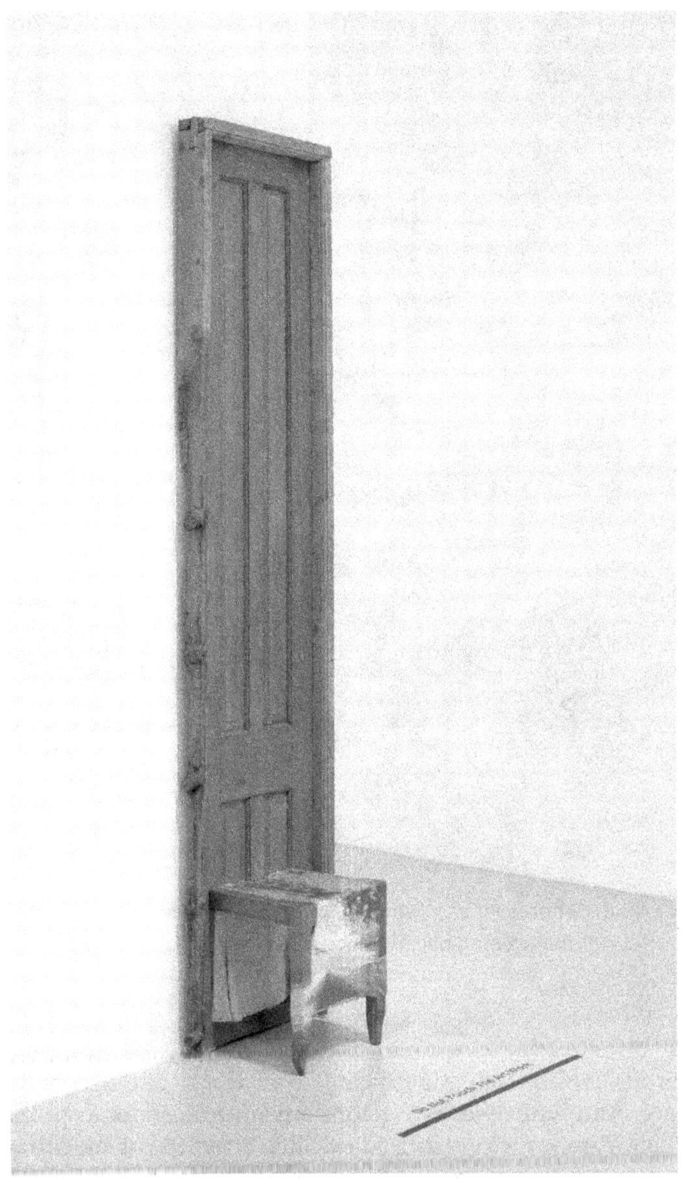

3.4 Doris Salcedo, *La Casa Viuda I*, 1992. Wood and fabric, 257.8 × 38.7 × 59.7 cm. Collection Worcester Art Museum, Worcester. Courtesy of Alexander and Bonin, New York.

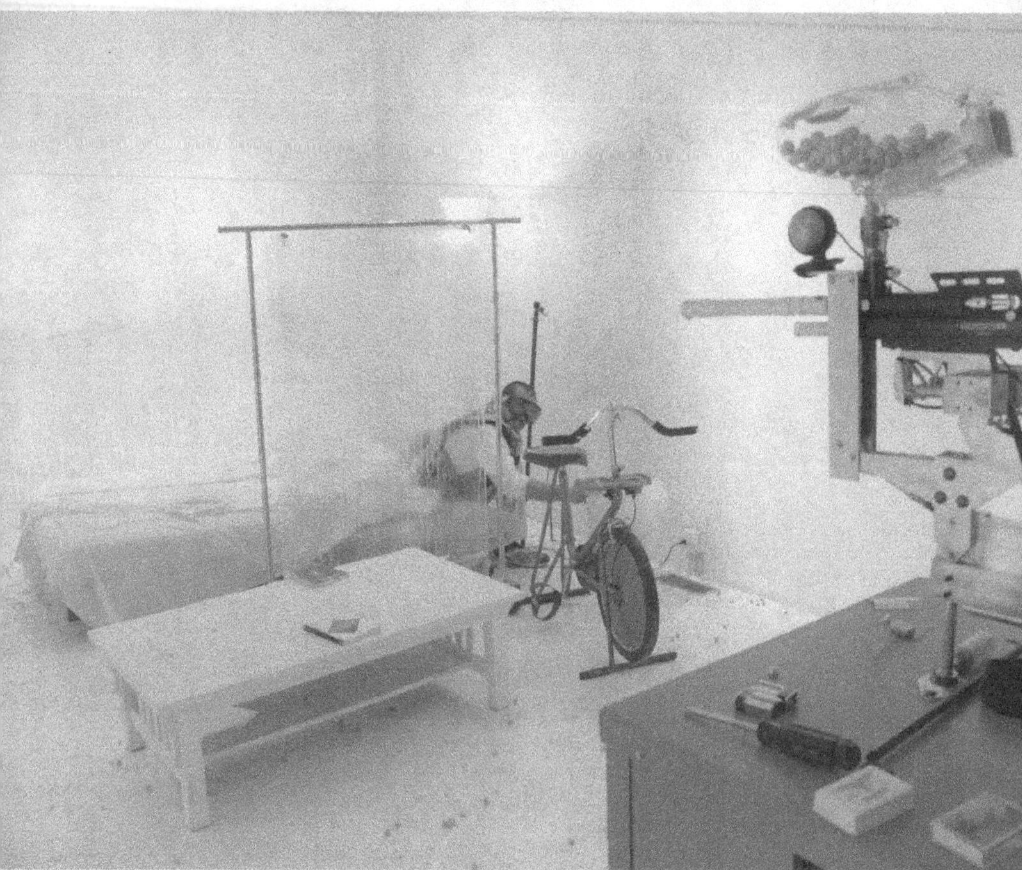

3.5 Wafaa Bilal, detail from *Domestic Tension*, performance, 2007. © Wafaa Bilal. Courtesy of the artist, Driscoll Babcock Galleries and Lawrie Shabibi Gallery.

of its purpose, fixed to an impermeable wall as if to underscore its own impotence. And while we, as viewers, are left to wonder as to the role of the chair – are we witnessing a last-ditch effort to bar the intruders? a lifeless body slumped against the door? – we are confronted with an unmistakable sense of terror and loss inscribed into the very fabric of the materials.

Recalling Santiago Sierra's obstructive installations and actions, the doors of *Casa Viuda* exist in the space of the gallery not as passages, but as barriers and blockages. The intimate space of silence that forms around these mute sculptures becomes, inevitably, a context in which the desire to experience the pain of another is constantly engaged and just as constantly frustrated. But to better explore the complex role of obstruction in activating the unhomely aesthetics of contemporary art, let us look at another contemporary art project that explores and conveys the visceral, corporeal ways in which war invades and violates the presumed safety of the home. The Iraqi artist Wafaa Bilal is intimately familiar with war's pernicious tendency to invade and violate the presumed safety of the home, having fled his homeland during the first Gulf War in 1991. In *Domestic Tension/Shoot an Iraqi* (2007), Bilal recreated the experience of living in a war zone when he spent thirty-one days and nights in Chicago's FlatFile Galleries. During this period, the artist was under twenty-four-hour live Web camera surveillance; visitors to his website were able to watch and converse with him online, and they were also free to aim and fire yellow paintballs with a remote controlled gun (reminiscent of the technology employed in the killing of the artist's brother). Restaging the experience of constant bombardment on civilian populations and broadcasting the ensuing wreckage in the intimate setting that he had constructed in the gallery, Bilal aimed, like Salcedo, to draw attention to the devastation that political friction wreaks on domestic settings. By the conclusion of the performance-installation, Bilal's room and personal effects had suffered substantial damage inflicted by an eager army of paintball snipers, and the artist himself was reduced to sleepless nights spent crouching behind the bed wearing a crash helmet – all of which amounted to a traumatic re-enactment of life under siege signalling the border between home and the world to be a dangerously porous space of conflict and negotiation. To the extent that Bilal invites his audience to play the role of perpetrator, he effectively forestalls any inclination to "act out" a position of over-identification with the artist/victim. Indeed the Web log of user comments reveals hundreds of trigger-happy participants, eager to indulge the artist's request (65,000 paintball bullets were fired during the installation), although perhaps the most subversive aspect of this project, and that which aligns it most convincingly with Kaja Silverman's notion of heteropathic identification, is the spontaneously assembled coalition of viewer-participants who took turns keeping the paintball gun aimed away from Bilal. Refusing the perpetrator role and denied access to the place of the victim, they transformed their own spectatorship into an opportunity for something akin to conscientious objection.[48]

Much like Santiago Sierra, Wafaa Bilal operationalizes a spectacle of suffering in order to expose hidden conditions of deprivation and exploitation (we also see this strategic spectacularization in Martha Rosler's *House Beautiful* collages, which in a different but not unrelated way also employed the screen to both reveal and challenge its alienating effects). What differentiates Salcedo's methodology (and this differentiation, I believe, is key to understanding Salcedo's unique intervention) is the difficulty with which the audience is able to occupy *any* stable identificatory position. Indeed, the artist expresses a profound mistrust of such aesthetic strategies: "I believe," states Salcedo, "that the major possibilities of art are not in showing the spectacle of violence but instead in hiding it … I want to be able to convert the audience into witnesses."[49] But bracketing for a moment Salcedo's imperative to refrain from visualizing violence (an issue to which I will return), I propose that the artist succeeds in transforming her audience into witnesses when our desire to inhabit the spaces of traumatic experience is challenged at every turn; the very tension between desire and failure is what enables the empathetically unsettling situation described by LaCapra as a "virtual, not vicarious, experience … in which emotional response comes with respect for the other and the realization that the experience of the other is not one's own."[50] In Salcedo's sculptural works, domestic references such as the chair serve to index a body that has been absented by violence; in essence, these objects – found and distorted – become archives of that which by its very absence simply cannot be represented, and yet demands acknowledgment and remembrance. This is manifested equally in Salcedo's early sculptural works and her later large-scale installations such as the Istanbul installation, which furthermore insist upon public acknowledgment of private suffering. Echoing theorizations of trauma as a politically charged experience that calls for collective response,[51] the Istanbul installation demands entry into the public archives of cultural memory. In so doing, Salcedo's work furthermore asks for a comprehensive revision of our very conception of the archive.

Domestic Disturbance, Public Archives

In *An Archive of Feelings*, theorist Ann Cvetkovich develops an approach to trauma that postulates the productive value of critical trauma cultures – "public cultures that form in and around trauma"[52] and through which new practices and publics are formed. Arguing that trauma theory tends to devalue private, localized experiences of suffering and loss, Cvetkovich suggests that cultural production – art, literature, performance, and activism – can mobilize affective investment in and around trauma that will facilitate political (rather than medical or therapeutic) responses. Such practices, which Cvetkovich acknowledges are often as ephemeral as the traumatizing experiences that generate them, must nevertheless be integrated into public culture as archival resources, thereby also revealing the need to reinvent the archive as "itself a form of mourning."[53] In her more recent large-scale projects, Doris Salcedo has exhibited a congruent interest in making private trauma a matter of public archivization. Since 2000, Salcedo's work has undergone a shift from "memory sculptures" (which, as defined by Andreas Huyssen, reject the public spaces of memorials and monuments for more intimate spaces of reflection)[54] towards large-scale, often site-specific, installations in galleries and public spaces. Two salient examples, both of which again employ the chair motif to evoke absent human presence, are *Tenebrae: Noviembre 6, 1985*, installed at the Cambden Arts Centre, London, in 1999–2000, and *Noviembre 6 y 7*, a performance-installation at the Palace of Justice in Bogotá, Colombia, in 2002, both of which reference the 1985 storming of the Colombian High Court by M-19 guerrillas, and the subsequent siege and battle which left over one hundred people dead, seventeen missing, and the building in flames. *Tenebrae* is an installation of thirteen upended lead-cast chairs, barely recognizable because of radically attenuated legs that extend across the expanse of the room, becoming barriers across the entranceway. *Noviembre 6 y 7*, a two-day performance marking the fifty-four hours of battle in 1985, entailed the glacially slow lowering of hundreds of wooden chairs down the facade of the Palace of Justice.

The argument can and has been made that these two works demonstrate not simply a move towards larger installations, but a shift in the artist's perspective from domestic trauma to the traumatizing condition of geopolitical displacement. For art historian Jill Bennett,

> Whereas Salcedo's work was formerly concerned with domestic space, it now deals with space as the locus of (dis)placement ... Whereas the works of the nineties were about belonging – in the sense that they suggested a process of inhabitation and invited us to inquire about their occupants – the later works give extension to a set of affects that dislocate. Unlike the domestic realm that imbricates memory, the non-site of these works has no

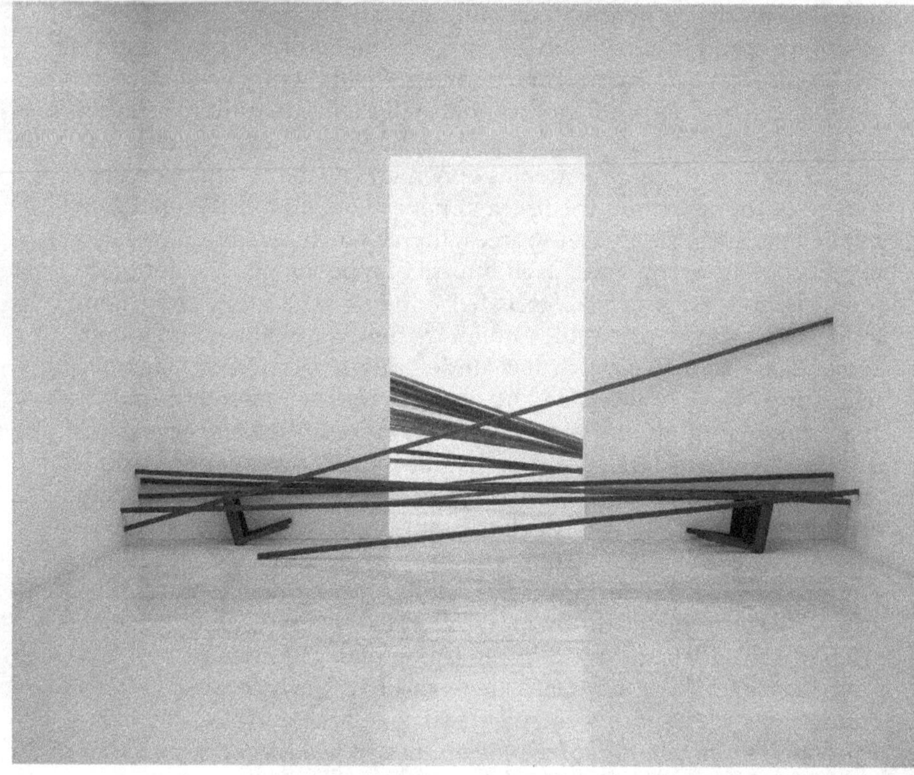

3.6 Doris Salcedo. *Tenebrae: Noviembre 7, 1985*. 1999–2000. Lead and steel in 39 parts, installed in two spaces: 163¾ × 207½ in. / 4.16 × 5.27 m (depth x width); 334½ × 260¼ in. / 8.5 × 6.61 m (depth x width). Courtesy of Alexander and Bonin, New York.

> human past. The sense of finding oneself in a world made strange, devoid of familiar reference points, is pushed to its limits now that Salcedo no longer incorporates signifiers of former inhabitants.[55]

But while Salcedo's art practice has certainly entered the public domain in an unprecedented way, and while projects since 2000 or so indeed involve a less intimate treatment of her subject matter in terms of both scale and material (as Bennett notes, lead-cast works such as *Tenebrae* remove all indexical traces of the human, including the artist's hand), it does not necessarily follow that the artist's recent works have shifted away from the issue of domestic unsettlement. This is not simply a rhetorical or semantic issue, but, rather, one with profound implications, if the point is (and it is) that issues of belonging can never be extricated from those of spatial displacement. Particularly, but not exclusively, in Colombia – where for decades, citizens' homes have been battlegrounds in the waging of the Dirty War, and where these invasions have led to massive internal displacement – belonging is inevitably (and especially in times of war) a precariously held condition, always in danger of succumbing to the condition of displacement. It is indeed this threat of dislocation that lurks in the shadows of the home that Freud characterized as the unhomely – rendering home, as Bhabha suggests in the epigraph to this chapter, a "territory of both disorientation and relocation, with all the fragility and fecundity implied by such a double take."[56] This double take, or dialectic if we prefer, is insightfully revealed in Salcedo's early works, which already constitute sustained reflection on displacement and the precarious occupation of space. Commenting on her own early works, Salcedo has stated that *La Casa Viuda* refers to "forced displacement ... to those millions of human beings who have no space," noting further that "humans are spatial beings, we need a place to eat, a place to write, to think, etc."[57] But, as Salcedo suggests, for those whose homes are violated by war, crime, and terror, these seemingly mundane rights are tenuously held. Home, then, is figured in Salcedo's early sculptures as a fragile, conditional site of belonging, and any efforts to make the home function as a stable, accessible archive for memories of this lost condition of belonging are bound, as these works reveal, to fail. As the title *Casa Viuda* implies, home can do little more than mourn the loss of its inhabitants.

Salcedo's large-scale works likewise render space a precarious entity, inoperative as a stable site of belonging and fragile as an archive (or widow) of human memory. At the same time, the very public nature of these installations reveals Salcedo's increasingly urgent commitment to the notion that just as violence in the public sphere infiltrates the presumedly safe realm of the domestic, so too must the intimately felt consequences of violence be attended to publicly, in such a way that Salcedo's installations come to function as public archives of loss. In installations like *Tenebrae* and *Noviembre 6 y 7*, the precarious nature of the archive as a home for loss continues to figure largely, again thanks to the saturated referential quality of the chair, whose capacity to recall the human body (or, more precisely, to mark the absence of the body) is again called upon to convey the body's fragility while haunting us with its absent presence. Thus the steel chairs of *Tenebrae*, prone and

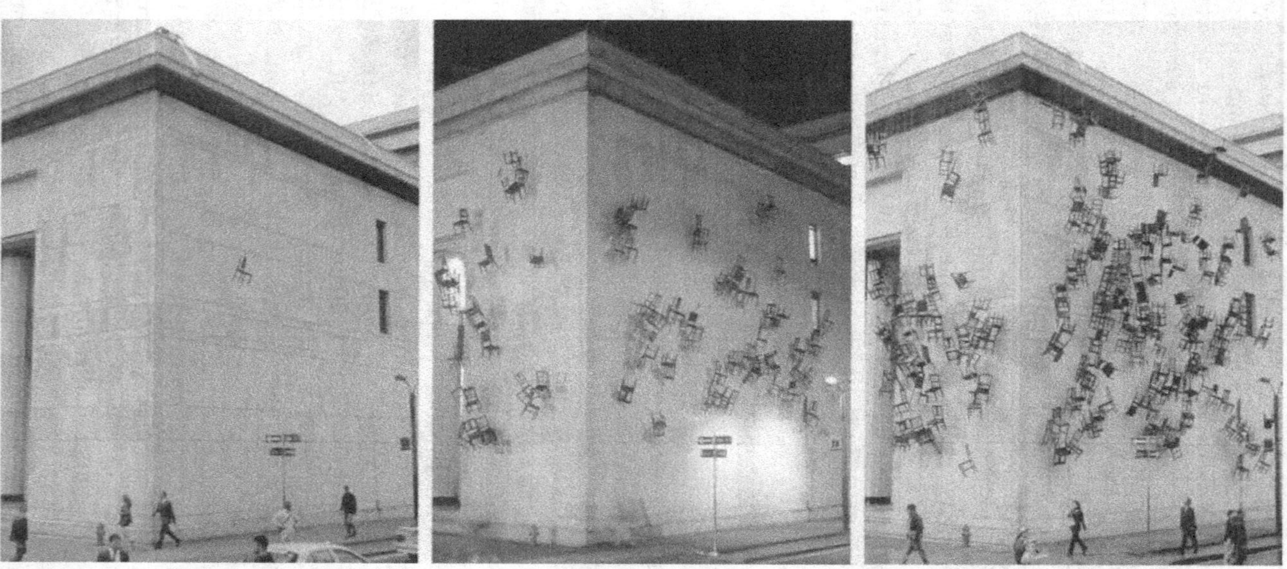

3.7 Doris Salcedo, *Noviembre 6 y 7*, Installation, Bogotá 2002. Photo: Sergio Clavijo. Courtesy of Alexander and Bonin, New York.

extended across the gallery floor, can be understood as metaphors for civilians caught in war's crossfire, attempting to flee but caught dead in their tracks. But the chairs themselves, exaggeratedly attenuated as they stretch across the space, also stretch any inclination to identify them as indexes, or even metaphors, of the human body. At the same time, the extended chairs function quite literally as barriers against any desire to inhabit the spaces of pain. Rather than offering a space for identification with the suffering of others, we as viewers are asked to relate to the work from our own mediated spectatorial positions.

The chairs that are slowly lowered down the facade of Bogotá's Palace of Justice in *Noviembre 6 y 7* bear similarly evocative (and less oblique) traces of human presence. For Mieke Bal, the chairs in this time-based installation form a sort of second shell, "the façade behind which the dark side of state power hid its terror" that, as they fall, bring this façade "down with them,"[58] but my own reading of the work (itself haunted by short-lived but searing public images of people falling and jumping from towers on 9/11) can register only human figures, tumbling to the earth in cinematic slow motion as if to escape a burning building. In a way that both recalls Gordon Matta-Clark's cuts and anticipates her own *Shibboleth* of 2007 – a giant crack in the floor of Tate Modern's Turbine Hall to which we will return in the following chapter – Salcedo here communicates a deep mistrust of architecture's capacity to shelter and protect that also mobilizes an affective registration of the precariousness with which we occupy these spaces – a sense of precariousness borne out by her own comments on the work: "The empty chairs are statements of absence allowing one to be aware of the fragility of those who were behind those walls seventeen years ago. Exposed and suspended on the stone façade, the empty chair emphasizes the vulnerability, not only of those who worked in the Palace of Justice, but of us all. This piece is vulnerable from within and unprotected on the exterior."[59] Here we can identify a forceful continuum emerging in Salcedo's practice, in which the precariousness of belonging, memory, and displacement continue to figure largely, though with an even greater sense of urgency, as these issues are now articulated as a violent confrontation between the public and the private. If there is an important conceptual distinction to be made between Salcedo's sculptures in the 1990s and the installations of the '00s and '10s, it is that her large-scale installations, particularly those sited in public places, take this confrontation – which inevitably begins with the violation of the public into private spaces – back to the public domain, where they become unhomely archives that function, and here I concur with Mieke Bal's reading, to "redefine monumentality."[60] Salcedo, writes Bal, "reconstitutes monuments as social spaces where intimacy and politics meet; where the ruptured intimacy of others, affectively experienced, cries out for political action."[61]

(Un)accommodating Memory

The transient nature of Salcedo's public installations further contributes to their capacity to redefine the function of public spaces of memory, and this ephemerality emblematizes my understanding of "melancholic archivization" – archival practices that, by contesting the archive's capacity to own and safeguard history, instead present the past as a Benjaminian flash of traces, which ideally activate both the archive's relationship with the past *and* the viewer's relation with the archive in the present. But what traces flash up to be seized in Salcedo's Istanbul installation? If we accept, as I have been insisting we must, that chairs in Salcedo's art practice function primarily as melancholic stand-ins for the absent human body, then this mass of chairs might be understood to connote a context of confinement. Although there are, somewhat shockingly, no street-side barriers or fencing around the installation, the chairs are so tightly enmeshed and intricately entwined that the flushness of the surface itself suggests the site as a holding tank of sorts, a prison with invisible bars. This reading would be in keeping with Salcedo's ongoing effort to visually articulate the vulnerable occupation of spaces of confinement, a pertinent example of which is *Neither*, a 2004 installation at London's White Cube Gallery that effected a transformation of the exhibition space into an ambiguous, indeed ethereal, site of incarceration. The installation, a room lined with gypsum board into which chain-link fencing has been embedded to produce a ghostly sort of compound, resembles, as one critic suggests, a refugee camp or detention centre[62] – increasingly ubiquitous places where detainees are reduced to what Giorgio Agamben calls "bare life"[63] and undergo what Judith Butler describes as a process of "desubjectivation" that leaves them unprotected by international protocol, unentitled to due legal process, and thus "something less than human ... an equivocation of the human."[64]

But if the Istanbul installation, like *Neither*, is a space of abject, even spectacular (to the extent that both installations also convey the condition of overexposure) confinement, its contents – hundreds of haphazardly deposited chairs – suggest an even bleaker set of associations. Given the genealogy that I have traced in which chairs function as

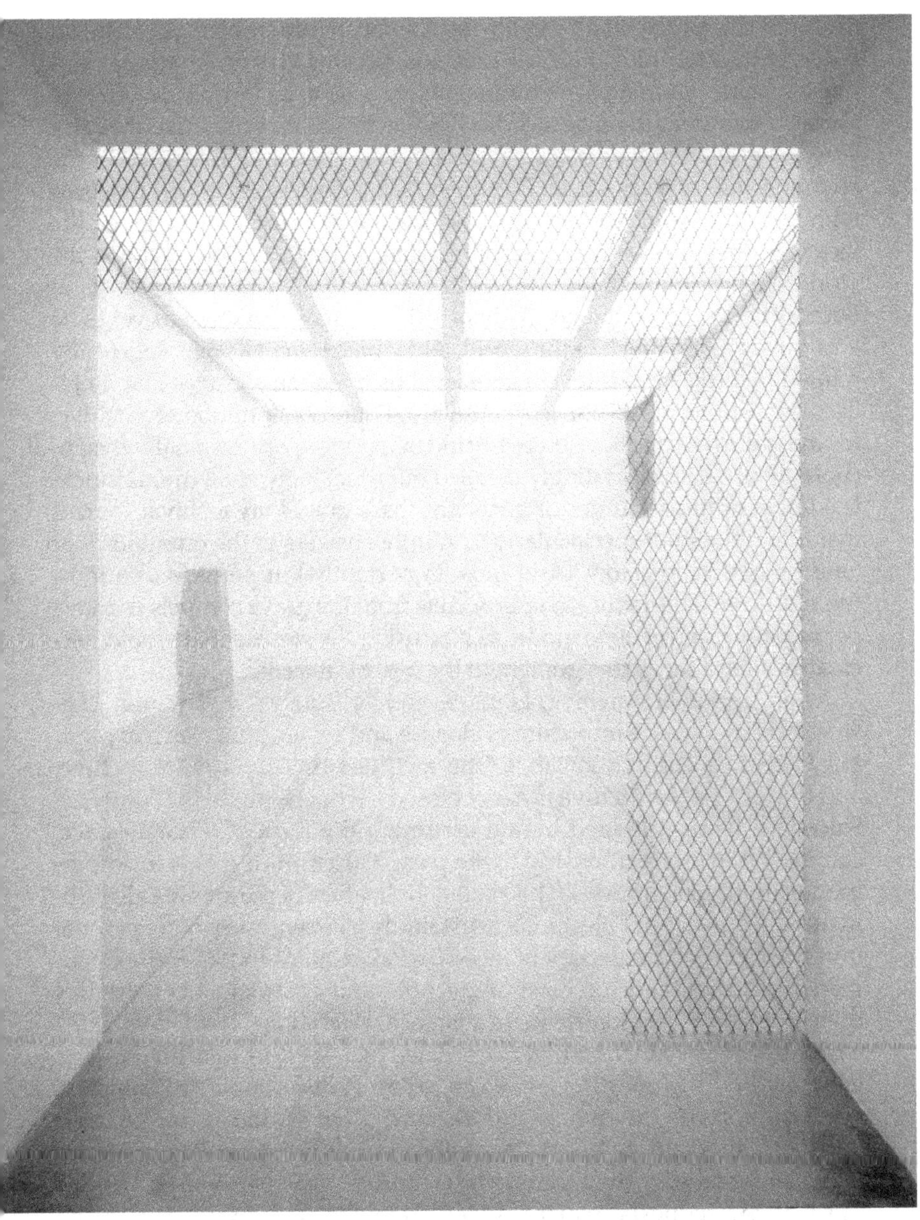

3.8 Doris Salcedo, *Neither*, 2004. Painted drywall and metal. 194½ × 291¼ × 590½ in. /494 × 740 × 1500 cm. Photo: Stephen White. Courtesy of Alexander and Bonin, New York

multiply referential stand-ins for the human figure, it becomes difficult *not* to encounter this jumble of 1,550 interlocking chairs not simply as a pile of chairs, but as a pile of human bodies – or, to be terribly precise, the abused, anonymous, emaciated bodies that haunt our collective memory bank of all-too familiar images (both photographic and imagined) of the countless mass graves – from Poland in 1945 to Rwanda in 1994 – that bear witness to the twentieth century's penchant for horror. Indeed, given the location of the installation in Istanbul, along with the curious fact that the work remains untitled, I am compelled to read the installation as a silent witness to the Armenian genocide of 1915 – a massacre that has yet to be acknowledged in much of the world, and which remains unapologetically refuted in Turkey.[65] It is this unspoken allusion to mass graves that mobilizes my reading of Salcedo's Istanbul installation as an unhomely archive, for mass graves can themselves be understood as quintessentially melancholic archives. Excruciatingly detailed but shockingly anonymous indexical traces of mass murder or genocide, mass graves are archival sources that themselves fail spectacularly to supply answers to the questions that haunt them: Who? How? And most importantly but perhaps also most futilely, Why? This failure to offer secrets from the grave compels us into a perpetually interrogative mode, as if refusing the closure that would necessarily attend their consignment to the historical record.

As an unhomely archive, Doris Salcedo's Istanbul installation likewise fails to coalesce into a site of closure and redemption. As if exploiting Derrida's observation that "the archivist produces more archive, and that is why the archive is never closed – it opens out to the future,"[66] Salcedo's archive, lodged in and assuming the form of a home-space, cannot stabilize a relationship to the past. It attempts but fails to accommodate its own memories. This melancholization of the archive also animates the practice of Palestinian artist Emily Jacir, whose neo-conceptual investigations of displacement faced by Palestinians in Israel, the Occupied Territories, and the diaspora, echoes and complements Salcedo's own anarchival project. Take, for instance, *Where We Come From* (2003), a multimedia installation that documents Jacir's effort to fulfil requests generated by the question, posed to exiled Palestinians, "If I could do anything for you, anywhere in Palestine, what would it be?" Armed with an American passport that afforded the artist relative mobility between Israel and the Occupied Territories, Jacir was able to realize most of the requests, which ranged from the mundane ("Go to the Israeli post office in Jerusalem and pay my phone bill") to the mournful ("Go to my mother's grave in Jerusalem on her birthday and place

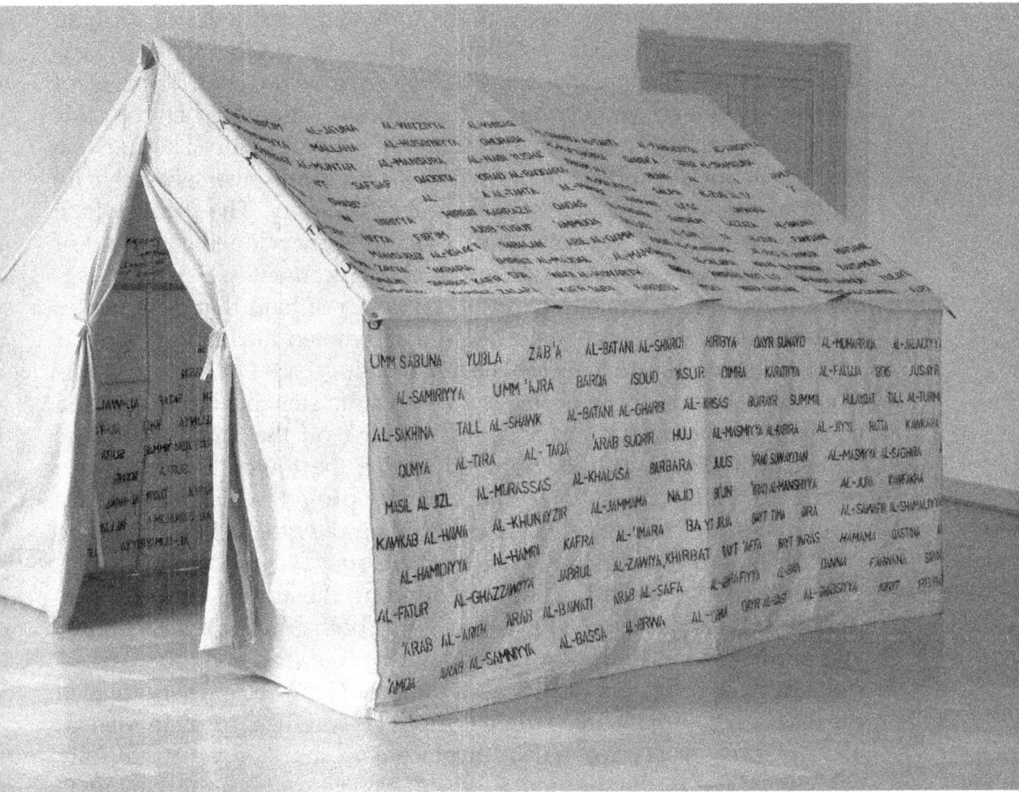

3.9 Emily Jacir, *Memorial to 418 Palestinian Villages which Were Destroyed, Depopulated and Occupied by Israel in 1948*, 2001. Refugee tent and embroidery thread, 8 × 10 × 12 feet. Photo: Stefan Rohner. © Emily Jacir. Courtesy of Alexander and Bonin, New York.

flowers and pray"). The recording of these actions (thirty-two mounted photographs, thirty framed texts and a video) attests to both a poetic longing for home and the everyday frustrations of being barred from it.[67] Itself a carefully assembled archive of loss and disenfranchisement, *Where We Come From*, rather than assuming the position of victim, instead conveys the fundamental experiential gap that separates the exiled or occupied Palestinian from the Western artist and audience, therefore sharing with Salcedo an insistence on bearing witness to traumatic experience in ways that unsettle processes of (over)identification.

Equally salient to this study of the unhomely aesthetics of contemporary art is Jacir's 2001 installation, *Memorial to 418 Palestinian Villages Destroyed, Depopulated and Occupied by Israel in 1948*. There is, of course, an immediate, jarring, and significant difference between this work and Salcedo's Istanbul installation: whereas Salcedo offers no title to anchor the subject of her work, Jacir's title conversely offers no room to manoeuvre *away* from the subject of hers. The piece, which draws explicitly on historian Walid Khalidi's encyclopedic account of the destruction of Arab villages and the displacement of 700,000 villagers during the 1948 takeover and occupation of land that now makes up parts of Israel,[68] consists of a large assembled burlap tent, similar to those once used to shelter Palestinian refugees.[69] On the tent's surface, the names of those destroyed villages are stencilled in pencil and stitched in thick black thread, as if warding off the threat that these names will disappear into oblivion as did the towns to which they refer. Like Wafaa Bilal's later *And Counting* project, which also evokes ceremonies and monumental spaces that employ the act of naming to memorialize the dead (the Vietnam Veterans' Memorial, the Names Project AIDS Quilt, and rituals surrounding the annual commemoration of 9/11, for instance), Jacir's project is both a memorial to what is lost and a preservation of what remains of that loss – in this case, an exactingly detailed list of 418 place names. Here, the preservation of detail is also an explicitly political project – a refusal to remain silent about a process of geopolitical displacement that has yet to be fully acknowledged in the international community, and a refusal, as well, to permit this memorial to stand in synecdochically for a non-localized, transcultural phenomenon of mobility and deterritorialization. Indeed, the precision of the work's title reveals the artist's effort to avoid such quixotic inclinations.[70]

But if Jacir's installation positions itself as an explicit defence against forgetting and in favour of home's critical status as a place of belonging, there is, at the same time, an implicit recognition of the ephemerality of memory and the provisionality of belonging. The medium of the refugee tent suggests itself as a transient and unstable home for loss, speaking both to the inaccessibility of the home that exists only in its traces, and to home's fragile position as a repository of history's traces. But the conditions of producing Jacir's memorial also speak to the contingencies inherent in any politics of location. Like *And Counting*, Jacir's was a communal effort – for several weeks, friends and colleagues were invited into Jacir's studio to contribute to the embroidery work. But when the work had not yet been completed by the opening of the work's inaugural exhibition at New York's PS1 in the spring of 2001, the tent was exhibited with some villages indicated only in ink-drawn outlines. While inadvertent, the incomplete nature of the memorial is also strongly evocative, suggesting that a stable and permanent collective memory of these places cannot be guaranteed, and suggesting as well that like this artwork in progress, the condition of Palestinian displacement remains unfinished business.

Elusive Archives

As an archive, Salcedo's Istanbul installation is frustratingly elusive, rendered so by Salcedo's rejection of spectacles of violence and suffering. To a certain degree, then, it is useful to align Salcedo's work with contemporary art practices – Alfredo Jaar's, for instance – that lament the image's impotence in the face of catastrophe, a reading that is given credence by Salcedo's resolute disinclination to visualize traumatic experience: "I'm not interested in the visual. I have constructed the work as invisibility, because I regard the non-visual as representing a lack of power. To see is to have power; it's a way of possessing ... What I'm addressing in the work is something which is actually in the process of vanishing."[71] Or, compare Salcedo's metonymic use of domestic furniture to the paintings of another Colombian artist, Ferdinand Botero, whose restagings of abuse photographs at Abu Ghraib prison in Iraq, while equally unsettling in their cartoon-like ferocity, nevertheless grant full visual access to bodies in pain. On the contrary, the human body in Salcedo's work is, as one critic observes, "just as absent and elusive as it would be in any memory of the past."[72]

But if Salcedo's aesthetic strategy can certainly be read in the context of recent scepticism in visual culture studies regarding the extent to which images are capable of generating an engagement with the suffering of others that goes beyond shock, catharsis, and the collective desire to spectacularize pain, there is something almost disingenuous about visual art's disavowal of the visual, invariably accompanied by visual manifestations of this very disavowal. On the contrary, I want to suggest that Salcedo's practice betrays a deep investment in pursuing the unique capacity of visual images to convey the affective, corporeal implications of traumatic experience. What Salcedo challenges is the spectacular use of imagery – the shock effect – which produces, she fears, at best a fleeting sense of outrage and at worst a premature sense of catharsis, even pleasure. Her work cannot, therefore, be considered simply as a facile rejection of imagery as a viable methodology for conveying difficult knowledge; in fact, I would instead align her practice, conditionally at least, with *defences* of imagery in the face of atrocity.

In his 2008 *Images in Spite of All*, art historian Georges Didi-Huberman engages with the ethics of representation through an examination of four controversial photographs that survived the Nazi concentration camp at Auschwitz in Poland. Taken surreptitiously by prisoners who were members of the Sonderkommando, they depict unclothed women being steered towards a gas chamber and gassed bodies being delivered to the crematorium. For Didi-Huberman, the survival of these images in spite of all asks us to acknowledge the necessity of imagining the Holocaust. Capitulation to the discourse of horror's unrepresentability, he suggests, is complicit with the Nazi project of making the tools of the extermination disappear, of "*obliterating every remnant*."[73] According to this provocative (and itself controversial) argument, images are neither deficient simulacra nor transparent documents, but rather traces whose very entry into the archive serve as reminders that "to bear witness is to tell *in spite of all* that which it is *impossible* to tell entirely."[74] Given the experiences that Salcedo seeks to examine in her work – the "bare life" of the camp inmate, the "negative space" of the immigrant, and the ongoing disappearances that are a common facet of a decades-long state of emergency in Colombia, where citizens continue to disappear without a trace – Salcedo's work is less about rejecting images than about building an archive that, however meagre, will constitute some kind of fragile memory bank.

And yet, Salcedo's melancholic attachment to the past also resists easy entry into the archives of public memory. In this respect, the Istanbul installation can be usefully compared to French artist Christian Boltanski's *Missing House* of 1990, whose formal similarities to Salcedo's installation are unmistakable, but whose divergent conceptual strategies underline the stakes and conditions of melancholic archivization. In East Berlin, Boltanski researched the history of an empty lot where a house destroyed during the Second World War once stood. On the walls of adjacent houses, Boltanski attached plates describing prior occupants of the house, and at a separate location in West Berlin he displayed documents concerning these (mostly Jewish) residents, some of whom had been deported to concentration camps during Nazi rule.[75] Like Salcedo, Boltanski employs the trope of home in order to activate it as a source of buried archival knowledge, while at the same time, as art historian John Czaplicka observes, demanding "that the viewer engage his or her imagination, knowledge, and memory in a process of completion."[76]

But whereas Boltanski's installation mines existing archives for lost and forgotten evidence, demanding precise and detailed recognition of the histories buried at this site (as Czaplicka further observes, Boltanski's task is to "follow the material presence and archival excerpts to reconstruct the past in the present"),[77] Salcedo declines to offer such a direct (if incomplete) conduit to the past. Instead, we are required to make our own meaning and draw our own conclusions. In Salcedo's work, home reveals itself as an unsettled space of archivization, just as the archive is revealed as a troubled home for loss.

The Future of the Unhomely Archive

Pondering the future of globalization in a post-9/11 world, Homi Bhabha proposes "unbuilding" as a paradigm for challenging the West's now largely discredited faith in progress:

> The times and places in which we live confront our sense of Progress with the image of the Unbuilt. The Unbuilt is not a place you can reach with a ladder ... The rubble and debris that survive carry the memories of other fallen towers, Babel for instance, and lessons of endless ladders that suddenly collapse beneath our feet. We have no choice but to place, in full view of our buildings, the vision of the Unbuilt – the foundation of *possible* buildings ... other alternative worlds.[78]

In a visceral way, Doris Salcedo's Istanbul installation conveys Bhabha's vision of the Unbuilt – a vision that reveals Western ideals of progress and modernity as a crumbling empire of collapsed ladders and fallen towers. Indeed, while I have argued that the installation's hundreds of chairs read as a sort of oblique anthropology of human suffering, the installation in its entirety also recalls something more akin to an archaeological ruin – Salcedo's work transforms immaterial traces of the past into material relics in the present. Importantly, what this also suggests is that Salcedo is less interested in acting out the moment of catastrophe than in rendering its charged affective repercussions available to those who would bear witness. Insightful in this respect is Jill Bennett's analysis of Salcedo's practice, which recognizes that her works align us "with the witnesses who live out the reality of loss in a context where pain is not contained in the single moment but is present in everyday life, in all interactions."[79] Salcedo conceives melancholia not simply as the failure to escape an unreconciled past, but as the carrying of that unsettled past into the present and for the future. Much like Lida Abdul's *Housewheel*, which opened this chapter, or Mona Hatoum's *Mobile Home*, which introduced this book, Salcedo's work resonates strongly with Bhabha's conception of the Unbuilt as the "foundation of *possible* buildings ... other alternative worlds." Her unhomely archives, produced out of the ruins of history, demonstrate what is perhaps contemporary art's unique contribution to the future of memory: a capacity to unsettle our collective relationship with the past while imagining a better future.

In this way, too, contemporary art is perhaps uniquely equipped to fulfil Derrida's mandate for the archive, which is to conceive of itself as an open question:

> The question of the archive is not, I repeat, a question of the past, the question of a concept dealing with the past which already might either be at our disposal or not at our disposal, an archivable concept of the archive, but rather a question of the future, the very question of the future, question of a response, of a promise and of a responsibility for tomorrow. The archive: if we want to know what this will have meant, we will only know tomorrow.[80]

Salcedo's unhomely archive, to recall Foster's (an)archival aesthetic, is likewise "founded on disaster" and "pledged against a ruin that it cannot forestall."[81] But it nevertheless points forward in time, asking us to recognize both the universality and the materiality of human precariousness in ways that might ideally mobilize heteropathically unsettling responses to the suffering of others. Such responses in turn possess the capacity to reshape our collective understanding of the past, the present, and indeed the future.

4
Biennial Culture's Reluctant Nomads

It seems proper that those who create art in a civilization of quasi-barbarism which has made so many homeless, which has torn up tongues and peoples by the root, should themselves be poets unhoused and wanderers across language. Eccentric, aloof, nostalgic, deliberately untimely.

George Steiner, *Extraterritorial*

Unfortunately, the world now seems divided between what Jacques Attali calls the rich and poor nomads: the nomadic elite who travel at will, expanding their world, and the disenfranchised poor who travel because they are desperate to improve their condition. However indigent artists may sometimes be, we in the art world are very distinct from those migratory laborers who cross borders illegally, return again and again, live on the margins, negotiate cultures because there is no other way to earn a living.

Carol Becker, "The Romance of Nomadism"

In October 2007, Doris Salcedo performed another sort of archaeological dig when she occupied the massive space of the Tate Modern's Turbine Hall with *Shibboleth*, a 548-foot fissure that snakes its way along the length of the floor, beginning as a hairline crack and at times gaping to expose what appears to be a bottomless crevasse, lined with concrete and chain link fencing. A complex meditation on the experience of immigration that simultaneously evokes the often treacherous experience of crossing borders and the "negative space" occupied by migrants within the increasingly policed borders of the European Union, the work seems determined to implicate the Tate itself in this rendering of gaping chasms and perilous border crossings, connecting the building to a colonial history of exclusion and exploitation that underpins the modernism celebrated within. In this respect, and to the extent that Salcedo employs the museum space as site, medium, *and* object of critical analysis of embedded social structures of power and injustice, *Shibboleth* can and has been justly identified as an heir to the genre of institutional critique associated with artists like Daniel Buren, Michael Asher, and Hans Haacke in the 1970s. Salcedo's work is deeply reminiscent of Haacke's *Germania* exhibit at the 1974 Venice Biennial (which, recall, saw the German Pavilion's interior marble floor smashed to bits), likewise a literal intervention into the fabric of an institutional space that sought to expose the cracks in its artifice of monumentality, neutrality, and universality.

But *Shibboleth* operates at another level, one that is deeply salient to the unhomely aesthetics of contemporary art. By directing her institutional critique towards the cultural, political, and geographical exclusions specific to the dislocating experience of migration, Salcedo's work also operates as an intervention into the "romance of nomadism" that arguably pervades the production and circulation of contemporary art – a romance that has only grown more passionate since the late 1990s, when art historian Carol Becker identified a tendency within the international art world to embrace an abstracted ideal of transnationalism while failing to attend to its lived realities.[1] In this way, I further suggest, Salcedo's intervention at the Tate Modern is emblematic of a contemporary version of institutional critique – one that targets not the grounded, venerable cultural institutions of the nineteenth and twentieth centuries, but rather the itinerant, situational "non-sites" of art production and reception in the twenty-first, now commonly grouped under the rubric of biennial culture (but which also include such phenomena as "relational" art and the de-institutionalization of art). The aim of the present chapter is to identify some aesthetic practices that critique biennial culture from within its nomadic model of art production and reception, and to analyse how this mode of critique – which I have found it useful to call "reluctant nomadism" – is harnessed to rethink the terms of contemporary art's engagement with questions of home and the unhomely in an age of unprecedented migration and mobility.

From the outset, it seems imperative not to confuse this set of critical aesthetic practices with a movement or genre that has been identified as the "new institutionalism" in contemporary art (and which, somewhat confusingly, has itself claimed the mantle of institutional critique). Epitomized by the emergence, in the early 2000s, of projects of Rirkrit Tiravanija, Andrea Fraser, and Carsten Höller (among others) characterized by discourses of transience, flux, and conviviality, the new institutionalism (often also called relational aesthetics) likewise promotes the transformation of institutional spaces (into open studios, laboratories, hang-outs, communal kitchens). Since its emergence, debate has emerged as to the legitimacy of relational art as the privileged model of institutional critique in the twenty-first century.[2] But if relational aesthetics, which favours flux over stasis and situation over site, constitutes a problematic legacy for institutional critique, it certainly seems to fall quite naturally into step with the emergence of biennial culture and its almost feverishly ambulatory ways. As art historian Claire Doherty already observed in 2004, "The biennial bears a resemblance to a circus blowing through town, floating its propensity for transient encounters. It's a natural home, then, for the new paradigms of artistic practice which have emerged concurrently with these new theorizations of place and engagement."[3] In contrast, the artists that I would like to consider articulate a self-reflexive discomfort with the artist's presumptive status as wandering nomad and the art institution's role as a platform or station along the way. Like Doris Salcedo, for whom the globalized artist's privileged mobility serves as a platform from which to address geopolitical issues of dislocation and displacement, these reluctant nomads – from Alfredo Jaar and Emily Jacir to Ursula Biemann and Yto Barrada – explore what it means to belong in a world in which the conceptual legitimacy of "home" is increasingly debased, even while home as lived reality is increasingly tenuous to much of the world's citizenry. In what follows, I address both biennial culture and its internalized critiques in the context of the ongoing global migration crisis, suggesting that the critical aesthetic practices of reluctant nomads offer sustained and useful deliberations on the concepts and conditions of local and global, centre and periphery, belonging and not belonging, home and its unmaking in contemporary art.

Biennial Culture and Its Discontents

Clearly, any definition of "biennial culture," or what the editors of an anthology on the topic call the "global biennial phenomenon,"[4] will be as heterogeneous and unruly as the phenomenon itself, whose breadth is global and whose conceptual concerns are largely dependent on the country in which the exhibition is mounted and the intellectual pursuits of the curator selected to lead it. In addition, biennial, triennial, and other large-scale international exhibitions fall under a wide variety of formats – from the Venice Biennale, which operates according to a model based on national pavilions, to the Liverpool Biennial, which invites international artists to engage directly with the city. Notwithstanding these challenges, the term "biennial culture" has largely come to stand for perennial large-scale international exhibitions, hosted by cities (often in order to boost international profile) and organized by guest curators around specific themes. Since the mid-1990s, debates regarding the "biennialization" of contemporary art have focused largely on the role of international exhibitions vis-à-vis multiple facets of globalization, sparked at least in part by the increasing frequency with which large-scale exhibitions have used their international podium to consider various facets of global culture. As Pamela M. Lee puts it, "the relay between contemporary art and globalization [is] by far the most important curatorial rubric of the last two decades,"[5] so it is not surprising that the stakes are high. On one hand, biennial culture has been praised for finally abandoning modernist myths of universality, instead embracing multiplicity, hybridity, the interstices, the West's peripheries, and so on. At their best, some insist, biennials offer "spaces of hope," even a "glimpse of a transnational utopia."[6] On the other hand, the rapid proliferation of biennials in all corners of the world has been vigorously disparaged as at best "conceptualized around certain curators' jet-set lifestyles,"[7] and at worst propelled by a "colonial logic [that simply] underwrites the expansion of the art world's traditional borders, as if the art world itself were gleefully following globalization's imperial mandate."[8]

One of the earliest, and still most cogent, analyses of both the virtues and limits of biennial culture derives from Carol Becker's response to the Johannesburg Biennial of 1997, themed "Trade Routes," arguably the first effort to assemble an international group of art professionals (artists, curators, and cultural theorists) to consider the socio-economic consequences of neoliberal globalization.[9] Applauding curator Okwui Enwezor's mandate to collectively imagine a seemingly imminent transnational future, Becker nevertheless chides the curatorial team for neglecting the geopolitical context in which the exhibition itself was staged. While the Truth and Reconciliation Commission hearings were in session, and while South Africa was grappling with both the legacy of apartheid and the future of the nation, the decision to formulate an international exhibition platform that sidestepped both the question of nation and its own geographical context was, Becker suggests politely, "unfortunate."[10] What Becker is observing here is a perhaps inevitable paradox that adheres to projects seeking to imagine a better world: the actually existing world can have the "unfortunate" effect of making such utopian ventures seem naive, even counterproductive. But what looked to many like naivety, even negligence,[11] was instead the product of a well-defined (and now, almost two decades later, well-rehearsed) reconceptualization of the terms and conditions of site-specificity as a model for artistic engagement – a rethinking that, having precipitated something of a rift in contemporary curatorial methodologies, deserves some unpacking here.

The battle over site-specificity as a model for socially engaged art has been waged on two fronts, both of which have profoundly affected how biennial culture has developed and, correspondingly, how this culture has responded to the complex set of problems attached to the current global order. First, a perceived tendency among artists to treat place anthropologically has been widely contested, perhaps most famously by Hal Foster, who, in his 1996 "The Artist as Ethnographer," problematizes art practices that "confirm rather than contest the authority of mapper over site."[12] For Foster, writing during one of the heydays of community-based art, such practices inevitably involve an "identitarian reduction" of places and their inhabitants that, he argues, "threatens to collapse new site-specific work into identity politics *tout court*."[13] Furthermore, as place itself has become an increasingly unstable epistemological category in both theory and practice, site-specific art has come under fire for advancing an outdated methodology that relies on nostalgic, essentializing visions of place and emplacement. Reinforced by the "nomadology" of Gilles Deleuze and Félix Guattari[14] along with conceptualizations of postmodernity's "non-places,"[15] critics of phenomenologically oriented site-specificity have instead advocated an understanding of site as "an intertextually coordinated, multiply located, discursive field of operation,"[16] notably in the practices of artists like Renée Green and Gabriel Orozco (characterized by art historian James Meyer as belonging to a contemporary breed of "artist-travellers").[17] Both Meyer and Miwon Kwon (also a critic of site-specificity) caution against universalizing valorizations of the nomadic condition; Kwon in particular is wary of the ways in which methodologies privileging instability and impermanence are "called forth to validate, even romanticize, the material and socioeconomic realities of an itinerant lifestyle."[18] But Kwon's main concern is with site-specific models that "reaffirm our sense of self, reflecting back to us an unthreatening picture of a grounded identity,"[19] and this critique has been carried into curatorial discourse in the form of international exhibitions that likewise posit "place" as a shifting signifier of dislocated identifications that can no longer be accommodated by static visions of site-specificity. Or, as Charlotte Bydler puts it bluntly, the question of location in the context of biennial culture is "hopelessly obsolete."[20]

The ongoing questions regarding site-specificity have occasioned two markedly divergent methodologies for curating large-scale international exhibitions. On one hand are those manifestations that privilege a concentrated attention to site, from the 5th Bucharest Biennale in 2011, whose mandate under the direction of curator Anne Barlow was to be "a form of agency within the city" with a "sustained local dimension,"[21] to the Liverpool Biennial of Contemporary Art, which positions itself as a series of sustained encounters between artists, residents, and the city itself (artists are usually invited to spend a significant period of time in the city, and to produce community-based commissioned works).[22] Liverpool's model, widely understood to have boosted the city's fledgling tourist economy since its inception in 2000, has also been widely disparaged by critics, who, in accord with Foster's critique of contemporary art's ethnographic impulse, remain unconvinced of the exhibition model's capacity to generate an engagement that is both meaningful and aesthetically rigorous, and unimpressed by the biennial's attention to site, described as "wide and shallow rather than narrow and deep – sightseeing rather than insight."[23]

As if in response to a loudening chorus of claims that site-sensitive international exhibitions such as the Liverpool Biennial are susceptible to overly anthropological, even neocolonial, approaches to site-specificity, the contrary impulse has been to renounce context altogether – to embrace the itinerancy of both the artist and the exhibition context as ideally decentred positions from which to examine how the interrelated spheres of mobility, migration, and globalization are currently reshaping the world. To a large extent, this shift away from site-specific or site-sensitive biennials has allowed curators to avoid any perceived tendency to anthropologize their host cities.[24] There is also little risk of indulging in essentialized, outdated notions of site when site itself is taken entirely off the curatorial menu. But there are risks associated with jettisoning attention to place, particularly in the context of art exhibitions that purport to address current models of globalism. For once the decision has been made to unmoor the international exhibition from its grounding in a specific locale, the biennial risks being transformed into precisely the paean to globalization's uneven processes of development and deterritorialization that its detractors fear it has already become.

The "theoretical transmigration"[25] so thoroughly endorsed by the nomadic culture of international exhibitions smacks of a romanticism that is uncannily familiar. Indeed, it would appear that biennial culture has supplied contemporary art with a convenient replacement for hackneyed, now mostly discredited, myths of the artist-sage, artist-madman, and artist-melancholic: artists who ride the biennial circuit are once again idealized as "poets unhoused and wanderers across language."[26] But whereas George Steiner's observation reflected a Frankfurt School–inspired unease at the prospect of making art after the horrors of the Second World War and its legacy of mass exile and displacement (identifying in the work of Joyce and Nabakov a literary lexicon for this collective unease), the romanticization of nomadism in contemporary art betrays a curious detachment from the current global crisis of migration. It is this perceived failure to address the vast gulf separating "rich nomads" from "poor nomads" that has instigated a backlash of sorts, arising especially from postcolonial theory.[27] As Edward Said already put it so eloquently in 1990, the contemporary situation demands that we "map territories of experience beyond those mapped by the literature of exile itself." We must, he concludes, "first set aside Joyce and Nabokov and think instead of the uncountable masses for whom UN agencies have been created."[28] Indeed, the limits of nomadology are acknowledged even by one of its most articulate advocates, Rosi Braidotti, who observes that "being nomadic, homeless, an exile, a refugee, a Bosnian rape-in-war victim, an itinerant migrant, an illegal immigrant, is no metaphor," but instead a devastatingly specific set of material conditions – "history tattooed on your body. One may be empowered or beautified by it, but most people are not; some just die of it."[29]

But the intention here is not to adjudicate whether the renunciation of site-specificity in biennial culture is capable of building a productive framework for responding to what Enwezor calls globalization's "multiple mutinies."[30] To do so would be to accept a dichotomy between "nomadism and sedentariness"[31] whose coherence is belied by the fact that any multinational exhibition, whether located in Liverpool or Kassel, Istanbul or Berlin, whether composed of twenty artists engaged in year-long, context-specific projects or two hundred artists flown in

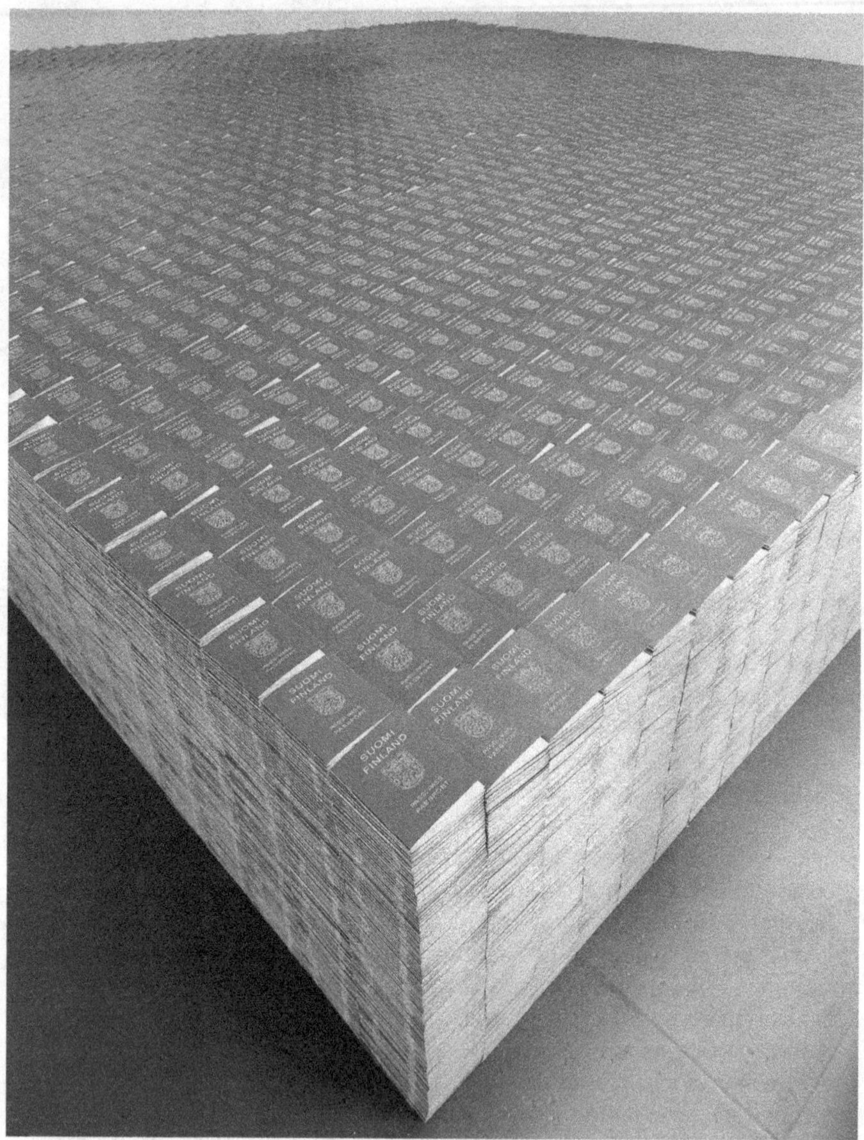

4.1 Alfredo Jaar, *One Million Finnish Passports*, 1995/2014. One million replicated Finnish passports, glass, 800 × 800 × 800 cm. Installation view from ARS 95, Ateneum Art Museum, Helsinki, Finland. © Alfredo Jaar. Courtesy of Galerie Lelong, New York.

hours before the event, is by inevitably a peripatetic venture, bound and indebted to the forces of globalization that it so frequently seeks to problematize. But if not even the most site-sensitive endeavours are capable of escaping the nomadic paradigm of biennial culture, is there a way instead to harness the logic, energy, and structural frameworks of nomadism to critique its very foundations?

Reluctant Nomads

Art critic Julian Stallabrass sees few, if any, avenues of criticality to be mapped in the modus operandi of biennial culture, which, he argues, "not only embodies but actively propagandizes the virtues of [neo-liberal] globalization."[32] To flesh out his critique of the culture of internationalism that biennial culture both reflects and propels, Stallabrass spotlights Alfredo Jaar's *One Million Finnish Passports*, a 1995 installation of one million passport replicas stacked like a minimalist floor sculpture and intended to recall the would-be immigrants who have been turned away at Finland's strictly guarded borders.[33] For Stallabrass, the work exemplifies biennial culture's privileging of mobility over national determination and "global capital" over "local concerns."[34] But let us agree (as I do) that international art exhibitions tend to perpetuate (while paradoxically condemning) a myth of unfettered mobility that validates, if unwittingly, the more pernicious world-is-flat, end-of-history, free-trade free-for-all underpinnings of the neoliberal capitalist brand of globalization. To map this critique, however, onto a project such as *One Million Finnish Passports* is to reduce the complexity of globalization into an oppositional paradigm whereby claims for transnational solidarity and entreaties to rich nations to share their bloated slices of the global pie are conflated with the interests of the multinational corporate elite. Far from advancing the cause of global capitalism, Jaar's project directly confronts the two-tiered nature of neoliberal globalization, characterized by an unprecedented and seemingly unrestricted global flow of wealth and goods that has precipitated a global migration crisis, which in turn, in a sort of anti-domino effect, has seen an unprecedented fortification of the borders of America and Europe. Checkpoints, border fences, remote satellite surveillance systems, and regressive immigration standards – these are not the antithesis, but rather the ugly underbelly, of free market globalism, and it is precisely this underbelly that Jaar seeks to expose.[35]

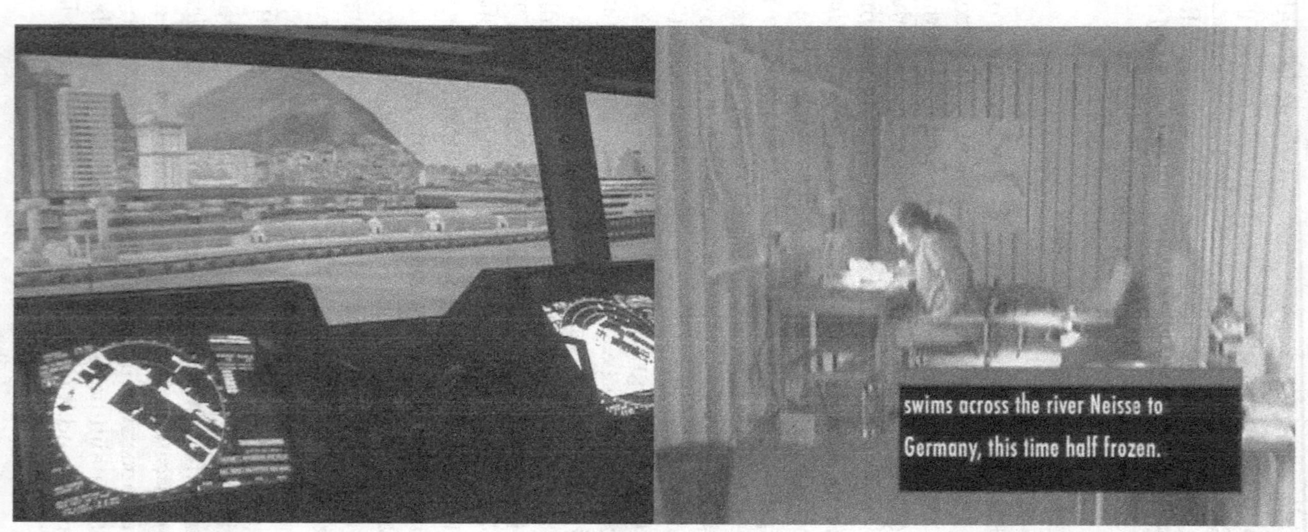

4.2 Ursula Biemann, *Contained Mobility*, 2004. Two-channel video, 20 min. Video still. Courtesy of the artist.

Swiss artist Ursula Biemann's video installation *Contained Mobility*, commissioned by the Third Liverpool Biennial in 2004, illustrates both the two-tiered nature of globalization and some of the aesthetic tactics that artists employ to uncover and map these processes. The installation recounts the troubled journey of a Russian asylum seeker named Anatol Zimmerman, whose life is thrown into chaos following a series of unfortunate incidents and who treks across the continent in desperate search of a new and better life. Following Zimmerman through illicit border crossings, police arrest, detention in a camp for asylum seekers, and eventually to Liverpool, where his future is left uncertain, the video finds a useful trope in the image of the shipping container, which, as Judith Butler observes, has come to symbolize the simultaneous conditions of dispossession and detention that mark the contemporary "paradigm of colonial violence."[36] Translating this contradictory logic into the syntax of visual culture, the installation tracks Zimmerman's passage with a synchronized double projection: one screen, an uninterrupted series of fluid video recordings, documents the smooth flow of goods across borders, while the other projects a shaky, disjointing sequence of images representing the uneasy migration of Zimmerman – described by the artist as an "itinerant body [who] moves through non-civil places, waits for status in off-social spaces, only to remain suspended in the post-humanist lapse."[37] In this way, *Contained Mobility* constitutes a deliberation on globalization that occludes neither the local context of Liverpool nor the culture of transnationalism in which the biennial is inevitably positioned, but instead engages self-reflexively in a critical appraisal of both the promises and perils of mobility today.

In their complex renderings of what is now often referred to as "global apartheid," Alfredo Jaar and Ursula Biemann join a growing number of artists whose meditations on the complex and often treacherous paths of transnational migration constitute an undermining from within the contemporary art world's ongoing narratives of transience and mobility. To a certain extent, these practices therefore align with James Meyer's conceptualization of the artist-traveller, which he divides into two groups: lyrical and critical nomads. In the practices of "lyrical nomads" such as Rirkrit Tiravanija and Gabriel Orozco, mobility is figured as a series of poetic, ephemeral everyday experiences that become fodder for aesthetic contemplation, the upshot being that the material conditions of these itinerant encounters are obscured. "Critical nomads," on the contrary (here, Renée Green is considered paradigmatic), address the discursive, historical, and institutional conditions of travel, and "expose these conditions as the historical ground of the practice itself."[38] Like Meyer's "critical nomads," the artists with whom this chapter (and indeed this book) is concerned are artist-travellers casting a critical gaze upon the material conditions of mobility and non-belonging. But the affinity breaks down in the details. In his examination of Renée Green's contribution to the 1993 multi-artist *Project Unité* at Le Corbusier's Unité d'Habitation housing complex in Firminy, France, Meyer explains that Green installed and slept in a tent inside the apartment she was assigned for the duration of the exhibition, alluding to "the nomad artist's plight of never having a home."[39] For Meyer, Green's project represents a significant intervention into the lyrical tendencies of the culture of nomadism, since "to be a working producer today is to be constantly on the move [and] working conditions are hardly optimum."[40] But without casting doubt on the accuracy of this observation, one must question the extent to which it (or Green's installation) critically intervenes in the romantic lyricism of nomadism, and conversely the extent to which it simply imbues the romance with a dose of melancholy. Indeed, I submit that a truly critical nomadic practice would need to expose not only the conditions that hinder the freedom and comfort of the artist-traveller, but also and importantly the conditions and hierarchies that undoubtedly expedite the artist's mobility in an era of tightly controlled transnational movement. It is this genre of criticality that informs what I am calling reluctant nomadism.

Reluctant nomads convey the risk that in our rush to embrace the language and logic of nomadism we forget or elide the very real dangers that attend to the geopolitical conditions of the migrant, the exile, the undocumented worker, the asylum seeker, and all those global citizens for whom deterritorialization is neither a trope for the fragmentation of the postmodern subject nor an opportunity to expand one's sphere of influence and marketability, but is instead an intensely corporeal state of impoverished marginalization. Recognizing, with Jacques Attali, an important distinction between rich nomads who "experience the world vicariously and safely" and poor nomads "seeking to escape from the destitute periphery,"[41] these artists insist on tracing, not transcending, the cultural, political, and geographical borders that define and confine our subjectivities. In their work, borders are underlined as dynamic social spaces – sites of both repression and transgression. And when this work is carried out, as it so often is, under the umbrella of large-scale perennial international exhibitions, they have the capacity to radically confront the romance of nomadism that biennial culture would seem to promote.

I am not the first to suggest that artists are taking on the task of casting a critical gaze towards the excesses and contradictions of neoliberal globalization, even from within biennial culture. Critic Marcus Verhagen has observed that artists who frequent the international exhibition circuit are increasingly challenging that system's embrace of, or at least collusion with, the logic of global markets. Noting that the most acclaimed works are often those that "put forward a critical appraisal of the biennial or pointedly detach themselves from it" (he mentions, for example, Santiago Sierra's intervention into the Spanish pavilion at the 2003 Venice Biennale, discussed in the second chapter),[42] Verhagen argues that these projects are too easily absorbed, disarmed, and recuperated by their institutional framework – an argument reminiscent of debates surrounding institutional critique in the 1980s. But Verhagen's critique obscures a real potential for critical efficacy in projects such as Sierra's. For while it is arguably true that "the biennial as a whole can't aspire to a cogent assessment of globalization because it is itself wholly shaped by global pressures,"[43] then surely artists within this system do possess the capacity, however limited, to challenge the romantic notions according to which biennial culture is able to elide these same global pressures. The artists whose work I align with the notion of reluctant nomadism are deeply embedded in the deterritorializing logic of such events. But while it would be convenient to proffer these practices, which take place in and around borders, checkpoints, and other contested sites of globalization, as further manifestations of biennial culture's imperial enterprise, I suggest instead that artists like Salcedo, Jaar, and Biemann operate both within and against the biennial system, employing what Mieke Bal terms a migratory aesthetic to critique – if complicitly – the celebratory nomadism of biennial culture.

Phantom Scenes

The problematics that attend to modelling a transnational framework for the circulation of contemporary art, and the extent to which this framework can be understood to both reflect globalization's excesses and challenge its exclusions, find an ideal case study in *The Unhomely: Phantom Scenes in Global Society*, Okwui Enwezor's 2006 International Biennial of Contemporary Art of Seville (BIACS II). Like Enwezor's previous large-scale exhibitions – Johannesburg in 1997 and Documenta

11 in 2002 – this exhibition paid sustained and thoughtful critical attention to both the existence and transgressions of geographic, cultural, and political borders in the rapidly globalizing spheres of art, economics, and politics. Here, ninety-one artists from thirty-five countries were invited to examine how the turmoils that seem to define the contemporary world – war, poverty, famine, and multiple refugee crises, to name a few – have transformed conventional modes of recognition – proximity, neighbourliness, and intimacy – into defamiliarizing modes of "non-recognition" – self-containment, xenophobia, and incarceration.[44] The curatorial program, in other words, sought to trace how and to what extent the vectors of contact that have materialized the long-awaited global village quickly fashioned that village into a place of fear, discrimination, and alienation, where the phantasmagoric nature of the international order is itself haunted with "phantom scenes" of conflict and confrontation that threaten our collective sense of safety and stability while radically reconfiguring the very nature of home.[45]

This exploration of the emergent global order and its destabilization of both the conceptual framework and material realities of home actually has its roots in Enwezor's 1997 Johannesburg Biennial, which likewise investigated the idea that "'Home' as a sign of stability is no longer easily sustainable."[46] Nine years after Enwezor's observation that "our cities and lives have been transformed by the ever changing direction of the compass as populations drift and masses of people are submitted to the most horrific methods of genocide, starvation, and cruelty,"[47] the stakes appeared to have multiplied. Ongoing conflict in the Middle East, unprecedented levels of state surveillance in cities and on borders around the world, sharply increasing rates of incarceration and detention, and refugee crises from Sudan to Afghanistan to Iraq (and now Syria) constitute what Enwezor, borrowing a term from postcolonial theorist David Scott, calls the "problem-spaces" in which the "multiple mutinies and upheavals that currently beset global society" are localized.[48] And indeed, the artworks represented at BIACS II – from Thomas Ruff's uncannily pixellated photographs of contemporary war zones to Harun Farocki's painstaking reconstruction of abuse in a California state prison using surveillance camera footage, and from Andreas Slominski's threateningly human-scaled animal traps to Lamia Joreige's intimate interviews with survivors of conflict in Lebanon – captured, in various ways, the "problem-spaces" that render our times and spaces unhomely.

Hence, insofar as *The Unhomely*'s mandate was to address the increasingly antagonistic expressions of belonging and unbelonging in the twenty-first century, it might be argued that the exhibition itself was a reluctant champion of the nomadic condition. Certainly, one of the problem-spaces identified within the curatorial framework was the current debate over art's proximity to society, and one of the exhibition's chief concerns was to contest the recuperation of "the romantic illusion of pure distance and total autonomy" in contemporary art, instead presenting a case for art's crucial role of articulating and intervening in contemporary conditions of upheaval by fashioning innovative modes of affiliation. Thus positioning art practices as integral, rather than peripheral, to global society's challenges, Enwezor successfully evaded the construction of a curatorial rhetoric that valorizes the romanticism of the "eccentric, aloof, nostalgic, deliberately untimely" itinerant artist.[49] But while promoting a rhetoric of proximity and neighbourliness, BIACS II, in almost programmatic form, itself became a problem-space whose own sense of neighbourliness was quickly called into question.

For Enwezor, it was important that BIACS II look "beyond the metaphor of the city"[50] towards a more global reflection on the complexities that define contemporary models and counter-models of adjacency; in this way it was hoped that the exhibition would circumvent the perceived tendency of location-specific biennials to "colonize" their host cities.[51] Thus, with a few modest exceptions (Yan Pei Ming's *Pirate Flags*, for example, silkscreened flags bearing images of children, skulls, and US dollars, were installed on a footbridge that crosses the city's Guadalquivir River, in order to create a visual "bridge" between the biennial's two main exhibition spaces, located on opposite sides of the river), the exhibiting artists refrained from any critical or sustained engagement with the local context.[52] But in an exhibition so attentive to questions of intimacy, proximity, and neighbourliness, the marked absence of attention to the city of Seville rendered BIACS itself something of an unhomely presence. Perhaps inevitably, Enwezor's insistence on transcending site-specificity left the exhibition vulnerable to censure, including a complaint among critics – a familiar refrain of late – that the biennial could have been held anywhere.[53] The seemingly deliberate alienation of the exhibition from its immediate context also prompted a lively local opposition that, with the rallying cry "BIACS, NO!" advertised its resistance to the parachute-in/parachute-out paradigm of international exhibitions with graffiti, postcards, YouTube videos celebrating the vibrancy of local culture, and a well-publicized anti-BIACS media event at Seville's most famous tourist attraction, the Giralda Tower.[54]

Swiss artist Thomas Hirschhorn's contribution to *The Unhomely* illuminates some of the stakes at play in the curatorial decision to eschew site-specificity. The site-specific installation *Re* (2006) was a sprawling room full of bookshelves, seating, video screens, and DIY signage, all covered in packing tape, intended to both document and reconstruct the artist's *Musée Précaire Albinet* (2004) – a fragile outdoor gallery in a working-class suburb of Paris built collaboratively with locals and temporarily displaying major works on loan from the Centre Georges Pompidou. On the streets of Paris, Hirschhorn's exhibit explored whether art can have a viable political impact and whether it can contribute to dismantling the artificial but seemingly intransigent borders of class and race. As the artist has explained, his practice (from the open-air museum in working-class Paris to the Gramsci Monument in a housing project in the Bronx in 2013) represents an effort to "cross from our stable, secure and safe space … in order to join the space of the precarious."[55] Reconstructed within the confines of the BIACS II exhibition space, however, the project – itself literally a phantom scene – appeared to abandon even the pretence of such an attempt. Phantoms also stalked the exhibition venues themselves. The exhibition was staged in two locations, both of which invite, indeed demand, analysis of Spain's principal role in the historical trajectory of globalization. The first, the Andalusian Centre for Contemporary Art located at the local Carthusian Monastery, was a favourite retreat of fifteenth-century explorer Christopher Columbus and, for several years after his death, the site of his remains. A prominent statue to Columbus is on permanent display on the gallery's grounds. The second location was the recently refurbished Royal Shipyards – coincidentally where many of the ships used to "discover" the Americas were built and launched. Given these historically loaded settings, the absence of attention to the disastrous consequences of the Western world's (and in this particular context, Spain's) propensity to test the limits of neighbourliness, proximity, and intimacy in the conquering and colonization of the Americas seemed to haunt the exhibition with its own barely repressed memories.

The absence of reflection, at least in the curatorial focus, on Seville's geographical position in the increasingly troubled southern region of Spain was likewise conspicuous. Spain's southern border has in recent years become a deadly battleground in Europe's war against undocumented migration; each year 300,000 to 500,000 hopeful migrants swim, hire inflatable rafts, or otherwise attempt to cross the Strait of Gibraltar from Morocco into Spain. Since the turn of the present century, thousands of people have been rescued and several thousand more are believed to have drowned, leading refugee aid organizations to refer to the Strait as the "largest mass grave of post-war Europe."[56] Those who do survive the treacherous crossing are likely to be captured by the sophisticated surveillance system that now blankets the entire coast. *The Unhomely* did acknowledge the proximity of North Africa with the organization of a film festival at Cinémathèque de Tanger in Morocco's second-largest city; the program, *Among the Moderns*, was intended to problematize the stereotypes that now plague representations of the Arab world while highlighting film and video production in the Maghreb region of North Africa. But this moment of transnational neighbourliness and collaboration only underscores biennial culture's tendency to trumpet its broadened boundaries of art production and reception while failing to acknowledge that the borders crossed so effortlessly by the presumably (white) Western biennial artists and audiences are relentlessly patrolled against incursions from the south, making it difficult to imagine that North African art audiences were offered equivalent access to the Seville exhibition. To wit, since the European Union enacted the Schengen Agreement in 1995, Moroccan citizens must now present a passport, a Schengen visitor visa, and a compelling justification to cross into Spain. As French-Moroccan artist Yto Barrada, represented at the Seville Biennial and the director of the Cinémathèque de Tanger, observes, the Strait of Gibraltar has become "legally a one-way strait"[57] – a situation only exacerbated by post-9/11 geopolitics of fear and hyper-surveillance. The Seville Biennial's cross-border logic seems to verify a prevailing suspicion regarding the opening of contemporary art to a postcolonial rhetoric that nevertheless operates according to neocolonial circuits. For while *The Unhomely* clearly reflected Enwezor's pioneering inclination to present a globalized roster of artists (of ninety-two participants, thirty-eight were born in and/or live in Asia, Africa, or South America), the exhibition's logistics revealed the presumption of an English-speaking Western audience, able to travel freely between Spain and Morocco[58] – suggesting that twenty years on, Gerardo Mosquera's critique of globalized art circulation, that "the world is practically divided between curating cultures and curated cultures,"[59] still rings true.

But while the questions raised by biennial culture's perceived failure to address, interpret, and respond to the repercussions of globalization in an appropriately self-reflexive manner are valid, indeed urgently needed, the answers are not necessarily as straightforward as, say, inviting more participation from local artists, hosting only interactive community art projects, or abandoning the biennial paradigm altogether in favour of a return to nineteenth-century exhibition models. One of Enwezor's curatorial mandates for BIACS II was to treat the relationship between North Africa and Europe as one of many "problem-spaces" associated with the current global order, and indeed two of the artists whose work will be discussed further – Ursula Biemann and Yto Barrada – investigate the Gibraltar region, a flashpoint in this relationship, in precisely this way. What I want to suggest is that the staging of BIACS II itself functioned productively as a problem-space, defined by David Scott as "an ensemble of questions and answers around which a horizon of identifiable stakes (conceptual as well as ideological-political stakes) hangs."[60] For if the curatorial outlook of the Seville Biennial seemed disinclined to reflect more than cursorily on either the complex (even unhomely) nature of Spain's southern border or the politics of belonging as they pertained to the exhibition's position within its socio-geographical context, it did create a space for reflection in its choice of artists, and it was precisely this slippage – between the curatorial message and artistic practices that I've identified under the rubric of reluctant nomadism – that revealed the exhibition to be a productive site of negotiation. Simultaneously enacting and challenging the romance of nomadism that pervades biennial culture and renders it relevant to debates over globalization's "phantom scenes," BIACS II demonstrated that large-scale international exhibitions, for all their apparent sins of geo-touristic ambition and corporate pandering, are perhaps uniquely positioned to unravel the intricately tangled relations between nations and nomads, borders and utopias, the West and its peripheries.

Mobility and Melanchronia

"There is no such thing as site specificity for exiles," writes art critic T.J. Demos, who draws on two key threads in contemporary political theory – Edward Said's notion that home is always a provisional entity for the exiled subject[61] and Giorgio Agamben's argument that the refugee constitutes the central figure of contemporary geopolitics[62] – in a close reading of the diasporic art practices of Emily Jacir, which, according to Demos, privilege mobility over "sitedness."[63] Particularly salient to Demos's claim is Jacir's 2003 *Where We Come From*, discussed briefly in chapter 3, which found the artist traversing Israel and the Occupied Territories to fulfil the wishes of Palestinians who, for various reasons, were barred from returning home. Demos is responding here to Lebanese critic Rasha Salti's accusation that the art world tends to recruit Jacir's work as representative of the universality of exile in a way that wilfully ignores the specifically Palestinian context to which her art responds. Jacir, Salti argues, has become wrongly labelled as "a paradigmatic 'exilic' artist, whose art is 'deterritorialized,' challenging 'site-specificity,' obsessively consumed with 'dislocation,' [such that] they dislocate Emily Jacir from the localized context of Palestinian artistic expression and practice to the universal worldliness of an emerging trend of 'diasporic artists,' perpetually tortured by permanent exile."[64] Demos counters that works like *Where We Come From* actually reconceive exile as a "corrosive force *against* the determination of nationality," belying the "retrograde resurrection of a nationalist framework to determine the meaning and significance of her art."[65]

Let us consider this claim in the context of an earlier work, *From Texas, with Love*. For this 2002 video, Jacir also posed a question, this time asking Palestinians living in the Occupied Territories to help her build a music playlist for an American road trip: "If you had the freedom to get in a car and drive for one hour without being stopped (imagine no Israeli military occupation; no Israeli soldiers, no Israeli checkpoints and roadblocks, no 'bypass' roads), what song would you listen to?"[66] Thus outfitted with musical accompaniment, Jacir drove through rural Texas for one hour without stopping – a journey that was feasible on the wide-open roads of the US south, but which would be unimaginable in the geographically restricted, closely policed and heavily barricaded Occupied Territories. But while this work, like *Where We Come From*, must certainly be understood as a critique of the forced immobility and deterritorialization endured by most Palestinians, it does not follow that Jacir's work proposes "a postnational basis of collective identification, one based upon the construction of a fluid culture of belonging."[67] Jacir's project, far from problematizing sitedness, instead challenges the very un-siting of collective identity in the practice and theorization of diasporic art – a challenge that Jacir herself articulates in relation to *From Texas, with Love*: "The ability to actually experience such a freedom in other countries is a painful marker and reminder of the impossibility of experiencing such a basic human right in Palestine."[68] Jacir's work, in other words, which juxtaposes her own privileged mobility with the imposed deterritorialization of exiled or occupied Palestinians, is congruent with the practice of self-reflexive, reluctant nomadism with which this chapter is concerned.

Jacir's practice also accords with Mieke Bal's thoughts on the aesthetics of site-specificity in the context of an increasingly internationally oriented art world. "Globalized art?" she asks. "What would such a term mean? This is not an art from nowhere, for such an art, I contend, does not exist. Since art making is a material practice, there is no such thing as site-unspecific art."[69] With this observation, Bal acknowledges two important facets of contemporary art practice: first, that art today is inextricably linked to the logic of the global marketplace; second, that the globalization (or, in the context of the present study, the biennialization) of art cannot and should not obscure the geopolitical nuances of its production, distribution, and reception. To respond to this apparent stalemate, Bal proposes "migratory aesthetics" as a way to conceptualize the "aesthetic encounter [that] takes place in the space of, on the basis of, and on the interface with, the *mobility* of people as a given, as central, and as at the heart of what matters in the contemporary, that is, 'globalized,' world."[70] In ways that echo Bal's observations, several artists represented at the 2006 Seville Biennial elaborated a set of positions vis-à-vis the culture of biennials that pose subtle but significant challenges to the exhibition's oblique self-narrative of postnational utopianism. What connects these artists – Cuban American neo-conceptual artist Tony Labat, French Moroccan photographer and video artist Yto Barrada, and Swiss video artist and curator Ursula Biemann – is that they each both enrich and are enriched by interaction with the concept of migratory aesthetics, the tenets of which are particularly suited to the task of unpacking and testing biennial culture's romantic attachment to nomadism.

In her elaboration of migratory aesthetics, Bal suggests that video art, which since its inception has been deeply invested in explorations of temporality, is uniquely apposite to explorations of migration's spatiotemporal complexities:

> Video is the medium of our time. It is also the medium of time; of time contrived, manipulated, and offered in different, multi-layered ways. Time no longer captured, as in the very first strips of celluloid, nor even "sampled" in bits separated by cuts; time is "framed," made to appear real but no longer indexically attached to the real time that it purportedly represents. Like filmic cinema, it offers images moving in time – slow or fast, interrupting and integrating. Similarly, and again, ... migration is the situation of our

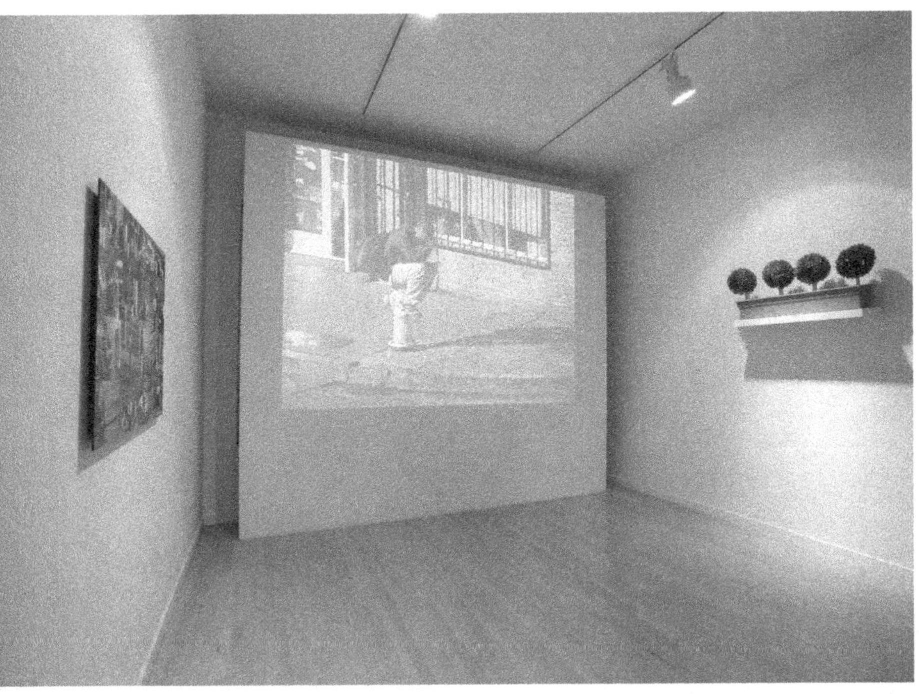

4.3 Tony Labat, *Day Labor: Mapping the Outside (Fat Chance Bruce Nauman)*, 2006. Surveillance station, 2-channel projection, LCD monitors, dimensions variable, installation detail. Courtesy of the artist and Anglim Gilbert Gallery, San Francisco.

> time. But it is also an experience of time; as multiple, heterogeneous – the time of haste and waiting; the time of movement and stagnation; the time of memory and of an unsetting, provisional present, with its pleasures and its violence. Video and migratory life have, thus, something in common. A complex, and sometimes confusing, challenging multitemporality characterizes both [and] video art can [therefore] contribute to a better understanding of migratory culture.[71]

It is therefore neither coincidental nor insignificant that one of the threads connecting the practices of Labat, Barrada, and Biemann is their privileging of video as a medium through which to explore mobility and migration. Consider Tony Labat's 2006 video installation *Day*

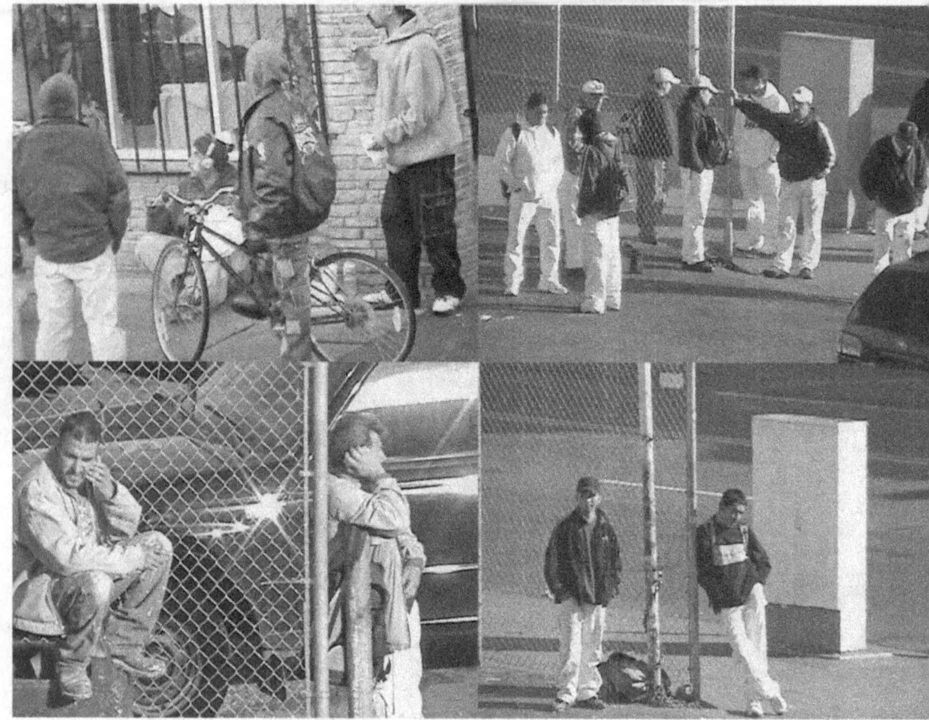

4.4 Tony Labat, *Day Labor: Mapping the Outside (Fat Chance Bruce Nauman)*, 2006. Surveillance station, 2-channel projection, LCD monitors, dimensions variable, installation detail. Courtesy of the artist and Anglim Gilbert Gallery, San Francisco.

Labor: Mapping the Outside (Fat Chance Bruce Nauman). For this work, Labat installed four surveillance cameras in the window of his San Francisco studio, which overlooks a parking lot where migrant labourers regularly convene, hoping to be called upon for temporary work. The installation includes two large projections – a four-split screening of edited footage from the surveillance cameras taken over several months, and a projection of video shot intermittently from a fifth, handheld camera.[72]

Labat's piece confirms in several interrelated ways Mieke Bal's contention regarding video's "eminent suitability" to the migrant experience. The use of video surveillance technology, for instance, reminds us (in a manner congruent with Biemann's *Contained Mobility*) that the migrant's life is under constant surveillance. It also conforms, at least in part, to Bal's observation that video's most significant contribution to migratory aesthetics is its capacity to express "temporal discrepancies and disturbed rhythms," particularly via techniques of cutting and distortion.[73] As Bal suggests, such discrepancies and disturbances are expressly felt by migratory subjects, "permanently on the move," who experience "the time of haste and waiting, the time of movement and stagnation; the time of memory and of an unsettling, provisional present, with its pleasures and its violence."[74] And certainly, Labat's installation both documents and rehearses this experience of multitemporality, or what Bal terms heterochrony, the multiple screens competing for our sensory attention to the various states of boredom, anticipation, and panic that measure the temporary worker's day.

But what emerges, even more forcefully, from the installation is a sense of temporality stalled. Notwithstanding sporadic episodes of relative hyperactivity (such as the unexpected arrival of a police cruiser), what the installation documents overwhelmingly is endless time spent waiting – playing cards, drinking coffee, napping, reading the paper, listening to music, leaning against a concrete wall with toes tapping. In fact the life of the migrant worker appears, from this footage, to be marked less by a heterochronic experience of time than an experience that I'd like to describe as *melanchronic*. In this way, a traumatic element is introduced that is reminiscent of Freud's concept of *Nachträglichkeit* or belated action.[75] Like the stalled temporality experienced by the patient who is unable to integrate, or "claim," a traumatic experience and is therefore bound perpetually to that traumatizing moment,[76] time stands still for the migrant (consider again Ursula Biemann's asylum seeker Anatol Zimmerman, suspended in a temporal realm of imprisoned mobility), for whom days turn into months waiting for papers or for work, waiting in refugee camps or at border checkpoints, waiting in detention centres to be sent back to a home that is unsustainable, only to begin the entire process anew.

What I find particularly interesting about *Day Labor*'s own investigation of the melanchronic experience of migration is how Labat piggybacks it onto video art's own history of investigating delayed temporality. The installation's subtitle, *Mapping the Outside (Fat Chance Bruce Nauman)*, is an explicit reference to Nauman's 2001 *Mapping the Studio I (Fat Chance John Cage)*, also a large-scale video installation

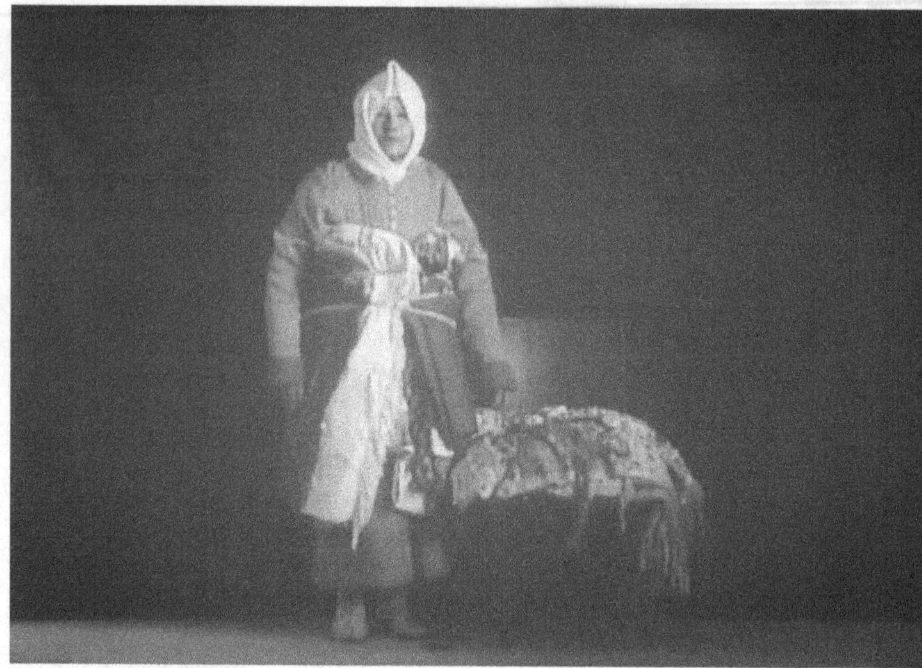

4.5. Yto Barrada, *La Contrebandière (The Smuggler)*, 2005 film, video, colour, mute 18 min. © Yto Barrada 2015. Courtesy of Pace Gallery, London; Sfeir-Semler Gallery, Hamburg, Beirut; and Galerie Polaris, Paris.

that documents surveillance video taken, in this case, inside the artist's studio. Nauman's work, which documents nocturnal activities in his studio (eerily calm except for the occasional appearance of a cat or mouse), is likewise a meditation on duration and ennui, as such, revisiting concerns that make Nauman a key figure in the early history of video art's temporal possibilities. For while it is true that the multi-temporal dimensions of video are key to its criticality in art and culture, it is video's capacity to express the banality of time that has enchanted artists since its inception in the late 1960s.[77] Tony Labat's intervention into these explorations is, I suggest, twofold. First, the work employs video art's relentlessly narcissistic gaze to cross-purposes, wresting the camera's lens away from self and towards the other in a move that renders the terms of video art's engagement with melanchronia decidedly relational.[78] But second (and more pertinently), like early video, which sought to both probe and disrupt conventional understandings of time, Labat's installation challenges contemporary culture's narratives of motion, speed, and acceleration. In so doing, he aptly conveys Alan Sekula's insightful observation that "a society of accelerated flows is also in certain key aspects a society of deliberately slow movements."[79] And it is in this way that Labat's aesthetic enunciation of melanchronia – which must also be considered his contribution to the unhomely aesthetics of contemporary art – constitutes an oblique aesthetic challenge to biennial culture's postmodern embrace of itinerancy as lifestyle.

Like Tony Labat, Yto Barrada – a photographer and video artist based in Tangier, Morocco – offers a radical take on what Enwezor calls the "complex nature of adjacency," in the process demanding a rethinking of the ethics and aesthetics of nomadism in a world increasingly delineated by closed and contested borders. And like Labat, Barrada employs a migratory aesthetic to convey the challenges of living between worlds. *The Smuggler*, first screened at BIACS II in 2006, is a silent eleven-minute video consisting of a slow, methodical, step-by-step demonstration of the process by which an elder Moroccan woman, identified only as T.M., prepares to smuggle textiles out of the town of Ceuta – a Spanish enclave inside the territory of Morocco. T.M. is one of hundreds of so-called "mule women" – residents of Ceuta and Melilla who don't require a visa to cross the border from Morocco and spend their days smuggling clothing and electronics.[80] In the video, T.M. prepares for her daily trek following the tradition of wrapping layer upon layer around her body, securing them with rope, then concealing them under her *djellaba* robe, as if illustrating Ursula Biemann's evocative observation that "the economic logic of the border inscribes itself onto every layer of the transforming, mobile female body."[81] On one hand, the smuggler's demeanour and facial expressions evince an unmistakably dignified desire to demonstrate the proper techniques for her trade. At another level, however, is revealed the routine daily struggle of fashioning a living in the Gibraltar region; the woman's diminutive frame seems to groan with every layer added, and at one point a young girl appears from beyond the frame to assist with the wrapping.

In *The Smuggler* the melanchronic aspects of the migratory experience are expressed in ways that both resemble and diverge from Tony Labat's work. Again, the video records a daily process that reveals the border to be a *temporally* liminal site of mundane, repetitive activities. But rather than exploiting video's capacity for lengthy recording,

Barrada instead employs the loop to reiterate the repetitive nature of the woman's livelihood; here, eleven minutes of drudgery become literally eternal. This again echoes the temporality of trauma, wherein time stands still in perpetual repetition, and indeed, time seems to stand still for the smuggler in multiple ways. The woman is filmed in front of a black backdrop, which adds a sense of timelessness to her performance; one quickly develops the impression that T.M. has been smuggling fabrics across the Spanish border, and will continue doing so, forever. The fleeting presence of the camera-shy young girl disrupts this temporal standstill to a certain extent, but it also signals another mode of timelessness, for the viewer is obliged to consider the possibility that the training is for her benefit, that she will one day carry on the burden (literally) of this borderline existence.

But as a critical strategy, this melanchronic restaging of migrant experience also conveys a spirit of subversive potential. Cultural theorist Jenny Edkins conceptualizes "trauma time" as a halted, disruptive temporality that interrupts the "smooth time" of hegemonic cultural narratives. Investigating the ways in which trauma impacts history, memory, and politics, Edkins suggests that trauma, "which refuses to take its place in history as done and finished with," has the capacity to "challenge sovereign power at its very roots" by insisting on bearing witness to that which cannot be integrated into national myths and narratives.[82] Thus in all its despondent, repetitive temporality, trauma can also be understood productively as the Barthesian *punctum* that both pricks the conscience of history and rewrites its future.[83] In the practices of Labat and Barrada, I see melanchronia operating in a parallel fashion, such that the traumatic is introduced into the ongoing narratives of unfettered mobility, uninterrupted speed, and infinitely crossable borders that circulate in, and indeed facilitate the existence of, international exhibition practices.

The Spatial Politics of Smuggling

Challenging normative narratives of smooth, rapid experiences of temporality, Yto Barrada's practice also challenges the spatial demarcation of borders. Troubling, if only implicitly, her own status as a binational, indeed international artist whose art world credentials grant her relatively easy border passage – and troubling, by association, the privileged status of the Western art tourist, whose access to Spain is likewise unimpeded – Barrada methodically outlines the borders that are otherwise elided by transnational exhibition practices. In this way, Barrada's practice can be usefully juxtaposed with Santiago Sierra's articulations of the Spanish-Moroccan border according to Irit Rogoff's observation that critical art practices can function to manifest "a kind of physical stamping of the terrain, an insistence on a border where everyone else is denying its existence."[84] Recall Sierra's *3000 Holes of 180 × 50 × 50 cm Each* (2002), which saw North African labourers digging coffin-sized holes on the Spanish coast facing Morocco. To a certain extent, Yto Barrada shares Sierra's determination to avow the existence of these otherwise elided borders; critics have noted that Barrada's photographs often feature roadblocks, holes, and other impassable geographies.[85] And yet these holes and obstructions also have a liberating dimension, exposing the materiality of the border in a way that also challenges its structural integrity. Barrada's ancient smuggler defiantly crosses and re-crosses the contested Spanish-Moroccan border, each passage underlining its contours while undermining its power to shape her movements and livelihood. As critic Nico Israel observes, "What at first appears absolutely impossible – overcoming a difference, bridging a treacherous strait – seems possible, if only for a fleeting instant, through art."[86]

Fortuitously, *The Smuggler* also resonates with Irit Rogoff's theorization of a "smuggling aesthetic," according to which "the notion of journey does not follow the logic of crossing barriers, borders, bodies of water but rather of sidling along with them seeking the opportune moment, the opportune breach in which to move to the other side."[87] For Rogoff, smuggling is a useful paradigm for critical art and curatorial practices because it privileges subversion over opposition:

> We have in recent years spoken much and often of not wanting to set up conflictual and binary engagements, of not wanting to have a fight with the art academy in the name of a progressive or revolutionary practice … or to waste time on battles between what is sanctioned "inside" the art institution versus what takes place more organically "outside" within the public sphere. Instead we have opted for a "looking away" or a "looking aside" or a spatial appropriation, which lets us get on with what we need to do or to imagine without reiterating that which we oppose. In theoretical terms we have moved from Criticism to critique to criticality to the actual inhabitation of a condition in which we are deeply embedded as well as being critically conscious. "Smuggling" exists in precisely such an illegitimate relation to a main event or a dominant economy without producing a direct critical response to it.[88]

This concept of smuggling as an illegitimate activity that relates critically (if not oppositionally) to a main event is particularly compelling in its twofold applicability to the thesis we are considering in this chapter: besides animating the border with her documentation of (literal) smuggling activities, Barrada also "smuggles" into the biennial context a subtle critique of the presumption of open borders that underwrites and even legitimizes its artistic offerings.

For Rogoff, the smuggling paradigm acknowledges the partiality of visibility by resisting the impulse to face dominant institutions and economies directly. Rogoff's insistence on "looking away" as a strategy for inhabiting a position of "partial knowledge"[89] is particularly salient to Yto Barrada's *Autocar – Tangier* (2004), a restrained and elusive series of four photographs that initially appear to be colourful geometric abstractions. In fact, the photographs depict logos painted on the backsides of tour buses that shuttle European tourists to and from North Africa. These logos, we learn, also function inadvertently as a series of coded messages, surreptitiously alerting teens and children as to the conditions according to which a particular company will unwittingly accommodate undocumented passage across the Strait. The logo pictured in *Autocar Figure 1*, for example, purportedly carries the following information: "Bus parks in front of the port near the ticket booth. 4 a.m. arrival in Tangier, 6 p.m. departure. Bring biscuits and dates, and plastic bag for shoes. They notice in Spain right away if your shoes are not clean. Bus goes onto Bismillah ferry, room for three small people [to hide] under the bus." The logo in *Figure 4* indicates that there is "one guard, but since he's in charge of the whole area, he can't check everything all the time. Climb in the middle of the planchas. Those who have papers go inside the bus."[90]

Like *The Smuggler*, the *Autocar* series operates as an insistent reminder of the perils of crossing borders: it is easy, and also immensely difficult, to visualize three small bodies crammed underneath a tour bus. But by mobilizing an instance in which the iconography of unobstructed global tourism is subversively transformed into a counter-iconography of illicit passage, the photographs indicate as well the (slim, costly, and dangerous) possibility of transgression. Thus, while Barrada's practice uncovers the troubled Gibraltar region as a complex site of economic hardship, physical struggle, and monotonous survival, what ultimately emerges in her work is a sense of borders breached. Like Doris Salcedo, Alfredo Jaar, and Tony Labat, Yto Barrada is clearly not seduced by what art historian Nikos Papastergiadis terms the contemporary

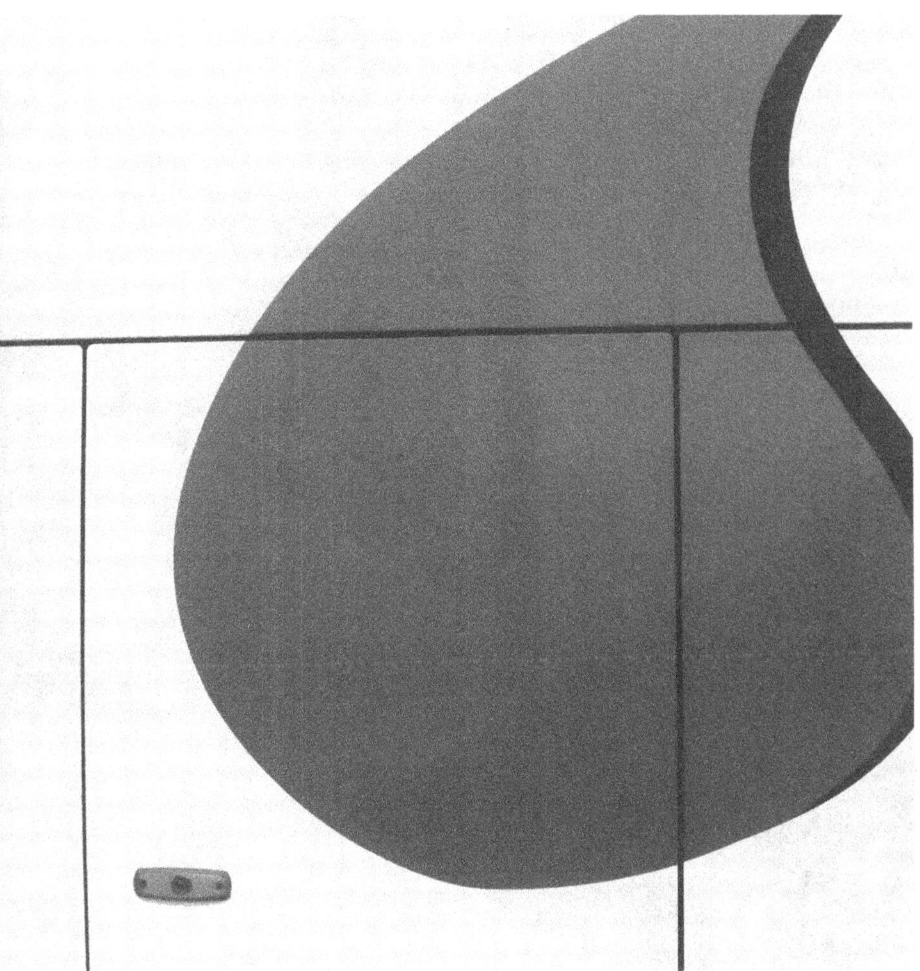

4.6. Yto Barrada, *Autocar – Tangier, Figure 1*, 2004. Chromogenic print, 88 × 88 cm (34⅝ × 34⅝ in.). © Yto Barrada 2015. Courtesy of Pace Gallery, London; Sfeir-Semler Gallery, Hamburg, Beirut; and Galerie Polaris, Paris.

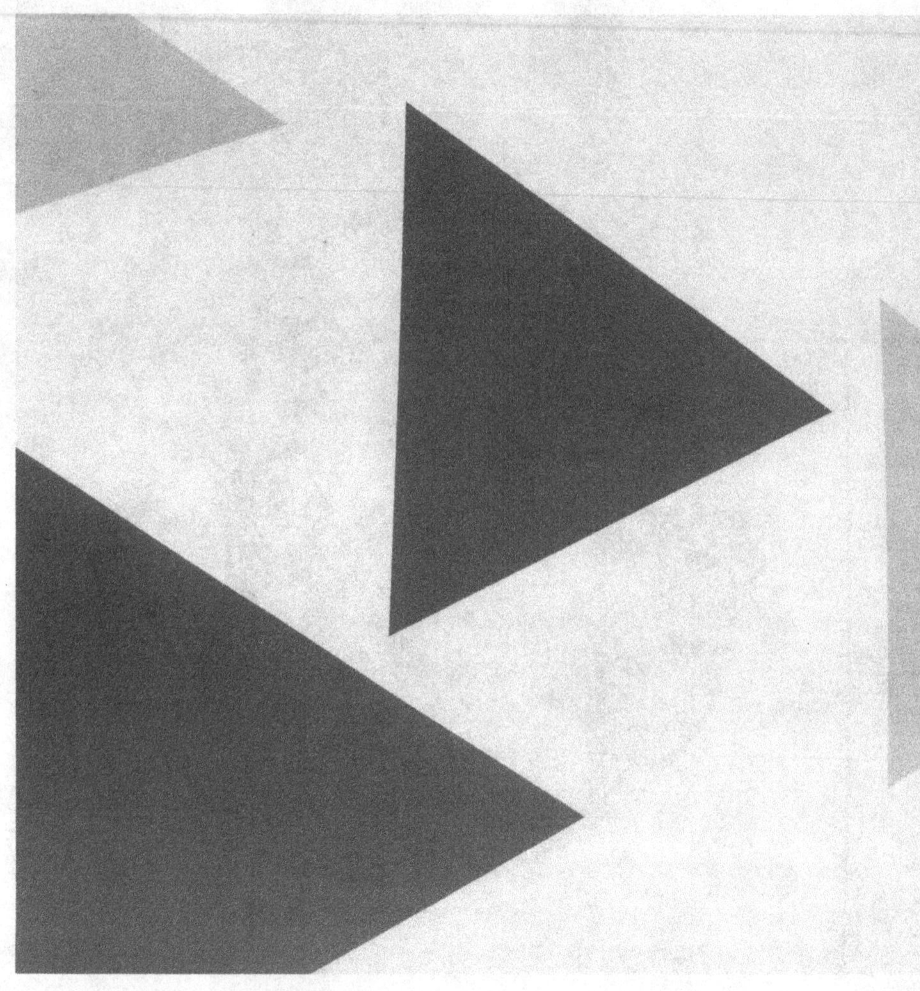

4.7. Yto Barrada, *Autocar – Tangier, Figure 2*, 2004. Chromogenic print, 88 × 88 cm (34⅝ × 34⅝ in.). © Yto Barrada 2015. Courtesy of Pace Gallery, London; Sfeir-Semler Gallery, Hamburg, Beirut; and Galerie Polaris, Paris.

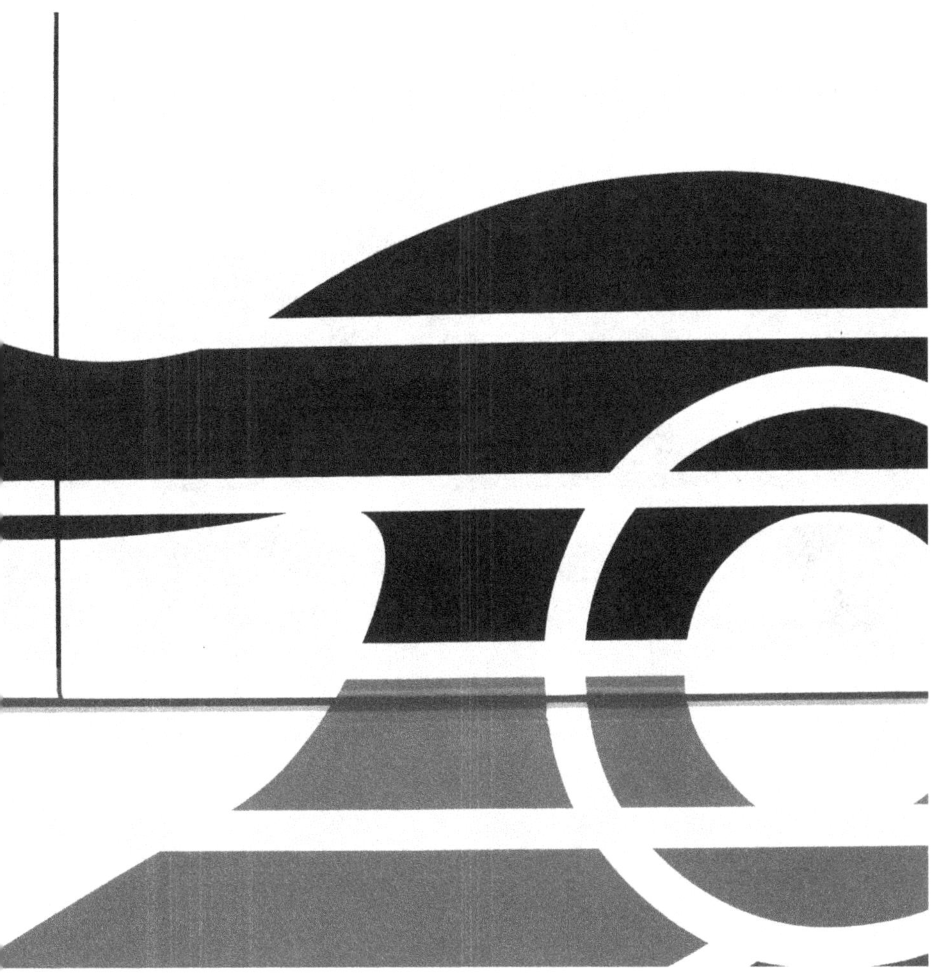

4.8. Yto Barrada, *Autocar – Tangier, Figure 3*, 2004. Chromogenic print, 88 × 88 cm (34⅝ × 34⅝ in.). © Yto Barrada 2015. Courtesy of Pace Gallery, London; Sfeir-Semler Gallery, Hamburg, Beirut; and Galerie Polaris, Paris.

4.9 Yto Barrada, *Autocar – Tangier, Figure 4,* 2004. Chromogenic print, 88 × 88 cm (34⅝ × 34⅝ in.). © Yto Barrada 2015. Courtesy of Pace Gallery, London; Sfeir-Semler Gallery, Hamburg, Beirut; and Galerie Polaris, Paris.

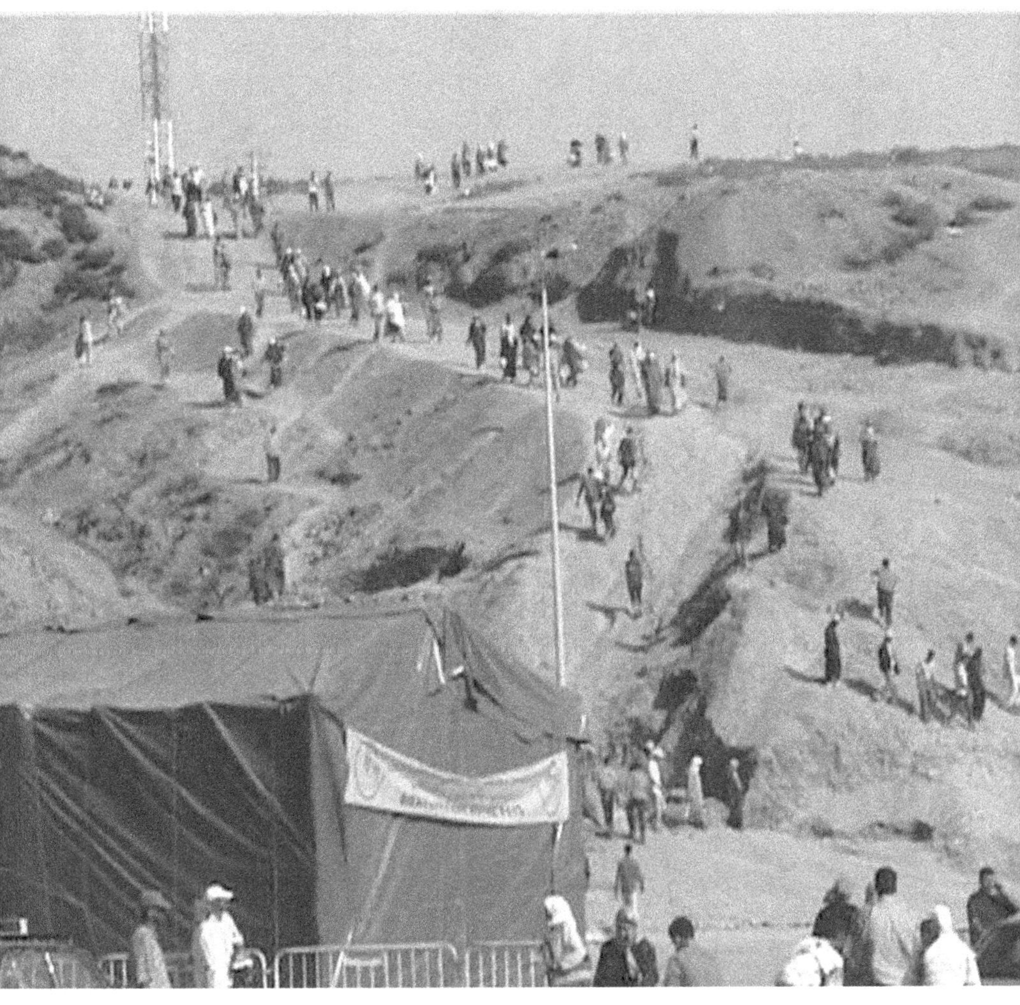

4.10 Ursula Biemann and Angela Sanders, *Europlex*, 2003. 20 min. Video still. Courtesy of the artist.

"fantasy of unrestricted mobility" (whether spatial or temporal) that both operationalizes and obscures "the violence of penetrating boundaries."[91] But in the artist's aesthetic rendering of these moments of subversive penetration, the contested Gibraltar Strait becomes imaginable as an interstitial site of both control and resistance, checkpoints and

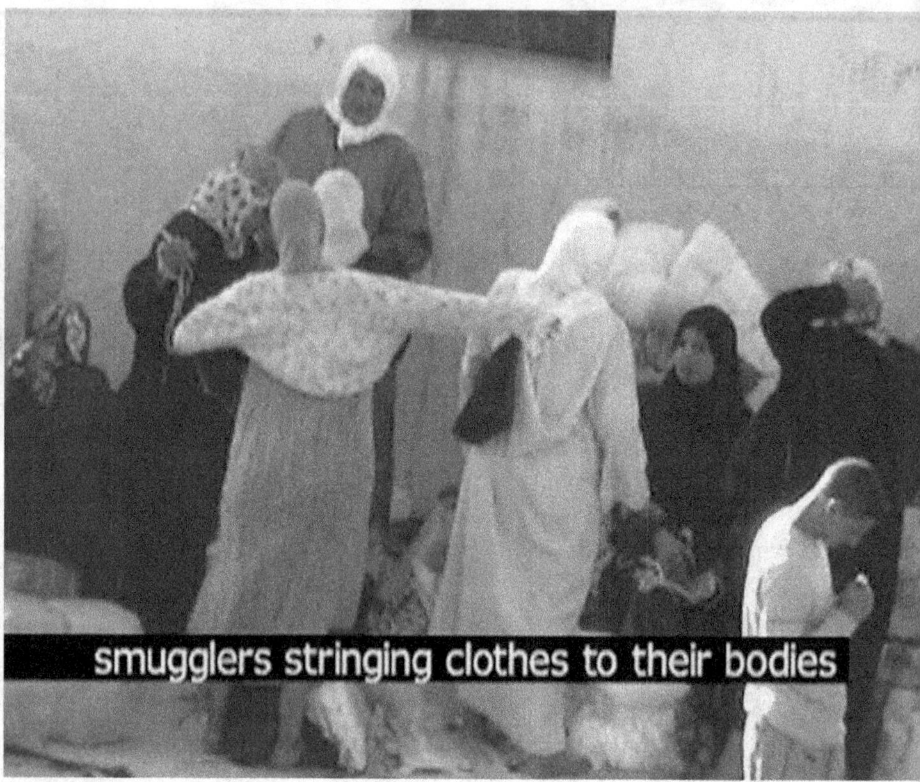

4.11 Ursula Biemann and Angela Sanders, *Europlex*, 2003. 20 min. Video still. Courtesy of the artist.

blindspots, borders and breaches. Or as the artist puts it, "What I am really unearthing, discovering, and learning to read are the strategies of resistance, the 'hidden transcripts' of people who are faced with superior power."[92] In the same instance, biennial culture under these terms becomes imaginable as a space where nomads and smugglers might ideally meet to negotiate and debate the conditions for a reconceived future of globalization.

Yto Barrada's work reveals the existence of borders in order to propose their susceptibility to transgression. This is also the proposition offered by Swiss artist Ursula Biemann, whose 2003 experimental ethnographic video essay *Europlex*, a collaboration with anthropologist Angela Sanders, is likewise concerned with the material and social

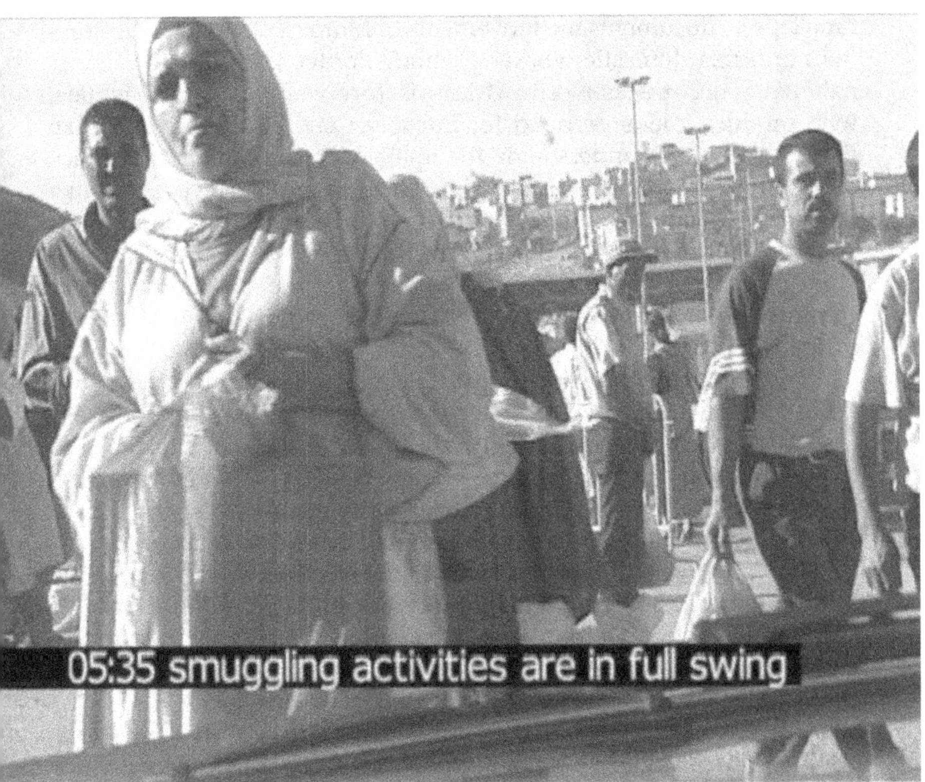

4.12 Ursula Biemann and Angela Sanders, *Europlex*, 2003. 20 min. Video still. Courtesy of the artist.

realities of the Spanish-Moroccan border area. A twenty-minute documentation of various activities that animate the border, *Europlex* articulates Biemann's Lefebvrian understanding of territorialization: "Territories," she suggests, "do not exist prior to contact and traffic. They are sustained through them. Appropriating and disciplining the restless movements of people and things: this is how space is made."[93] The video actually consists of three separately composed films, or "border logs," each of which focuses on a specific intersection of economy, geography, and gender. "Border Log I," subtitled "smuggling: a cartography of struggle," watches as women like Yto Barrada's T.M. "transform their bodies into vehicles of commerce"[94] by concealing goods and fabrics under their dresses. "Border Log II," or "domesticas living in a time lapse," documents the movements of Moroccan women who cross the border as domestic workers, while "Border Log III," "the transnational zone," tracks North African factory workers, mostly female, who produce goods destined for European and Asian markets. Like Barrada, Biemann understands the Spain-Morocco border as a space of both repression and transgression, struggle and survival. And, like Barrada, Biemann works to expose the material, embodied dimensions of the global market, which, as Imre Szeman observes, are "still too often passed over in discussions that focus on the spectrality of new communications technologies, the disembodied circulation of finance capital, and so on."[95]

What renders *Europlex* such a fitting exemplar of migratory aesthetics is the way in which Biemann challenges the rhetoric of disembodiment that attaches to both economic and cultural discourses of globalization by tracking and charting the movement of bodies back and forth across the border; her own smuggling tactics once again reveal the border as both a temporally and spatially liminal space. "Border Log II," for instance, spotlights the curious fact that the domestic workers who live in the Moroccan town of Tétuan, but work in the Spanish enclave of Ceuta, cross not only a border, but also a time zone (with a two-hour lag) each day. To convey the complex spatio-temporal dimensions that characterize the lives of these "permanent time travellers,"[96] the video employs advanced digital editing techniques that allow for a dense layering of video and audio tracks. The technical complexity of the work fulfils two functions: first, video's non-linear, non-logical dimensions are exploited to emphasize what Mieke Bal calls "the anti-narrative thrust of heterochrony" in the migratory experience.[97] But the video's complexity – stacked moving and still images, running text, and elaborate soundtrack – also signals Biemann's intention to underscore what she identifies as migrant women's high-tech competence as dynamic participants in the cross-border micro-economies of Gibraltar. As she observes, "many of them use the same state-of-the-art technologies of transportation and communication as high-tech businessmen do, in order to get to where they are."[98]

This last point is particularly relevant in understanding Biemann's migratory aesthetic. For Biemann, as for Barrada, the border represents both tightly controlled movement and the daily potential for subversion. Expressing impatience with representations of migrant women "in images of need, poverty, and helplessness, placed in humanitarian and development discourses, or in scenarios of exploitation,"[99] Biemann instead populates her video essay with images of women – smugglers, *domesticas*, and factory workers alike – who animate the border area in a way that corresponds to Michel de Certeau's notion of the itinerary: the unstructured and unauthorized mode of travel that subverts both the logic and authority of the official map.[100] The smugglers of "Border Log I" in particular, followed by a hand-held video camera as they create a kind of geopolitical network of desire lines[101] from Morocco into the "grey trade" zone outside Ceuta, develop itineraries that both demarcate and challenge the space of the border. In the tracing of this network of desire lines, neither designed nor authorized but rather worn away gradually by people finding the most expedient distance between two points, Biemann's migratory aesthetic offers a model for site sensitivity that is neither anthropological nor indifferent, neither melancholic nor transcendent, neither nostalgically sedentary nor romantically nomadic.

Transgressive Mobility, Radical Relations

In different ways, the artists in this chapter each reveal the embodied materiality of border spaces only to trace how bodies circulate within and against the logic of these spaces, compelling them to admit a certain porosity. To this extent, these artists agree with Okwui Enwezor's characterization of borders as "problem-spaces" of generative tension. Somewhat more provocatively, however, the borders in these works can furthermore be understood as traumatized spaces. Jenny Edkins proposes that trauma, rather than being understood as injury, might be productively conceived as itself a form of border crossing, "something to do with the crossing of distinctions we take for granted, the distinctions between psyche and body, body and environment, for example."[102] For Edkins, trauma understood in this light becomes a way to imagine the possibility of "radical relationality," which she conceptualizes in a way that cuts to the heart of the unhomely aesthetics of contemporary art practices: "We prefer to think of buildings as solid, of home as a place of safety, of ourselves as separate from our neighbours, and of our bodies as made of living flesh not inorganic atoms. A traumatic event demonstrates how untenable, or how insecure, these distinctions and these assumptions are. It calls for nothing more or less than the recognition of the radical relationality of existence."[103] Trauma, in other words, undermines the presumed impermeability of self–other borders much in the same way that the smugglers and temporary workers documented in contemporary video projects destabilize the presumed infallibility of national borders. Resonating also with Kristeva's understanding of the foreigner as a "scar" that tears across the presumption of a coherent relationship between human and citizen, troubling conventions of home and homeland and demanding new models of relationality,[104] the reluctant nomads of contemporary art treat the troubled borders of global society as wounded spaces that also, subversively, suggest the potential for suture..

Consider, for instance, the fate of Doris Salcedo's *Shibboleth*. On an October evening in 2007, hundreds of Londoners convened in Tate Modern's Turbine Hall to participate in a mobile clubbing flash mob.[105] At precisely 7:01 p.m., this motley assembly of friends and strangers, each wearing a personal music player with earphones, turned on their music of choice and began dancing on and around Salcedo's *Shibboleth* in utter, joyous silence. I began this chapter by describing the fissure that Salcedo tore into the Turbine Hall, and suggested that the work, which sought to materialize the enormous pressures and barriers that confront the contemporary immigrant, offered a way to begin thinking of a new model for institutional critique – one that counters the romance of nomadism in the transnational circulation of contemporary art with a sustained deliberation on the often traumatizing aspects of mobility and migration. I conclude with this work as well, because I believe it also provides, if somewhat inadvertently, a way to begin thinking how art can become a vehicle for forging itineraries out of maps, desire out of despair, and hope out of catastrophe. Of all the art practices that have been discussed in this book, *Shibboleth* is perhaps the most literal manifestation of a wounded space of stranger relations. Much like the artists who challenged the elision of borders underwriting the Seville Biennial of 2006, Salcedo likewise undermines the art world's "glimpse of a transnational utopia"[106] that, in order to function, must remain blind to its less than utopian context and conditions of production and circulation. Salcedo's crack in the floor of the Tate Modern has since been cemented over, but it still exists under the surface: the point is not to perform a kind of cosmetic surgery that will repair this wounded borderspace so as to imagine that the wound never existed, but instead to remain ever vigilant to its vulnerability. But it is also significant that of all the art practices discussed in this book, *Shibboleth* is perhaps the most formally related to Gordon Matta-Clark's building cuts. Like Matta-Clark's cuts, Salcedo's crack manages to let the light in. For consider how Salcedo reconfigured Turbine Hall. Rather than building an imposing fence or otherwise insuperable barrier to act out the difficult crossing of borders, Salcedo's negative space instead offers an infinitely transgressible border zone. Indeed, it seems to invite violation. Salcedo's *Shibboleth*,

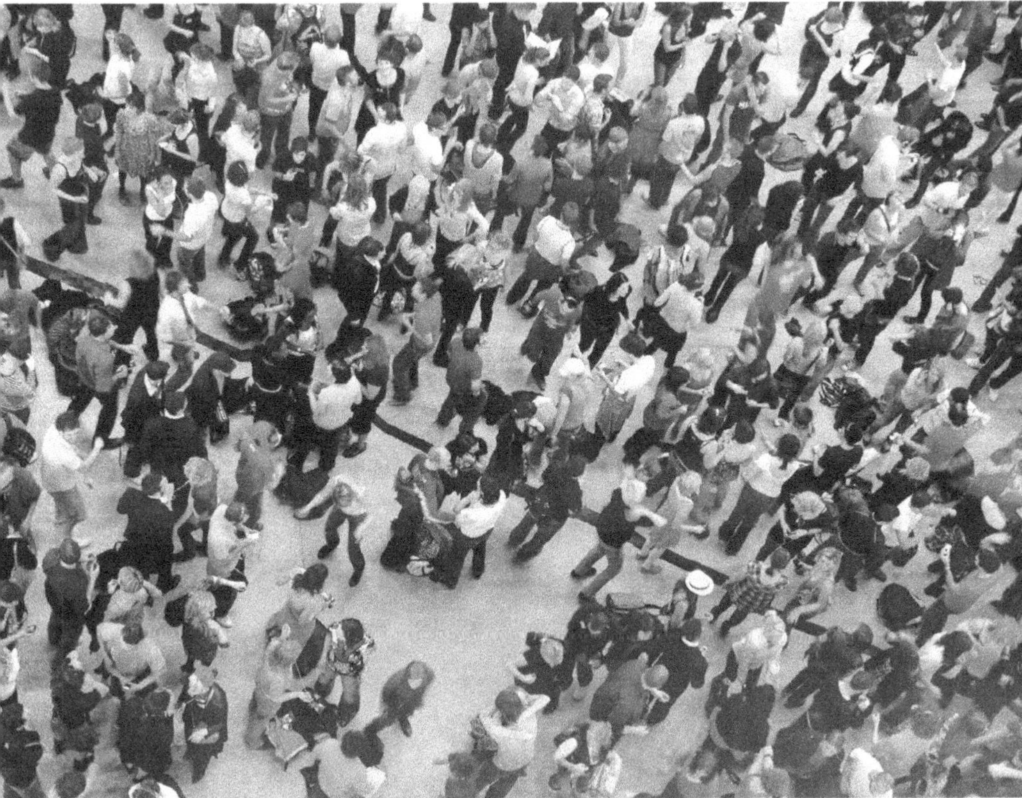

4.13 Dean Ayres, *Dancing on the Edge*, 2007. © Dean Ayres. Courtesy of the artist.

in other words, creates the opportunity to transform a wounded space into a site for the performance of radical relationality – an opportunity that was seized by London's mobile clubbers.[107]

Engaging a migratory aesthetic to both convey and perform instances of mobilized subjectivity, reluctant nomads occupy a position that indulges in neither an uncritical romanticization of itinerancy nor a nostalgic attachment to static notions of place. Instead, they draw attention to the mobile subjects whose activities and itineraries are constantly activating spaces of belonging and unbelonging, transforming them into zones of subversive economics and radical relations. In the process, these artists exemplify what I have theorized as the unhomely aesthetic that prevails in contemporary art practice and contemplates the global politics of borders, belonging, and the unhomely nature of contemporary global society.

The exile, Edward Said observes, "knows that in a secular and contingent world, homes are always provisional."[108] It is this knowledge that animates the reluctant nomadism of contemporary art practices, and indeed, Said's observation cuts to the heart of this book's central concern with contemporary art's capacity to reveal the provisionality (but also the tenacity) of home as both concept and material site. In the artworks discussed in these chapters, the desire to reconstruct, remember, or return home is articulated as simultaneously impossible and imperative, while the borders and boundaries between states and subjects are constantly challenged. It is this challenge that constitutes what I have argued is contemporary art's unique capacity to generate an ethics of witnessing that can adequately respond to the questions of home and belonging in an increasingly unhomely world. Home, in the process, emerges as a series of fragments weighted with violent loss, fragile memory, and impossible return.

Notes

Introduction: Unmaking Home

1 Homi K. Bhabha, "The World and the Home," *Social Text*, no. 31/32 (1992): 144.
2 Judith Butler, *Precarious Life: The Powers of Mourning and Violence* (London and New York: Verso, 2004), 40.
3 See E. Ann Kaplan, *Trauma Culture: The Politics of Terror and Loss in Media and Literature* (New Brunswick, NJ: Rutgers University Press, 2005); Didier Fassin and Richard Rechtman, *The Empire of Trauma: An Inquiry into the Condition of Victimhood*, trans. Rachel Gomme (Princeton, NJ: Princeton University Press, 2009); and Anne Rothe, *Popular Trauma Culture: Selling the Pain of Others in the Mass Media* (Rutgers, NJ: Rutgers University Press, 2011).
4 This is the conclusion reached by Andreas Huyssen in *Present Pasts: Urban Palimpsests and the Politics of Memory* (Stanford, CA: Stanford University Press, 2003), 8.
5 UN Refugee Agency, *UNHCR Global Trends 2013*, June 2014, http://www.unhcr.org/5399a14f9.html.
6 Giorgio Agamben, "Beyond Human Rights" (1993), in *Radical Thought in Italy: A Potential Politics*, ed. Paolo Virno and Michael Hardt (Minneapolis: University of Minnesota Press, 1996), 160.
7 Ibid., 163.
8 The Environmental Justice Foundation predicts up to 150 million climate refugees by 2050. See their 2009 report, *No Place Like Home: Where Next for Climate Refugees?* http://ejfoundation.org/report/no-place-home-where-next-climate-refugees. The growing body of analysis includes Jane McAdam, ed., *Climate Change and Displacement: Multidisciplinary Perspectives* (Oxford and Portland: Hart, 2012) and Etienne Piguet, Antoine Pécoud, and Paul de Guchteneire, eds, *Migration and Climate Change* (Paris,

Cambridge, and New York: UNESCO and Cambridge University Press, 2011).

9 See Slavoj Žižek's insightful observations on how 9/11 shattered "the symbolic coordinates which determine what we experience as reality," in *Welcome to the Desert of the Real: Five Essays on 11 September and Related Dates* (London and New York: Verso, 2002), 16.

10 Susan Buck-Morss, *Thinking Past Terror: Islamicism and Critical Theory on the Left* (New York: Norton, 2003), 71.

11 By 2007, an astonishing 27 per cent of the global refugee population originated in Afghanistan. In 2008, the non-profit lobbying organization International Rescue Committee (IRC) estimated that over four million Iraqi civilians had been displaced by the five-year conflict. See UN Refugee Agency, *2007 Global Trends: Refugees, Asylum-seekers, Returnees, Internally Displaced and Stateless Persons,* June 2008, http://www.unhcr.org/4852366f2.html; and International Rescue Committee, *Iraqi Refugees in Dire Straits*, March 2008, http://www.rescue.org.

12 Irit Rogoff, *Terra Infirma: Geography's Visual Culture* (London and New York: Routledge, 2000), 9.

13 Ibid., 10.

14 Notable group exhibitions of the past few years include *Homebodies* (Museum of Contemporary Art Chicago, 2013), *There's No Place Like Home* (Tate Modern, 2013), and *Domestic Utopias* (ngbk, Berlin, 2013).

15 See, for instance, Nicolas Bourriaud, *The Radicant* (New York: Lukas & Sternberg, 2009); Jennifer Johung, *Replacing Home: From Primordial Hut to Digital Network in Contemporary Art* (Minneapolis; London: University of Minnesota Press, 2012); Kobena Mercer, ed., *Exiles, Diasporas and Strangers* (Cambridge and London: MIT Press, 2008); and Marsha Meskimmon, *Contemporary Art and the Cosmopolitan Imagination* (London and New York: Routledge, 2011).

16 Bourriaud, *The Radicant*, 40.

17 Johung, *Replacing Home*, xiv.

18 Ibid., 163.

19 Bourriaud, *The Radicant*, 52. Emphasis added.

20 Doreen Massey, *Space, Place and Gender* (Minneapolis: University of Minnesota Press, 1994), 61–2.

21 See Roger I. Simon, "A Shock to Thought: Curatorial Judgment and the Public Exhibition of 'Difficult Knowledge,'" *Memory Studies* 4, no. 4 (October 2011): 432–49.

22 Butler, *Precarious Life*, xiv.

23 See especially Cathy Caruth, *Listening to Trauma: Conversations with Leaders in the Theory and Treatment of Catastrophic Experience* (Baltimore: Johns

Hopkins University Press, 2014); Cathy Caruth, *Unclaimed Experience: Trauma, Narrative, and History* (Baltimore: Johns Hopkins University Press, 1996); and Shoshana Felman and Dori Laub, *Testimony: Crises of Witnessing in Literature, Psychoanalysis, and History* (New York: Routledge, 1992).

24 See Huyssen, *Present Pasts*; Jenny Edkins, *Trauma and the Memory of Politics* (Cambridge and New York: Cambridge University Press, 2003); and Roger Luckhurst, *The Trauma Question* (London: Routledge, 2008).

25 Caruth, *Listening to Trauma*, xv.

26 See especially Jill Bennett and Rosanne Kennedy, *World Memory: Personal Trajectories in Global Time* (Basingstoke and New York: Palgrave Macmillan, 2003); Stef Craps, *Postcolonial Witnessing: Trauma out of Bounds* (Basingstoke and New York: Palgrave Macmillan, 2012); and Ogaga Ifowodo, *History, Trauma, and Healing in Postcolonial Narratives: Reconstructing Identities* (New York: Palgrave Macmillan, 2013).

27 David Johnson, "Theorizing the Loss of Land: Griqua Land Claims in Southern Africa, 1874–1998," in *Loss: The Politics of Mourning*, ed. David L. Eng and David Kazanjian (Berkeley, Los Angeles, and London: University of California Press, 2003), 293.

28 Judith Butler, "After Loss, What Then?" in Eng and Kazanjian, *Loss*, 468.

29 Sigmund Freud, "Mourning and Melancholia" (1917), in *The Standard Edition of the Complete Psychological Works of Sigmund Freud*, ed. James Strachey (London: Hogarth Press and the Institute of Psycho-analysis, 1958), 14:249.

30 Ibid.

31 Eng and Kazanjian, *Loss*, 3.

32 Aristotle, *Problemata* 30.1.54, reprinted in Raymond Klibansky, Erwin Panofsky, and Fritz Saxl, *Saturn and Melancholy: Studies on Natural Philosophy, Religion, and Art* (New York: Basic Books, 1964), 18. The authorship of the *Problemata* (likely not Aristotle himself) remains contested.

33 See also Jennifer Radden, ed., *The Nature of Melancholy from Aristotle to Kristeva* (New York: Oxford University Press, 2000); and Stanley Jackson, *Melancholia and Depression: From Hippocratic Times to Modern Times* (New Haven, CT: Yale University Press, 1986). On the historical association between art and melancholia as read through the figure of Albrecht Dürer's engraving *Melencolia I* (1514), see Klibansky, Panofsky, and Saxl, *Saturn and Melancholy*.

34 Leigh Gilmore, "Autobiography's Wounds," in *Just Advocacy? Women's Human Rights, Transnational Feminisms, and the Politics of Representation*, ed. Wendy S. Hesford and Wendy Kozol (New Brunswick, NJ, and London: Rutgers University Press, 2005), 106. See also Jonathan Flatley, *Affective Mapping: Melancholia and the Politics of Modernism* (Cambridge and London: Harvard University Press, 2008).

35 Bhabha, "The World and the Home," 144.
36 Eng and Kazanjian, *Loss*, 5.
37 Kathrin Rhomberg and Erzen Shkololli, *Petrit Halilaj: Kosovo Pavillion/Venice Biennale* (Köln: Walther Konig, 2014).
38 Judith Butler, *Dispossession: The Performative in the Political. Conversations with Athena Athanasiou* (Cambridge, UK; Malden, MA: Polity Press, 2013).
39 Roger I. Simon and Claudia Eppert, "Remembering Obligation: Pedagogy and the Witnessing of Testimony of Historical Trauma," *Canadian Journal of Education/Revue canadienne de l'éducation* 22, no. 2 (1997): 178.
40 See Dominick LaCapra, *Writing History, Writing Trauma* (Baltimore: Johns Hopkins University Press, 2001).
41 Patricia Yaeger, "Consuming Trauma; or, the Pleasures of Merely Circulating," in *Extremities: Trauma, Testimony, and Community*, ed. Nancy K. Miller and Jason Tougaw (Urbana: University of Illinois Press, 2002), 29.
42 Edouard Glissant, "For Opacity," in *Poetics of Relation* (Ann Arbor: University of Michigan Press, 1997).
43 Jill Bennett, *Empathic Vision: Affect, Trauma, and Contemporary Art* (Stanford, CA: Stanford University Press, 2005), 65.
44 Pierre Nora, "Between Memory and History: Les lieux de mémoire," *Representations* 26, no. 1 (1989): 7–24.
45 Butler, *Precarious Life*, 74, 29, 91.
46 Butler, *Dispossession*, 4–5. Emphasis added.
47 Ibid., 3.
48 Ibid., 68.
49 Sigmund Freud, "The Uncanny" (1919), in *The Standard Edition of the Complete Psychological Works of Sigmund Freud*, ed. James Strachey (London: Hogarth Press and the Institute of Psycho-analysis, 1955), 17:222. In both cases, Freud is referring to Sanders's German Dictionary of 1860.
50 Ibid., 226.
51 Freud, "The Uncanny," 241, 245. Here Freud is drawing on Schelling's definition of the *unheimlich* as "everything that ought to have remained … secret and hidden but has come to light." Friedrich Wilhelm Joseph Schelling, *Philosophy of Mythology*, trans. Eric Randolf Miller (Darmstadt: Wissenschaftliche Buchgesellschaft, [1835] 1966), 649.
52 Bhabha, "The World and the Home," 141. Bhabha is responding in part to Julia Kristeva's geopolitical rendering of the uncanny, which argues that Freud "teaches us how to detect foreignness in ourselves." See Julia Kristeva, *Strangers to Ourselves*, trans. Leon S. Roudiez (New York: Columbia University Press, 1991), 191.
53 Ibid.

54 Kristeva, *Strangers to Ourselves*, 97–8.
55 The Greek translation, for instance, is *xenoi*, or foreign, and in French the term translates similarly to *étranger*.
56 Kristeva, *Strangers to Ourselves*, 191, 192.
57 Ibid., 195.
58 Bhabha, "The World and the Home," 141.
59 Bhabha's project parallels, as he acknowledges, Kristeva's effort to translate the Freudian uncanny into a politics of stranger relations. Bhabha, however, reprimands Kristeva for speaking "perhaps too hastily of the pleasure of exile," particularly in her earlier essay "Women's Time." See Homi K. Bhabha, "DissemiNation: Time, Narrative and the Margins of the Modern Nation," in *The Location of Culture* (London and New York: Routledge, 1994), 140.
60 Ibid., 149.
61 Anthony Vidler, "A Dark Space," in *Rachel Whiteread: House*, ed. James Lingwood (London: Phaidon Press, 1995), 71.
62 Ibid., 72.

1 An Unhomely Genealogy of Contemporary Art

1 Kerwin Lee Klein, "On the Emergence of Memory in Historical Discourse," *Representations*, no. 69, Special issue: Grounds for Remembering (Winter 2000): 127.
2 Huyssen, *Present Pasts*, 13, 27. On the compression of space and time in postmodernity, see David Harvey, *The Condition of Postmodernity: An Enquiry into the Origins of Cultural Change* (Cambridge, MA: Blackwell, 1990).
3 Huyssen, *Present Pasts*, 25.
4 Ibid., 28.
5 Ibid., 24–7.
6 Ibid., 6.
7 That nostalgia is a "romance with one's own fantasy" is acknowledged by Svetlana Boym in her otherwise spirited reclamation of the sentiment. Svetlana Boym, *The Future of Nostalgia* (New York: Basic Books, 2001), xiii.
8 Rogoff, *Terra Infirma*, 155.
9 Ibid., 14.
10 Ibid.
11 Ibid., 3.
12 Huyssen, *Present Pasts*, 111.
13 Ibid., 120.
14 Ibid., 111. See also Christine Ross's *The Past Is the Present; It's the Future Too: The Temporal Turn in Contemporary Art* (London and New York: Bloomsbury Academic, 2013), which argues for contemporary art's capacity to

rethink the modernist regime of teleological historicity in favour of more fluid understandings of temporality.

15 See Maryanne Kowaleski and P.J.P. Goldberg, eds, *Medieval Domesticity: Home, Housing and Household in Medieval England* (Cambridge and New York: Cambridge University Press, 2011); and Michael McKeon, *The Secret History of Domesticity: Public, Private, and the Division of Knowledge* (Baltimore: Johns Hopkins University Press, 2005).

16 Witold Rybczynski, *Home: A Short History of an Idea* (New York: Viking Penguin, 1986), 199.

17 Charles Baudelaire, "The Painter of Modern Life" (1863), trans. Jonathan Mayne, in *The Painter of Modern Life and Other Essays* (London: Phaidon, 1964), 11.

18 See Wendy Parkins, ed., *William Morris and the Art of Everyday Life* (Newcastle: Cambridge Scholars Publishing, 2010).

19 For an insightful feminist analysis of the treatment of domestic space in French impressionist painting, see Griselda Pollock, "Modernity and the Spaces of Femininity," in *Vision and Difference: Femininity, Feminism and the Histories of Art* (London: Routledge, 1988). But see also Aruna D'Souza and Tom McDonough, eds, *The Invisible Flâneuse? Gender, Public Space, and Visual Culture in Nineteenth-Century Paris* (Manchester and New York: Manchester University Press, 2006), for revisionist perspectives on the intersections between gender, modernity, and the public sphere in impressionist painting.

20 Christopher Reed, introduction to *Not at Home: The Suppression of Domesticity in Modern Art and Architecture*, ed. Christopher Reed (London: Thames and Hudson, 1996), 16.

21 For analysis and insight into surrealism's interest in home as the realm of the uncanny, see Jane Alison, ed., *The Surreal House* (New Haven, CT: Yale University Press, 2010); Anthony Vidler, *The Architectural Uncanny: Essays in the Modern Unhomely* (Cambridge, MA: MIT Press, 1992); and Hal Foster, *Compulsive Beauty* (Cambridge, MA: MIT Press, 1993).

22 On Le Corbusier's idea of the house as a "machine for living in," see *Towards a New Architecture*, trans. Frederick Etchells (London: Architectural Press, [1927] 1970).

23 Jane Alison, "The Surreal House," in Alison, *The Surreal House*, 14.

24 Roberto Matta Echaurren, "Mathématique sensible – Architecture du temps," *Minotaure* (Paris), no. 11 (May 1938): 43.

25 Tristan Tzara, "D'un certain automatisme du goût," *Minotaure* (Paris), nos. 3–4 (December 1933).

26 Katharine Conley, "Safe as Houses: Anamorphic Bodies in Ordinary Spaces," in *Angels of Anarchy: Women Artists and Surrealism*, ed. Patricia Allmer (Munich and New York: Prestel, 2009), 46.

27 Rosalind E. Krauss, "Sculpture in the Expanded Field," *October*, no. 8 (Spring 1979).
28 Ibid., 34.
29 Martin Heidegger, "The Letter on Humanism" (1947), in *Basic Writings*, ed. David Krell (San Francisco: Harper Books, 1993), 243.
30 T.J. Demos, *The Exiles of Marcel Duchamp* (Cambridge and London: MIT Press, 2007), 38. See also Irit Rogoff's *Terra Infirma*, 36–72, for an insightful reading of how the suitcase is mobilized in contemporary art practices to signify both displacement and belonging.
31 Demos, *Exiles*, 225.
32 The German term has no direct equivalent in English, and refers to both home and homeland.
33 Theodor Adorno, "On the Question, 'What Is German?'" (1965), *New German Critique* (Special issue on *Heimat*), no. 36 (Fall 1985): 121. George Steiner identifies a similar rationale for the "unhomeliness" of postwar literature (such as that of Joyce, Conrad, Kafka, and Nabakov) in *Extraterritorial: Papers on Literature and the Language Revolution* (Harmondsworth: Penguin, 1972), 21.
34 Christine Poggi, "Vito Acconci's Bad Dream of Domesticity," in Reed, *Not at Home*, 237.
35 See Katharina Eck, "Protective Buildings, Exposed Bodies: The Femme-Maison Imagery in the Art of Louise Bourgeois," *Women's Studies* 41, no. 8 (December 2012): 904–24.
36 Betty Friedan, *The Feminine Mystique* (New York: W.W. Norton, 1963).
37 See Faith Wilding, *By Our Own Hands: The Women Artist's Movement, Southern California 1970–1976* (Santa Monica, CA: Double X, 1977), 25–30.
38 Arlene Raven, "Womanhouse," in *The Power of Feminist Art: The American Movement of the 1970s, History and Impact*, ed. Norma Broude and Mary D. Garrard (New York: H.N. Abrams, 1994), 61. See also Miriam Schapiro, "The Education of Women as Artists: Project Womanhouse," *Art Journal* 31, no. 3 (Spring 1972); and Temma Balducci, "Revisiting *Womanhouse*: Welcome to the (Deconstructed) Dollhouse," *Woman's Art Journal* 27, no. 2 (Fall/Winter 2006). For documentation of the project, see http://www.womanhouse.net.
39 Wilding, *By Our Own Hands*, 25.
40 Freud, "The Uncanny," 241.
41 That said, hooks also decries the extent to which the appropriation of white bourgeois sexist norms has transformed "that subversive homeplace into a site of patriarchal domination of black women by black men." See bell hooks, "Homeplace: A Site of Resistance," in *Yearning: Race, Gender, and Cultural Politics* (Toronto: Between the Lines, 1990), 47.

42 For Rosler's own analysis of the California women's art movement, see Martha Rosler, "The Private and the Public: Feminist Art in California," *Artforum* (September 1977). For an astute analysis of the relationships between homelessness, urban policy, and gentrification in New York, see Neil Smith, *The New Urban Frontier: Gentrification and the Revanchist City* (London and New York: Routledge, 2005).
43 This may be the reason the exhibition was notoriously cancelled six weeks ahead of its scheduled opening by Guggenheim New York's director Thomas Messer, who referred to the work as "an alien substance [that] violates the supreme neutrality of the work of art." In "Guest Editorial," *Arts Magazine* 45, no. 8 (Summer 1971): 4–5.
44 Rosalyn Deutsche, *Evictions: Art and Spatial Politics* (Cambridge, MA, and London: MIT Press, 1996), 49.
45 Ibid., 105.
46 Dick Hebdige, "The Machine Is Unheimlich: Wodiczko's Homeless Vehicle Project," in *Krzysztof Wodiczko*, ed. Duncan McCorquodale (London: Black Dog, 2011), 148–9.
47 Michel Foucault, "Nietzsche, Genealogy, History," in *The Foucault Reader*, ed. Paul Rabinow (New York: Pantheon Books, 1984), 83.
48 The exhibition is documented and analysed in Brian Wallis, ed., *If You Lived Here: The City in Art, Theory, and Social Activism. A Project by Martha Rosler* (New York: New Press, 1991), a volume published as part of the project. See also Nina Möntmann, "(Under)Privileged Spaces: On Martha Rosler's 'If You Lived Here,'" *e-flux journal* 9 (October 2009): 1–15.
49 Hebdige, "The Machine Is Unheimlich," 148.
50 In Benjamin H.D. Buchloh, "A Conversation with Martha Rosler," in *Martha Rosler: Positions in the Life World*, ed. Catherine de Zegher (Birmingham: Ikon Gallery; Vienna: Generali Foundation; Cambridge, MA, and London: MIT Press, 1999), 50.
51 The collages were designed for black-and-white reproduction (primarily as photocopies) in non-art contexts, and were first exhibited as colour photographs at Simon Watson Gallery in 1991, during the first Gulf War.
52 Wendy Kozol's *Life's America: Family and Nation in Postwar Photojournalism* (Philadelphia: Temple University Press, 1994) is a comprehensive and fascinating study of how middle-class domesticity is staged in *Life*.
53 Laura Cottingham, "The War Is Always Home: Martha Rosler," in *Bringing the War Home: Photomontages from the Vietnam War Era* (New York: Simon Watson, 1991), n.p.
54 Martha Rosler, "Here and Elsewhere," *Artforum International* 46, no. 3 (November 2007): 50.
55 Beatriz Colomina, *Domesticity at War* (Cambridge, MA: MIT Press, 2007).

56 Ibid., 12.
57 Ibid., 19.
58 Ibid., 56. See also *Atomic Dwelling: Anxiety, Domesticity and Postwar Architecture*, ed. Robin Schuldenfrei (London and New York: Routledge, 2012), an edited collection of essays that investigate various facets of the troubled (but also mutually informed) relationship between postwar domestic architecture and the collective anxiety associated with the Cold War. Dianne Harris's *Little White Houses: How the Postwar Home Constructed Race in America* (Minneapolis and London: University of Minnesota Press, 2013) is also relevant here. Harris details how the iconographies of dwelling and domesticity in postwar America normalized and reinforced increasingly pervasive ideological assumptions of white home ownership.
59 See Steve Edwards, *Martha Rosler: The Bowery in Two Inadequate Descriptive Systems* (London: Afterall Books, 2012).
60 Jacques Rancière, *The Future of the Image*, trans. Gregory Elliot (London: Verso, 2007), 57.
61 See Brian Massumi, "Introduction: Like a Thought," in *A Shock to Thought: Expression after Deleuze and Guattari*, ed. Brian Massumi (New York: Routledge, 2002).
62 See Michael J. Arlen, *Living-Room War* (Syracuse, NY: Syracuse University Press, 1997).
63 Sigmund Freud, "Screen Memories" (1899), in *The Standard Edition of the Complete Psychological Works of Sigmund Freud*, vol. 3, ed. James Strachey (London: Hogarth Press and the Institute of Psycho-analysis, 1962).
64 Marita Sturken, *Tangled Memories: The Vietnam War, the AIDS Epidemic, and the Politics of Remembering* (Berkeley, Los Angeles, and London: University of California Press, 1997), 8.
65 Ibid.
66 See especially Butler, *Dispossession*.
67 This idea was coined by architectural historian Charles Jencks in *The Language of Post-Modern Architecture* (New York: Rizzoli, 1977), 9.
68 For context, see Alexander Von Hoffman, "Why They Built Pruitt-Igoe", in *From the Tenements to the Taylor Homes: In search of an Urban Housing Policy in Twentieth-Century America*, edited by John F. Bauman, Roger Biles, and Kristin M. Szylvian (University Park: Pennsylvania State University Press, 2000), 180–205.
69 Gordon Matta-Clark, undated and unaddressed proposal, c. 1974, Archive of the Estate of Gordon Matta-Clark on deposit at the Canadian Centre for Architecture, Montreal (hereafter GMC Archive).
70 For analysis of Gordon Matta-Clark's challenge to modernism in architecture, see James Attlee, "Towards Anarchitecture: Gordon Matta-Clark and Le Corbusier," *Tate Papers* (spring 2007), http://www.tate.org.uk/

download/file/fid/7297, and Philip Ursprung, "Gordon Matta-Clark and the Limits to Architecture," translated by Steven Lindberg, in *Gordon Matta-Clark. Moment to Moment: Space*, edited by Hubertus von Amelunxen, Angela Lammert, and Philip Ursprung (Berlin: Verlag fur Moderne Kunst, 2013), 28–43. But see also Stephen Walker's *Gordon Matta-Clark: Art, Architecture and the Attack on Modernism* (London and New York: I.B. Tauris, 2009), which argues for a more complicated relationship between Matta-Clark and his architectural predecessors.

71 In Donald Wall, "Gordon Matta-Clark's Building Dissections," *Arts Magazine* 50, no. 9 (May 1976): 78.

72 Pamela M. Lee, *Object to Be Destroyed: The Work of Gordon Matta-Clark* (Cambridge: MIT Press, 1999), 116.

73 In Lisa Le Feuvre, "Skyhooks and Dragon Buildings. About Hot Air – What Can It Do?," in James Attlee and Lisa Le Feuvre, *Gordon Matta-Clark: The Space Between* (Tucson, AZ: Nazraeli Press, 2003), 57.

74 Gordon Matta-Clark, "An Old Man Crossing," draft manuscript, undated, GMC Archive. Even these smaller-scale works have garnered renewed attention in the past decade. *Open House*, for instance, was recreated at New York's David Zwirner Gallery in 2007, while *Garbage Wall* was reconstructed in 2009 by the Pulitzer Foundation for the Arts, and again in 2012 for EXPO CHICAGO.

75 Anthony Vidler, "'Architecture-to-Be': Notes on Architecture in the Work of Matta and Gordon Matta-Clark," in *Transmission: The Art of Matta and Gordon Matta-Clark*, ed. Betti-Sue Hertz (San Diego: San Diego Museum of Art, 2006), 59. Judith Russi Kirschner also identifies parallels between Matta's proposal for an "*architecture du temps*" and Matta-Clark's own disorienting architectural spaces, in "Non-u-ments," *Artforum International* 24, no. 2 (October 1985): 104–06.

76 Bhabha, "The World and the Home," 141.

77 In Lisa Bear, "*Splitting*: The Humphrey Street Building," *Avalanche* (December 1974): 36.

78 Gordon Matta-Clark, "Étant d'art pour locataire," draft manuscript, Paris, 1975, GMC Archive.

79 In Wall, "Gordon Matta-Clark's Building Dissections," 76.

80 In Joan Simon, "Interviews," in Mary Jane Jacob, *Gordon Matta-Clark: A Retrospective* (Chicago: Museum of Contemporary Art, 1985), 33.

81 Thomas Crow, "Survey," in *Gordon Matta-Clark*, ed. Corinne Diserens (London: Phaidon, 2003), 82. Yve-Alain Bois instead invokes Bataille's notion of the informe to describe the vertiginous effect of Matta-Clark's cuts, in which "one suddenly realized that one could not differentiate between the vertical section and the horizontal plane." "Threshole," in Yve-Alain Bois

and Rosalind E. Krauss, *Formless: A User's Guide* (New York: Zone Books, 1997), 191.

82 See Lee, *Object to Be Destroyed*, esp. ch. 3, "On Matta-Clark's 'Violence'; Or, What is a 'Phenomenology of the Sublime'?," 114–61.

83 Ibid., 116, 45, 60.

84 This response is recalled by the IAUS exhibition's curator Andrew McNair in Jacob, *Gordon Matta-Clark: A Retrospective*, 96.

85 Melvin Kaufman, letter to Gordon Matta-Clark, 9 February 1975, GMC Archive.

86 In Judith Russi Kirschner, "Interview with Gordon Matta-Clark" (1978), in *Gordon Matta-Clark*, ed. Maria Casanova (Valencia, Spain: IVAM Centro Julio Gonzàlez, 1993), 394.

87 Maud Lavin, "Gordon Matta-Clark and Individualism," *Arts Magazine* 58, no. 5 (January 1984): 141.

88 Lee, *Object to Be Destroyed*, 24. Italics in original.

89 Ibid., 28.

90 See Attlee, "Towards Anarchitecture," n.p.

91 See Jacob, *Gordon Matta-Clark: A Retrospective*, 99.

92 Dan Graham, "Gordon Matta-Clark," *Parachute*, no. 43 (June/July/August 1986): 24–25).

93 Huyssen, *Present Pasts*, 111.

94 See Bruce Jenkins, *Conical Intersect* (New York: Afterall Books, 2011) and Peter Muir, *Gordon Matta-Clark's Conical Intersect: Sculpture, Space, and the Cultural Value of Urban Imagery* (Burlington, VT: Ashgate Publishing, 2014).

95 Matta-Clark quoted in Florent Bex, "Interview with Gordon Matta-Clark, Antwerp, September 1977," in *Gordon Matta-Clark* (Antwerp: International Culturel Centrum, 1977), 12.

96 Jean Baudrillard, "The Beaubourg Effect: Implosion and Dissuasion" (1977), trans. Rosalind E. Krauss and Annette Michelson, *October*, no. 20 (spring 1982): 7, 5.

97 Huyssen, *Present Pasts*, 118.

98 I use this term advisedly. As Pamela Lee notes in regards to the fact that Matta-Clark's "anarchitecture" is sometimes linked to the postmodern architectural practices of Zaha Hadid, Frank Gehry and others, "the word 'deconstruction' is often sloppily linked to his work, as if to appeal to literal disassembling of buildings as well as the theoretically acute notion of 'deconstructivist' architecture" (*Object to Be Destroyed*, 215).

99 James Attlee, "Flame, Time and the Elements," in *Gordon Matta-Clark: The Space Between*, ed. James Attlee and Lisa Le Feuvre (Tucson, AZ: Nazraeli Press, 2003), 88.

100 These include large Matta-Clark retrospectives at the Whitney Museum of American Art (2007) and the SMS Contemporanea in Siena (2008). Monographs produced in the past dozen years include Corinne Diserens, ed., *Gordon Matta-Clark* (London: Phaidon, 2003); Gloria Moure, ed., *Gordon Matta-Clark: Works and Collected Writings* (Madrid: Museo nacional centro de arte Reina Sofía, 2006); Lorenzo Fusi and Marco Pierini, eds., *Gordon Matta-Clark* (Milan: Silvano Editoriale, 2008); Stephen Walker, *Gordon Matta-Clark: Art, Architecture and the Attack on Modernism* (London and New York: I.B. Tauris, 2009); and Hubertus von Amelunxen, Angela Lammert, and Philip Ursprung, eds., *Gordon Matta-Clark. Moment to Moment: Space* (Berlin: Verlag fur Moderne Kunst, 2013).

101 Matta-Clark died of cancer in 1978 at the age of 35.

102 Jeffrey Kastner, Sina Najafi, and Frances Richard, eds., *Odd Lots: Revisiting Gordon Matta-Clark's "Fake Estates."* (New York: Cabinet Books, 2005). For analysis of both projects, see Johung, *Replacing Home*, 33–66.

103 Christine Macel and Valérie Guillaume, eds., *Airs de Paris* (Paris: Centre Pompidou, 2007).

104 In 1974, the group exhibited their ideas at a SoHo studio and in a two-page spread in *Flash Art*. For elaboration, see Mark Wigley, "Anarchitectures," in *Gordon Matta-Clark. Moment to Moment: Space*, ed. Hubertus von Amelunxen, Angela Lammert, and Philip Ursprung (Berlin: Verlag fur Moderne Kunst, 2013), 12–26.

105 The film was shot on 16-mm film and transferred to DVD.

106 Mike Hoolboom, *Practical Dreamers: Conversations with Movie Artists* (Toronto: Coach House Books, 2008), 301.

107 Vito Acconci, "Beyond Sculpture: Function, Commodity, and Reinvention in Contemporary Art," *ArtLab23* 1, no. 2 (fall 2006), http://artlab23.sva.edu/issue1vol2/contents/acconci.html.

108 Yve-Alain Bois, "Threshole," in Yve-Alain Bois and Rosalind E. Krauss, *Formless: A User's Guide* (New York: Zone Books, 1997), 191.

109 Acconci, "Beyond Sculpture," n.p.

110 In Bryant Rousseau, "The ArchRecord Interview: Vito Acconci," *The Architectural Record* (June 2007), http://www.architecturalrecord.com/articles/6524-the-archrecord-interview-vito-acconci?v=preview.

111 Jean-Paul Sartre, *Being and Nothingness: A Phenomenological Essay on Ontology*, trans. Hazel E. Barnes (New York: Washington Square Press, 1957), 325.

112 Petra Kuppers, *The Scar of Visibility: Medical Performances and Contemporary Art* (Minneapolis and London: University of Minnesota Press, 2007), 76.

113 Ibid.
114 Friend's book, *No Place Like Home: Echoes from Kosovo* (San Francisco: Midnight Editions, 2001), documents this project and adds post-war portraits of refugees in Macedonia.
115 See Friend, *No Place Like Home*, 12. The exhibition is documented at http://www.melaniefriend.com.
116 Melanie Friend, "Homes and Gardens: Documenting the Invisible," *Home Cultures* 4, no. 1 (2007): 97.
117 See Abigail Solomon-Godeau, "Lament of the Images: Alfredo Jaar and the Ethics of Representation," *Aperture*, no. 181 (winter 2005).
118 In Tim Griffin, "Domesticity at War: Beatriz Colomina and Homi K. Bhabha in Conversation," *Artforum International* 45, no. 10 (summer 2007): 444–45.
119 Ibid., 444.
120 Ibid.
121 Rosler, "Here and Elsewhere," 50.
122 Joseph Masco, *The Theater of Operations: National Security Affect from the Cold War to the War on Terror* (Durham, NC: Duke University Press, 2014).
123 See Julie Bosman and Matt Apuzzo, "In Wake of Clashes, Calls to Demilitarize Police," *New York Times*, 14 August 2014.
124 Radley Balko, "Rise of the Warrior Cop," *Wall Street Journal*, 7 August 2013. For elaboration, see Balko's *Rise of the Warrior Cop: The Militarization of America's Police Forces* (New York: PublicAffairs, 2013). See also the American Civil Liberties Union's report, *War Comes Home: The Excessive Militarization of American Policing* (June 2014), https://www.aclu.org, and for a global perspective, see Mark Neocleous, *War Power, Police Power* (Edinburgh: Edinburgh University Press, 2014).
125 Jody Berland and Blake Fitzpatrick, "Introduction: Cultures of Militarization and the Military-Cultural Complex," *TOPIA: Canadian Journal of Cultural Studies*, Special Issue: Cultures of Militarization, no. 23–24 (2010): 9–27.
126 See Pippa Oldfield, ed., *Bringing the War Home* (London: Impressions Gallery, 2010).
127 See Nina Berman, *Homeland* (London: Trolley Books, 2008) and Dora Apel, *War Culture and the Contest of Images* (Newark, NJ: Rutgers University Press, 2012).
128 Berland and Fitzpatrick, 9–10.
129 Heather Diack, "Too Close to Home: Rethinking Representation in Martha Rosler's Photomontages of War," *Prefix Photo* 7, no. 2 (November 2006): 59.

130 On September 21, 2001, Bush encouraged Americans to "Get down to Disney World in Florida. Take your families and enjoy life, the way we want it to be enjoyed." Cited in Elaine Tyler May, "Echoes of the Cold War: The Aftermath of September 11 at Home," in *September 11 in History: A Watershed Moment?*, ed. Mary L. Dudziak (Durham, NC: Duke University Press, 2003), 44.
131 In Christy Lange, "Bringin' It All Back Home," *Frieze*, no. 95 (November-December 2005): 96.
132 Martha Rosler, "Martha Rosler," *Photography Quarterly*, no. 96 (2007): 30–33.
133 In Lange, "Bringin' It All Back Home," 96.
134 Homi K. Bhabha, "Halfway House," *Artforum International* 35, no. 9 (May 1997): 125.

2 The Art of Longing and Belonging

1 Bhabha, "DissemiNation," 149, 39.
2 See D.W. Winnicott, *Playing and Reality* (London: Routledge, 1971); Judith Lewis Herman, *Trauma and Recovery: From Domestic Abuse to Political Terror* (New York: Basic Books, 1992); and Kristeva, *Strangers to Ourselves*, 1991.
3 Krzysztof Wodiczko, "Designing for a City of Strangers," in *Krzysztof Wodiczko*, ed. Duncan McCorquodale (London: Black Dog, 2011), 250.
4 Krzysztof Wodiczko, *Critical Vehicles: Writings, Projects, Interviews* (Cambridge, MA, and London: MIT Press, 1999), 131.
5 Ibid., 105.
6 See Norbert Wiener, *Cybernetics, or Control and Communication in the Animal and the Machine* (Cambridge, MA: MIT Press, 1965).
7 Bertolt Brecht, *Brecht on Theatre: The Development of an Aesthetic*, trans. and ed. John Willett (London: Methuen, 1978).
8 Krzysztof Wodiczko, "*Mouthpiece (Porte-Parole)*," in McCorquodale, *Krzysztof Wodiczko*, 228.
9 Julia Kristeva, *Powers of Horror: An Essay on Abjection*, trans. Leon S. Roudiez (New York: Columbia University Press, 1982).
10 Kristeva, *Strangers to Ourselves*, 192.
11 Krzysztof Wodiczko, "Open Transmission," in *Architecturally Speaking: Practices of Art, Architecture, and the Everyday*, ed. Alan Read (London and New York: Routledge, 2000), 90.
12 Ibid., 93.
13 See Nicholas Royle, *The Uncanny* (New York: Routledge, 2003), 5.

14 Rosalyn Deutsche, "Sharing Strangeness: Krzysztof Wodiczko's *Ægis* and the Question of Hospitality," *Grey Room* no. 6 (Winter 2002): 38.
15 Krzysztof Wodiczko, "*Ægis: Equipment for a City of Strangers*" (1999–2000), in McCorquodale, *Krzysztof Wodiczko*, 254.
16 Ibid.
17 Ibid., 255-6.
18 See, chiefly, Ernesto Laclau and Chantal Mouffe, *Hegemony and Socialist Strategy: Towards a Radical Democratic Politics* (London: Verso, 1985).
19 Krzysztof Wodiczko, "Interrogative Design" (1994), in McCorquodale, *Krzysztof Wodiczko*, 245.
20 Hebdige, "The Machine Is Unheimlich," 150.
21 Wodiczko, in Patricia C. Phillips, "Creating Democracy: A Dialogue with Krzysztof Wodiczko," *Art Journal* 62, no. 4 (Winter 2003): 37, 38.
22 Wodiczko, "*Ægis*," in McCorquodale, ed., *Krzysztof Wodiczko*, 255-56.
23 In Phillips, "Creating Democracy," 35.
24 Ben Highmore, *Michel de Certeau: Analysing Culture* (London and New York: Continuum, 2006), 171.
25 In Nancy Princenthal, "Forty Ways of Looking at a Stranger," *Art in America* 91, no. 12 (December 2003): 43.
26 See "Critical Guests: Krzysztof Wodiczko in Conversation with John Rajchman," in *Krzysztof Wodiczko: Guests*, ed. Bożena Czubak (Warsaw: Zacheta National Gallery of Art, 2009), 11–12. "Fearless Speech" is the title given posthumously to a series of lectures that Foucault gave at UCal Berkeley in 1983 on the theme of parrhesia – a Greek concept roughly equivalent to the contemporary idea of speaking truth to power. See Michel Foucault, *Fearless Speech*, ed. Joseph Pearson (Los Angeles: Semiotext(e), 2001).
27 Wodiczko, "Critical Guests," 10.
28 Herman, *Trauma and Recovery*, 237.
29 In *Art 21: Art in the Twenty-First Century*, season 3, program 9, episode: "Power."
DVD, produced by Catherine Tatge (Alexandria, VA: PBS Home Video, 2005).
30 In Elise S. Youn and María J. Prieto, "Interview with Krzysztof Wodiczko: Making Critical Public Space," 11 April 2004, http://architecturalinterviews.blogspot.ca/2009/12/interview-with-krzysztof-wodiczko.html.
31 Ibid.
32 Winnicott, *Playing and Reality*, 3.
33 Cited in Krzysztof Wodiczko, "Voices of Mouthpiece" (1994–6), in McCorquodale, *Krzysztof Wodiczko*, 243.
34 In Dan Cameron, "An Interview with Krzysztof Wodiczko," thespleen.com, 23 October 2000, http://www.art-omma.org/NEW/past_issues/theory/07_An%20Interview%20With%20Krzysztof%20Wodiczko.htm.

35 See Wodiczko, "Interrogative Design," in McCorquodale, *Krzysztof Wodiczko*, 245.

36 Ann McCoy, "In Conversation: Krzysztof Wodiczko with Ann McCoy," *The Brooklyn Rail*, February 2014, http://www.brooklynrail.org/2014/02/art/krzysztof-wodiczko-with-ann-mccoy.

37 *Maquiladora* is the term used to refer to the approximately 6,000 foreign-owned factories (usually American) operating in free-trade zones on the US-Mexico border. They employ mainly women, and are routinely accused of imposing low wages, forced overtime, and unhealthy working conditions. For an astute analysis of the gendered politics of the *maquiladora* industry, see Melissa W. Wright, *Disposable Women and Other Myths of Global Capitalism* (New York: Routledge, 2006). See also Doreen J. Mattingly and Ellen R. Hansen, ed., *Women and Change at the US-Mexico Border: Mobility, Labor and Activism* (Tucson: University of Arizona Press, 2008), for an overview of the intersections of labor, globalization, and gender at the border.

38 For elaboration, see Sanford Levinson, *Written in Stone: Public Monuments in Changing Societies* (Durham, NC, and London: Duke University Press, 1998); Robert S. Nelson and Margaret Olin, eds, *Monuments and Memory, Made and Unmade* (Chicago and London: University of Chicago Press, 2003); and James E. Young, *The Texture of Memory: Holocaust Memorials and Meaning* (New Haven, CT: Yale University Press, 1993).

39 Deutsche, "Krzysztof Wodiczko's Homeless Projection," in McCorquodale, *Krzysztof Wodiczko*, 132.

40 See Jacques Rancière, *Dissensus: On Politics and Aesthetics*, ed. and trans. Steven Corcoran (London and New York: Continuum, 2010).

41 In McCoy, "In Conversation," 2014.

42 MIT TechTV, *Tijuana Projection*, http://video.mit.edu/watch/tijuana-projection-4295/.

43 Luiza Nader, "Migratory Subjects: Memory Work in Krzysztof Wodiczko's Projections and Instruments," in *Memory and Migration: Multidisciplinary Approaches to Memory Studies*, ed. Julia Creet and Andreas Kitzmann (Toronto: University of Toronto Press, 2011), 251.

44 Youn and Prieto, "Interview with Krzysztof Wodiczko," n.p.

45 Ibid.

46 Wodiczko, " Pomnikoterapia," n.p.

47 Huyssen, *Present Pasts*, 9.

48 Dori Laub, "Bearing Witness, or the Vicissitudes of Listening," in Felman and Laub, *Testimony*, 57.

49 Ibid, 237.

50 Ewa Lajer-Burcharth, "The Global Wanderer," in McCorquodale, *Krzysztof Wodiczko*, 2012.
51 Wodiczko, cited in Phillips, "Creating Democracy," 34.
52 Nicolas Bourriaud, *Relational Aesthetics*, trans. Simon Pleasance and Fronza Woods (Dijon: Les presses du réel, 2002), 3.
53 Nicolas Bourriaud, "Berlin Letter about Relational Aesthetics" (2001), in *Contemporary Art: From Studio to Situation*, ed. Claire Doherty (London: Black Dog Publishing, 2004), 44.
54 Wodiczko, in *Art 21*, DVD.
55 Jacques Rancière, "Problems and Transformations in Critical Art," in *Participation*, ed. Claire Bishop (Cambridge: MIT Press, 2007), 90.
56 This is a term used by Bourriaud to describe the environments constructed by practitioners of relational aesthetics such as Rirkrit Tiravanija.
57 Claire Bishop, "Antagonism and Relational Aesthetics," *October*, no. 110 (Fall 2004): 69.
58 Ibid., 71.
59 Santiago Sierra, cited in Martin Herbert, "Material Witness," *Artforum International* 43, no. 1 (September 2004): 210.
60 Claire Bishop, "Delegated Performance: Outsourcing Authenticity," *October* 140 (Spring 2012): 91–112.
61 Bishop, "Antagonism and Relational Aesthetics," 70.
62 See, for example, Carlos Jiménez, "Santiago Sierra: Or Art in a Post-Fordist Society," *Art Nexus* 3, no. 56 (April-June 2005), and Juan Albarrán, "Beyond an Ethics of Labor: Geometry, Commodity, and Value in the Oeuvre of Santiago Sierra," in *Santiago Sierra: Sculpture, Photography, Film*, ed. Dirk Luckow and Daniel Schreiber (Köln: Snoeck, 2013), 31–44.
63 Claire Bishop, *Installation Art: A Critical History* (New York: Routledge, 2005), 123.
64 Judith Butler, "After Loss, What Then?" in *Loss*, ed. David L. Eng and David Kazanjian (Berkeley, Los Angeles, and London: University of California Press, 2003), 468.
65 LaCapra, *Writing History, Writing Trauma*, 70.
66 Rosa Martinez, "Interview to Santiago Sierra," in *Santiago Sierra: Pabellón de España, 50a Bienal de Venecia / Spanish Pavilion, 50th Venice Biennale*, ed. Rosa Martinez (Madrid: Turner, 2003), 23.
67 Francis Alÿs, "A Thousand Words: Francis Alÿs Talks About *When Faith Moves Mountains*," *Artforum International* 40, no. 10 (summer 2002): 147.
68 *When Faith Moves Mountains* was produced in 2002 in coordination with the third Bienal Iberoamericana de Lima.

69 Alÿs, "A Thousand Words," 147.
70 Statistics indicate that the number of deaths associated with attempts to cross into Europe by sea has increased expentially since 2002. Between January and September 2014, up to 3,072 migrants are believed to have died in the Mediterranean out ot a total of 4,077 migrant deaths worldwide. 2014 has been the deadliest year on record for the Mediterranean route: a huge leap compared to the 700 migrant deaths recorded in 2013. This far exceeds the previous record of 1,500 deaths that occurred on this route during the 2011 Arab Spring. Tara Brian and Frank Laczko, *Fatal Journeys: Tracking Lives Lost during Migration* (Geneva: International Organization for Migration, 2014), http://www.iom.int/files/live/sites/iom/files/pbn/docs/Fatal-Journeys-Tracking-Lives-Lost-during-Migration-2014.pdf.
71 Teresa Margolles, "Santiago Sierra," *Bomb*, no. 86 (Winter 2003–4): 65.
72 Schelling, *Philosophy of Mythology*, 649.
73 Freud, "The Uncanny," 241.
74 Deutsche, "Krzysztof Wodiczko's Homeless Projection," 132.
75 *Lights in the City* was produced for the 1999 Mois de la Photo in Montreal. See Pierre Blache, Marie-Josée Jean, and Anne-Marie Ninacs, eds, *Le mois de la photo à Montréal 1999: Le souci du document* (Montreal: VOX Centre de diffusion de la photographie, 1999).
76 In Patricia C. Phillips, "The Aesthetics of Witnessing: A Conversation with Alfredo Jaar," *Art Journal* 64, no. 3 (2005): 22.
77 Ibid.
78 See Solomon-Godeau, "Lament of the Images," 2005.
79 Ibid.
80 Alfredo Jaar, cited in Solomon-Godeau, "Lament of the Images," 42.
81 In Montreal, where the homeless population is approximately 10,000, homeless residents are routinely ticketed for loitering, sleeping in the Metro, and other by-law offences. See Justin Douglas, "The Criminalization of Poverty: Montreal's Policy of Ticketing Homeless Youth for Municipal and Transportation By-Law Infractions," *Appeal* 16 (2011): 49–64.
82 Pac Pobric, "Brother, Can You Spare Some Screen Time?" *The Art Newspaper*, online version, 20 October 2014.
83 Santiago Sierra, cited in Ana Maria Guasch, "Santiago Sierra: A New Mode of Cultural Activism," in *Otredad y mismidad: arte público / Otherness & Selfness: Public Art*, ed. Aldo Sánchez (Puebla, Mexico: Galería de arte contemporáneo y diseño, 2003), 34.
84 Santiago Sierra, "A Thousand Words: Santiago Sierra," *Artforum International* 41, no. 2 (October 2002): 130.

85 Julian Stallabrass, *Art Incorporated: The Story of Contemporary Art* (Oxford: Oxford University Press, 2005), 41.
86 In Martinez, "Interview to Santiago Sierra," 169.
87 Coco Fusco, "The Unbearable Weightiness of Beings: Art in Mexico after NAFTA," in *The Bodies that Were Not Ours, and Other Writings* (London: Routledge, 2001), 67.
88 Bishop, *Installation Art*, 120. See Michael Fried, "Art and Objecthood," *Artforum International*, no. 5 (June 1967): 12–23.
89 In Margolles, "Santiago Sierra," 69.
90 The eighteen-foot-high US–Mexico barrier now runs 650 miles. For a history of the contentious structure, see Rachel St John, *Line in the Sand: A History of the Western US-Mexico Border* (Princeton, NJ: Princeton University Press, 2011).
91 Wodiczko, "Interrogative Design," in McCorquodale, *Krzysztof Wodiczko*, 245.
92 Cited in Marc Spiegler, "When Human Beings Are the Canvas," *ARTnews* (June 2003): 97.
93 Mark Selzer, "Wound Culture: Trauma in the Pathological Public Sphere," *October*, no. 80 (Spring 1997): 3–26; Eric Cazdyn, *The Already Dead: The New Time of Politics, Culture, and Illness* (Durham, NC: Duke University Press, 2012).
94 Pip Day, "Scene of the Crime," *ArtReview* 1, no. 11 (2003): 76.
95 Cited in Spiegler, "When Human Beings Are the Canvas," 96.
96 Cuauhtémoc Medina, "Customs," in *Santiago Sierra: Pabellón de España, 50a Bienal de Venecia / Spanish Pavilion*, 50th Venice Biennale (Madrid: Turner, 2003), 233.
97 Jörg Heiser, "Good Circulation," *Frieze*, no. 90 (April 2005): 82.
98 Rogoff, *Terra Infirma*, 122. Haacke's installation was produced in association with *The Finiteness of Freedom*, an international exhibition organized by the cultural department of the Berlin Senate in 1990. See Giovanni Anselmo, ed., *Die Endlichkeit der Freiheit Berlin 1990 – Ein Ausstellungprojekt in Ost und West* (Berlin: Edition Hentrich, 1990).
99 Sierra, in Martinez, "Interview to Santiago Sierra," 181.
100 See Katya García-Antón, "Buying Time," in *Santiago Sierra: Works 2002–1990* (Birmingham: Ikon Gallery, 2002), 15.
101 Christine Ross, *The Aesthetics of Disengagement: Contemporary Art and Depression* (Minneapolis and London: University of Minnesota Press, 2006), 63.
102 In Margolles, "Santiago Sierra," 65. Claire Bishop also observes the recurring motif of obstruction in Sierra's work, but, curiously, she attributes

it solely to his acknowledgment of antagonisms between the "mutually exclusive" social and aesthetic spheres "after a century of attempts to fuse them" ("Antagonism and Relational Aesthetics," 78).

103 Freud, "Mourning and Melancholia," 244, 46.

104 Gilmore, "Autobiography's Wounds," 106. Emphasis added.

105 LaCapra, *Writing History, Writing Trauma*, 151.

106 David Eng and David Kazanjian, introduction to *Loss: The Politics of Mourning* (Berkeley: University of California Press, 2003), 3.

107 Kristeva, *Strangers to Ourselves*, 195.

3 Unhomely Archives

1 "Les images de la maison marchent dans les deux sens: elles sont en nous autant que nous sommes en elles." Gaston Bachelard, *The Poetics of Space*, trans. Maria Jolas (Boston: Beacon Press, 1994), xxxvii.

2 Kaja Silverman, *The Threshold of the Visible World* (London and New York: Routledge, 1996), 189.

3 In Charles Merewether, "An Interview with Doris Salcedo," in *Unland: Doris Salcedo: New Work* (San Francisco: San Francisco Museum of Modern Art, 1999), n.p.

4 Edward W. Said, "Reflections on Exile," in *Out There: Marginalization and Contemporary Cultures*, ed. Russell Ferguson et al. (New York: New Museum of Contemporary Art; Cambridge, MA: MIT Press, 1990), 365.

5 See Dan Cameron, ed., *International Istanbul Biennial: Poetic Justice* (Istanbul: Istanbul Foundation for Culture and Arts, 2003). Salcedo's installation was located at Yemeniciler Caddesi No. 66, Persembepazari, Karaköy.

6 According to Salcedo's representatives at Alexander and Bonin Gallery in New York, the chairs were held in place by a metal framework. The artist declined to explain how the flush effect was achieved, although the Istanbul Biennial organization confirms that a scaffold was built, and the piece installed by local mountain climbers. The chairs were purchased locally.

7 Doris Salcedo, "Proposal for a Project for the 8th International Istanbul Biennial," 2003, reproduced in Achim Borchardt-Hume, ed., *Doris Salcedo: Shibboleth* (London: Tate Publishing, 2007), 99.

8 Jacques Derrida, *Archive Fever: A Freudian Impression*, trans. Eric Prenowitz (Chicago: University of Chicago Press, 1996), 1. As Derrida notes, "This name apparently coordinates two principles in one: the principle according to nature or history, *there* where things *commence* … but also the principle according to the law, *there* where men and gods *command*, there where authority, social order are exercised, in this place from which order

is given" (1). Therefore, Derrida concludes, "There is no political power without control of the archive" (4). Italics in original.

9 Diana Taylor, *The Archive and the Repertoire: Performing Cultural Memory in the Americas* (Durham, NC, and London: Duke University Press, 2003), 20.

10 Hal Foster, "2003: Archival Aesthetics," in *Art since 1900: Modernism, Antimodernism, Postmodernism*, ed. Hal Foster et al. (New York: Thames and Hudson, 2004), 665.

11 The practice of French artist Pierre Huyghe, such as his reconstruction of the 1975 film *Dog Day Afternoon* in his two-channel video *The Third Memory* (1999), is considered paradigmatic here. See Nicolas Bourriaud, *Postproduction: Culture as Screenplay: How Art Reprograms the World*, trans. Jeanine Herman (New York: Lukas and Sternberg, 2002).

12 Hal Foster, "An Archival Impulse," *October*, no. 110 (Fall 2004): 5.

13 Ibid.

14 Ibid., 9.

15 Ibid., 22.

16 Ibid.

17 Hal Foster, *The Return of the Real: The Avant-Garde at the End of the Century* (Cambridge, MA: MIT Press, 1996), 166.

18 Ibid.

19 Butler, "After Loss, What Then?" 468.

20 Ibid.

21 Foucault, "Nietzsche, Genealogy, History," 81. Contrast this with Foucault's definition of the archive as a set of discursive practices that circumscribe the "law of what can be said." In *The Archaeology of Knowledge*, trans. A.M. Sheridan (London: Tavistock, 1972), 129.

22 While the goal was to achieve 100,000 tattooed dots, Bilal's own corporeal limit was reached at 25,000, although the artist has stated his intention to complete the project in the future.

23 Derrida, *Archive Fever*, 91.

24 In Marguerite Feitlowitz, "Interview with Doris Salcedo," *Crimes of War Project Magazine*, August 2001, http://margueritefeitlowitz.com/publications/interview-with-doris-salcedo/.

25 On Oklahoma's "Field of Empty Chairs," see Marita Sturken, *Tourists of History: Memory, Kitsch, and Consumerism from Oklahoma City to Ground Zero* (Durham, NC, and London: Duke University Press, 2007), esp. 110–16.

26 This is not to suggest that worn chairs necessarily merit the loaded indexical status or authenticity of experience that attends to them, but simply that this status does adhere, in a way that recalls what Mieke Bal observes as the over-determined indexical effect of worn shoes in Holocaust exhibits (Bal here is writing in the context of an earlier Salcedo work, *Atrabiliarios* of

1992–7, an installation of women's shoes installed in wall niches shrouded in animal skin). See Mieke Bal, *Of What One Cannot Speak: Doris Salcedo's Political Art* (Chicago: University of Chicago Press, 2010), 60–74.

27 One could easily write an art history of the chair, whose rich set of associations has made it a perennial favourite, especially among contemporary artists, from Joseph Beuys' *Fat Chair* (1964) and Joseph Kosuth's *One and Three Chairs* (1968) to Ai Weiwei's *Fairytale Chairs*, an installation of 1,001 Qing Dynasty wooden chairs at Documenta 12 in 2007 and, more recently, Ai's *Bang*, an installation of 886 antique stools at the 2013 Venice Biennale.

28 Walter Benjamin, "Theses on the Philosophy of History," in *Illuminations*, ed. Hannah Arendt, trans. Harry Zohn (New York: Schocken Books, 1969), 255.

29 See Chris Townsend, "When We Collide: History and Aesthetics, Space and Signs, in the Art of Rachel Whiteread," in *The Art of Rachel Whiteread*, ed. Chris Townsend (London: Thames and Hudson, 2004).

30 See Nancy Princenthal, "Silence Seen," in Nancy Princenthal, Carlos Basualdo, and Andreas Huyssen, *Doris Salcedo* (London: Phaidon, 2000), 77–78, for elaboration on this theme.

31 In Princenthal, Basualdo, and Huyssen, *Doris Salcedo*, 12.

32 Salcedo also links her work to the non-site of Robert Smithson, which resonates even more with her large-scale exhibitions: "I'm using Robert Smithson's idea of 'non-site' in a Third World way, to demonstrate the experience of displaced people – people who have been pushed off their land for political reasons." In "Doris Salcedo," *Flash Art*, no. 171 (Summer 1993): 97.

33 Joan Rzadkiewicz, "Early Memory and the Reconditioned Object: Doris Salcedo, Robert Gober, Clay Ketter, Miroslaw Balka, Luc Tuymans, *The Unthought Known*," *Etc. Montreal*, no. 59 (September-November 2002): 62.

34 Nancy Princenthal, "Silence Seen," 78.

35 Wodiczko, "Critical Guests," 10.

36 Giorgio Agamben, *Remnants of Auschwitz: The Witness and the Archive*, trans. Daniel Heller-Roazen (New York: Zone Books, 1999), 34.

37 LaCapra, *Writing History, Writing Trauma*, 41–2.

38 Ibid., 41, 27.

39 Silverman, *The Threshold of the Visible World*, 4.

40 Ibid., 185.

41 Silverman borrows, but radically revises, terminology developed by German philosopher Max Scheler, who argues that idiopathic identification "self-despotizes," while in heteropathic identifications, "the one self is entirely 'lost' in the other." See Scheler's *The Nature of Sympathy*, trans. Peter Heath (London: Routledge and Kegan Paul, 1954), 24–5.

42 Silverman, *Threshold of the Visible World*, 84, 85.

43 Ibid., 185, 4.
44 Ibid., 84.
45 Ibid., 185.
46 Bennett, *Empathic Vision*, 65.
47 Olga M. Viso, "Doris Salcedo: The Dynamic of Violence," in *Distemper: Dissonant Themes in the Art of the 1990s* (Washington, DC: Hirshhorn Museum and Sculpture Garden, 1996), 90.
48 See Wafaa Bilal and Kari Lydersen, *Shoot an Iraqi: Art, Life and Resistance under the Gun* (San Francisco: City Lights, 2008), for documentation and reflection.
49 Cited in Santiago Villaveces-Izquierdo, "Art and Mediation: Reflections on Violence and Representation," in *Cultural Producers in Perilous States: Editing Events, Documenting Change*, ed. George E. Marcus (Chicago and London: University of Chicago Press, 1997), 238.
50 LaCapra, *Writing History, Writing Trauma*, 40.
51 See especially Ann Cvetkovich, *An Archive of Feelings: Trauma, Sexuality, and Lesbian Public Cultures* (Durham, NC, and London: Duke University Press, 2003).
52 Ibid., 9.
53 Ibid., 238.
54 "[Memory sculpture] is an artistic practice that remains clearly distinct from the monument or the memorial. Its place is in the museum or the gallery rather than in public space. Its addressee is the individual beholder rather than the nation or community." Huyssen, *Present Pasts*, 110.
55 Jill Bennett, "*Tenebrae* after September 11: Art, Empathy, and the Global Politics of Belonging," in *World Memory: Personal Trajectories in Global Time*, ed. Jill Bennett and Rosanne Kennedy (Basingstoke and New York: Palgrave Macmillan, 2003), 191–92.
56 Homi K. Bhabha, "Halfway House," *Artforum International* 35, no. 9 (May 1997): 11.
57 In Feitlowitz, "Interview with Doris Salcedo," n.p.
58 Bal, *Of What One Cannot Speak*, 25.
59 Doris Salcedo, "Proposal for a Project for the Palace of Justice, Bogotá," 2002, reproduced in *Doris Salcedo: Shibboleth*, 83.
60 Bal, *Of What One Cannot Speak*, 25.
61 Mieke Bal, "Earth Aches: The Aesthetics of the Cut," in *Doris Salcedo: Shibboleth* (London: Tate Publishing, 2007), 55.
62 Edlie L. Wong, "Haunting Absences: Witnessing Loss in Doris Salcedo's *Atrabiliarios* and Beyond," in *The Image and the Witness: Trauma, Memory and Visual Culture*, ed. Frances Guerin and Roger Hallas (London and New York: Wallflower Press, 2007), 184.

63 Giorgio Agamben, *Homo Sacer: Sovereign Power and Bare Life*, trans. Daniel Heller-Roazen (Stanford, CA: Stanford University Press, 1998), esp. 119–80.
64 Butler, *Precarious Life*, 74.
65 From 1914 to 1918, up to 1.5 million Armenians were killed during deportation from Turkey. For a comprehensive survey of the historical, political, and cultural dimensions of the genocide and its aftermath, see Richard G. Hovannisian, ed., *The Armenian Genocide in Perspective* (New Brunswick, NJ: Transaction Publishers, 1986).
66 Derrida, *Archive Fever*, 68.
67 Within a year, the situation in Palestine had already worsened to the extent that the artist's own mobility was no longer ensured. As Jacir stated at the time, "It is now May 2004 and … I can no longer move freely through the borders with my American passport. I cannot make the project *Where We Come From* today." See Emily Jacir, Roland Wäspe, and Andreas Baur, *Emily Jacir* (Nürnberg: Verlag für Moderne Kunst, 2008), in which this and other projects are documented.
68 Walid Khalidi, ed., *All That Remains: The Palestinian Villages Occupied and Depopulated by Israel in 1948* (Washington: Institute for Palestine Studies, 1992).
69 The United Nations Relief and Works Agency used these large tents in Palestinian refugee camps in Jordan, Lebanon, Syria, Gaza, and the West Bank until 1968, when construction began on more permanent shelters and facilities. The total number of registered Palestinian refugees (defined as Palestinians displaced as a result of the 1948 Arab–Israeli conflict and their direct descendents) is approximately twelve million. See United Nations Relief and Works Agency for Palestine Refugees in the Near East homepage, http://www.un.org/unrwa/english.html.
70 Jacir acknowledges her intention was to forestall such efforts, noting that the exact subject of the work is "unavoidable, it's there in the title." Cited in Chiara Gelardin, "Memories in Exile," *Museo Contemporary Art Magazine*, no. 6 (2003), http://www.columbia.edu/cu/museo/6/jacir/.
71 In Princenthal, Basualdo, and Huyssen, *Doris Salcedo*, 26.
72 Huyssen, *Present Pasts*, 111.
73 Georges Didi-Huberman, *Images in Spite of All: Four Photographs from Auschwitz*, trans. Shane B. Lillis (Chicago and London: University of Chicago Press, 2008), 21. Italics in original.
74 Ibid., 105. Italics in original. Didi-Huberman's polemic is directed against a group of French scholars, including filmmaker Claude Lanzmann, who viewed the exhibition of these photographs at the 2001 exhibition *Mémoire des camps* at Hôtel de Sully in Paris (and indeed all photographic documentation of the Holocaust) as a kind of senseless, scandalous spectacle. See

Claude Lanzmann, "Le monument contre l'archive?" *Les cahiers de médiologie*, no. 11 (2001).

75 The project was part of the *Finitude of Freedom* exhibition of international artists responding to the reunification of East and West Germany (mentioned briefly in the preceding chapter as the exhibition that also hosted Hans Haacke's *Freedom Is Now Simply Going to Be Sponsored – Out of Petty Cash*).

76 John Czaplicka, "History, Aesthetics, and Contemporary Commemorative Practice in Berlin," *New German Critique*, no. 65 (Spring/Summer 1995): 168.

77 Ibid.

78 Homi K. Bhabha, "Democracy De-Realized," in *Democracy Unrealized: Documenta11_ Platform1*, ed. Okwui Enwezor et al. (Ostfildern-Ruit, Germany: Hatje Cantz, 2002), 363–4. Italics in original.

79 Jill Bennett, "Art, Affect, and the 'Bad Death': Strategies for Communicating the Sense Memory of Loss," *Signs* 28, no. 1 (Autumn 2002): 346.

80 Derrida, *Archive Fever*, 36.

81 Foster, "An Archival Impulse," 5, n. 8.

4 Biennial Culture's Reluctant Nomads

1 Carol Becker, "The Romance of Nomadism: A Series of Reflections," *Art Journal* 58, no. 2 (Summer 1999): 22–9. In the epigraph to this chapter, Becker is referring to Jacques Attali, *Millennium: Winners and Losers in the Coming World Order*, trans. Leila Conners and Nathan Gardels (New York: Times Books/Random House, 1991).

2 The contours of these debates are traced in Shannon Jackson, *Social Works: Performing Art, Supporting Publics* (Oxon and New York: Routledge, 2011), and Gerald Raunig and Gene Ray, eds, *Art and Contemporary Critical Practice: Reinventing Institutional Critique* (London: MayFlyBooks, 2009).

3 Claire Doherty, "The New Situationists," in *Contemporary Art: From Studio to Situation*, ed. Claire Doherty (London: Black Dog Publishing, 2004), 8. See also Caroline A. Jones, "Biennial Culture: A Longer History," in *The Biennial Reader*, ed. Elena Filipovic, Marieke Van Hal, and Øvstebø Solveig (Ostfildern: Hatje Cantz, 2010), 71.

4 Elena Filipovic, Marieke Van Hal, and Solveig Øvstebø, eds, *The Biennial Reader: An Anthology on Large-Scale Perennial Exhibitions of Contemporary Art* (Ostfildern: Hatje Cantz, 2010).

5 Pamela M. Lee, *Forgetting the Art World* (Cambridge, MA: MIT Press, 2012), 3. Witness a selection of curatorial themes in the past decade: "Not

Only Possible, but Also Necessary: Optimism in the Age of Global War" (Istanbul, 2007); "Integration and Resistance in the Global Era" (Havana, 2009), "What a Wonderful World" (Gothenburg, 2010), "Rewriting Worlds" (Moscow, 2011), "Intense Proximity" (Paris Triennale, 2011), "The Unexpected Guest" (Liverpool, 2012), and "All Our Relations" (Sydney, 2012).

6 Simon Sheikh, "Markers of Distinction, Vectors of Possibility: Questions for the Biennial," *Open*, The Art Biennial as a Global Phenomenon 16 (2009): 79, and Carlos Basualdo, "Launching Site: Interview with Rosa Martinez," *Artforum International* 37, no. 10 (Summer 1999): 39.

7 Jen Budney, "Politics in Aspic: Reflections on the Biennale of Sydney and Its Local Effects," *FUSE*, January 2007, 10.

8 Pamela M. Lee, "Boundary Issues: The Art World under the Sign of Globalism," *Artforum International* 42, no. 3 (November 2003): 165.

9 Arguably, it was Enwezor's 2002 Documenta 11, a sprawling multi-city series of lectures, symposia, and exhibitions that rendered the "deterritorialization" of the international art circuit a global phenomenon.

10 Becker, "The Romance of Nomadism," 26.

11 See Brenda Atkinson and Candice Breitz, eds, *Grey Areas: Representation, Identity and Politics in Contemporary South African Art* (Johannesburg: Chalkham Hill Press, 1999); and Jen Budney, "Who's It For? The 2nd Johannesburg Biennial," *Third Text*, no. 42 (Spring 1998).

12 Foster, *Return of the Real*, 197.

13 Ibid., 198. Debates concerning the ethnographic dilemma of site-specific practices are played out in Claire Bishop, *Artificial Hells: Participatory Art and the Politics of Spectatorship* (London and New York: Verso Books, 2012); Alex Coles, ed., *Site-Specificity: The Ethnographic Turn* (London: Black Dog Publishing, 2000); Nick Kaye, *Site-Specific Art: Performance, Place and Documentation* (London and New York: Routledge, 2013); Grant H. Kester, *Conversation Pieces: Community and Communication in Modern Art* (Berkeley and New York: University of California Press, 2004); and Miwon Kwon, *One Place after Another: Site-Specific Art and Locational Identity* (Cambridge and London: MIT Press, 2004).

14 Gilles Deleuze and Félix Guattari, *Nomadology: The War Machine*, trans. Brian Massumi (New York: Semiotext(e), 1986). The rich and complex theorization of nomadology in the work of Deleuze and Guattari is beyond the scope of this chapter in which I am instead concerned with how philosophical investigations of nomadic subjectivity have been reduced to formulaic visions of the artist-wanderer.

15 Marc Augé, *Non-Places: Introduction to an Anthropology of Supermodernity*, trans. John Howe (New York: Verso, 1995).

16 Miwon Kwon, "The Wrong Place," in *Contemporary Art: From Studio to Situation*, ed. Claire Doherty (London: Black Dog Publishing, 2004), 30.
17 James Meyer, "Nomads: Figures of Travel in Contemporary Art," in *Site-Specificity: The Ethnographic Turn*, ed. Alex Coles (London: Black Dog Publishing, 2000), 11.
18 Kwon, "The Wrong Place," 31.
19 Kwon, *One Place after Another*, 163. Kwon here is responding directly to Lucy Lippard's place-based counter-argument to the nomadic model of art practice, in *The Lure of the Local: Senses of Place in a Multicentered Society* (New York: New Press, 1997).
20 Charlotte Bydler, "The Global Art World, Inc.: On the Globalization of Contemporary Art," in Filipovic, Van Hal, and Solveig, *The Biennial Reader*, 381.
21 http://www.biennialfoundation.org/2011/06/the-5th-bucharest-international-biennial-for-contemporary-art-generated-by-pavilion-journal-for-politics-culture-set-for-25-may-22-july-2012-under-the-curatorship-of-anne-barlow-ukusa-re/.
22 Curator and critic Claire Doherty identifies three precedents for the predominance of place in biennial culture: large-scale public art projects such as Mary Jane Jacobs's *Culture in Action* of 1994, research-based public programs such as Artangel in London, and the artist-in-residence tradition. For Doherty, all three models represent an outmoded understanding of place. Claire Doherty, "Curating Wrong Places ... Or Where Have All the Penguins Gone?" in *Curating Subjects*, ed. Paul O'Neill and Søren Andreasen (London: Open Editions, 2007), 101–3.
23 Declan McGonagle, cited in Claire Doherty, "Location Location," *Art Monthly*, no. 281 (November 2004): 9. See also Pryle Behrman, "In Search of the Ideal Biennale," *Art Monthly*, no. 301 (November 2006): 5–8; Thomas Wulffen, "Liverpool Biennale," *Kunstforum International*, no. 173 (November-December 2004): 384–6; and Nikos Papastergiadis and Meredith Martin, "Art Biennales and Cities as Platforms for Global Dialogue," in *Festivals and the Cultural Public Sphere*, ed. Gerard Delanty, Liana Giorgi, and Monica Sassatelli (Oxon and New York: Routledge, 2011), 45–62.
24 The neocolonial charge is perhaps stickler. The trend, advanced largely by Enwezor, to use biennials as a context in which to tap the wealth of the world's art peripheries has been critiqued, as Paul Ardenne notes, as the West's ploy to use "its art biennials as a way of externalizing its art and aesthetics in very much the same way as it does its economic activity, by relocating and turning globalization into profit." In "From Biennale to Banal? Schmooze and Globalization," *Art Press*, no. 291 (June 2003): 43.
25 Becker, "The Romance of Nomadism," 28.

26 George Steiner, *Extraterritorial: Papers on Literature and the Language Revolution* (New York, 1971), 11.
27 Tim Cresswell's critique of what he terms "nomadic metaphysics" and concomitant espousal of a "politics of mobility" is paradigmatic in this respect. See *On the Move: Mobility in the Modern Western World* (New York: Routledge, 2006).
28 Said, "Reflections on Exile," 357–9.
29 Rosi Braidotti, *Metamorphoses: Towards a Materialist Theory of Becoming* (Cambridge: Polity Press, 2002), 3. Braidotti's feminist appropriation of Deleuzian nomadism is based, in a nutshell, on the notion that "mobility is one of the aspects of freedom, and as such it is something new and exciting for women: being free to move around, to go where one wants to is a right that women have only just started to gain." In *Nomadic Subjects: Embodiment and Sexual Difference in Contemporary Feminist Theory* (New York: Columbia University Press, 1994), 256.
30 Okwui Enwezor, "The Unhomely: Phantom Scenes in Global Society," in *The Unhomely: Phantom Scenes in Global Society* (Seville: Foundation for the International Biennial of Contemporary Art of Seville, 2006), 13.
31 Kwon, *One Place after Another*, 166.
32 Stallabrass, *Art Incorporated*, 37.
33 According to Jaar, one million is the number of migrants that Finland would accept if its immigration policies matched those of its European neighbours. As if acknowledging this fact as a threat, the Finnish government ordered the "passports" closely guarded during their showing at the Museum of Contemporary Art in Helsinki and had them destroyed shortly thereafter. See http://www.alfredojaar.net.
34 Stallabrass, *Art Incorporated*, 30.
35 On what Brian Massumi refers to as late capitalism's "checkpoint" logic, see Mary Zournazi, "Navigating Movements: A Conversation with Brian Massumi," in *Hope: New Philosophies for Change* (London and New York: Routledge, 2003), 228–31.
36 Butler, *Dispossession*, 23. See also Brian Holmes, "Do Containers Dream of Electric People? The Social Form of Just-in-Time Production," *Open*, (Im) Mobility: Exploring the Limits of Hypermobility, 21 (2011): 30–44, for an insightful reading of the shipping container in Biemann's work.
37 Ursula Biemann, "*Contained Mobility*," 2004, http://www.vtape.org/video?vi=6885.
38 Meyer, "Nomads," 17.
39 Ibid., 23.
40 Ibid.

41 Attali, *Millennium*, 105, 5.
42 Marcus Verhagen, "Biennale Inc.," *Art Monthly*, no. 287 (June 2005): 2.
43 Ibid., 3.
44 Enwezor, "The Unhomely," 14.
45 Consider, for example, how the machinations of the US war on terror transformed "homeland" into a term laden with connotations of security, defence, and suspicion.
46 Okwui Enwezor, "Trade Routes," in *Trade Routes: History and Geography. 2nd Johannesburg Biennale 1997*, ed. Okwui Enwezor (Johannesburg: Thorold's Africana Books, 1997), 8.
47 Ibid.
48 Enwezor, "The Unhomely," 12–13. See David Scott, *Conscripts of Modernity: The Tragedy of Colonial Enlightenment* (Durham, NC: Duke University Press, 2005), whose concept of "problem-spaces" is elaborated below.
49 Steiner, *Extraterritorial*, 21.
50 In Paul Achiaga, "Okwui Enwezor [Interview]," *El Cultural* (Madrid), October 2006, http://www.elcultural.es/historico_articulo.asp?c=18937.
51 Luis Sánchez-Moliní, "La BIACS que viene," e-sevilla.org, 9 September 2006, http://e-sevilla.org/index.php?name=News&file=article&sid=832.
52 Nor was the exhibition contextualized within its own internal history. No continuity was attempted or established with Harold Szeman's First Seville Biennial in 2004 – a trend that continued in 2008 with Peter Weibel's third instalment, an exhibition of international new media art that also marked the final instalment of BIACS.
53 See, for instance, Martin Herbert, "2nd Seville Biennial," *Frieze*, no. 104 (January-February 2007): 103.
54 The third iteration of BIACS, curated by Peter Weibel in 2008, was even more dogged by controversy, especially regarding the cost of mounting the exhibition and the failure to remunerate participating artists.
55 Quoted in Hal Foster, "Towards a Grammar of Emergency," *New Left Review* 68 (March-April 2011): 107. See also Anna Dezeuze, *Thomas Hirschhorn: Deleuze Monument* (London: Afterall Books, 2014), for an insightful reading of precariousness in Hirschhorn's practice.
56 Helmut Dietrich, "Das Mittelmeer Als Neuer Raum Der Abschreckung: Flüchtlinge Und Migrantinnen an Der Südlichen Eu-Außengrenze," Forschungsgesellschaft Flucht und Migration e.V., Berlin, 24 April 2007, http://www.ffm-berlin.de/mittelmeer.html.
57 Yto Barrada, *A Life Full of Holes: The Strait Project* (London: Autograph ABP, 2005), 57. The Schengen Agreement abolished "internal" borders between participating EU nations and harmonized external border controls.

58 The question of language is telling here. All text at the exhibition was provided in Spanish and English, rather than languages spoken by neighbours in Portugal, Italy, or Morocco. Also interestingly, films and videos in languages other than Spanish or English were invariably translated into English only.

59 Gerardo Mosquera, "Some Problems in Transcultural Curating," trans. Jaime Flórez, in *Global Visions: Towards a New Internationalism in the Visual Arts*, ed. Jean Fisher (London: Kala Press and The Institute of International Visual Arts, 1994), 135.

60 Scott, *Conscripts of Modernity*, 4.

61 Said, "Reflections on Exile," 365.

62 "Only in a world in which the spaces of State have been perforated and topographically deformed and in which the citizen has been able to recognize the refugee that he or she is – only in such a world is the political survival of humankind today thinkable." Agamben, "Beyond Human Rights," 165.

63 T.J. Demos, "Life Full of Holes," *Grey Room*, no. 24 (Summer 2006): 82.

64 Rasha Salti, "Emily Jacir: She Lends Her Body to Others to Resurrect an Absent Reality," *Zawaya* (Beirut), no. 13 (Fall 2004–Winter 2005); cited in Demos, "Life Full of Holes," 79.

65 T.J. Demos, "Desire in Diaspora: Emily Jacir," *Art Journal* 62, no. 4 (Winter 2003): 79. Emphasis added.

66 Ibid., 76.

67 Demos, "Life Full of Holes," 80.

68 Cited in ibid., 76.

69 Mieke Bal, "Lost in Space, Lost in the Library," in *Essays in Migratory Aesthetics: Cultural Practices between Migration and Art-Making*, ed. Sam Durrant and Catherine M. Lord (Amsterdam and New York: Rodopi, 2007), 25.

70 Ibid., 23–4.

71 Mieke Bal, "Heterochrony in the Act: The Migratory Politics of Time," in *Art and Visibility in Migratory Culture*, ed. Mieke Bal and Miguel Hernández-Navarro, Thamyris/Intersecting: Place, Sex and Race, vol. 23 (Amsterdam and New York: Rodopi, 2011), 211–12.

72 In three months of shooting, Labat recorded 672 hours of surveillance footage and twelve hours with the handheld camera.

73 Bal, "Heterochrony in the Act," 210.

74 Ibid., 203.

75 Freud's concept of *Nachträglichkeit* elaborates the idea that a traumatic event becomes fixed in memory, a process that affords it its power over the subject. In "Project for a Scientific Psychology I" (1895), in *The Standard Edition*

of the Complete Psychological Works of Sigmund Freud, ed. James Strachey (London: Hogarth Press and the Institute of Psycho-analysis, 1974), 1:353–4.

76 For elaboration, see Caruth, *Unclaimed Experience*, and Michael S. Roth, "Hysterical Remembering," *Modernism/Modernity*, no. 3 (May 1996): 4–5.

77 See Christine Ross, "The Temporalities of Video: Extendedness Revisited," *Art Journal* 65, no. 3 (Fall 2006): 83.

78 On the narcissistic gaze of early video art, see Rosalind Krauss's germinal essay, "Video: The Aesthetics of Narcissism," *October*, no. 1 (1976): 50–64.

79 Allan Sekula, *Fish Story* (Dusseldorf: Richter Verlag, [1995] 2002), 50. *Fish Story*, both a book and a photographic series, documents the geopolitical and socio-economic implications of the global shipping trade.

80 See Suzanne Daley, "A Borderline Where Women Bear the Weight," *New York Times*, 31 March 2014, A1.

81 Ursula Biemann and Angela Sanders, *Europlex* (Zurich: Women Make Movies, 2003), 20 minutes, colour, VHS/DVD.

82 Jenny Edkins, *Trauma and the Memory of Politics* (Cambridge and New York: Cambridge University Press, 2003), 59, 230.

83 In *The Return of the Real*, Hal Foster considers Barthes's *punctum* and Lacan's *tuché* as analogous expressions of trauma's missed encounter with the Real (132).

84 Rogoff, *Terra Infirma*, 122.

85 See especially Nico Israel, "Border Crossings: A Portfolio by Yto Barrada," *Artforum International* 45, no. 2 (October 2006): 246–7, on Barrada's series of photographs entitled *A Life Full of Holes: The Strait Project* (1998–2003).

86 Ibid., 247.

87 Irit Rogoff, "'Smuggling': A Curatorial Model," in *Under Construction: Perspectives on Institutional Practice*, ed. Vanessa Müller and Nicolaus Schafhausen (Köln: Walther Konig, 2006), 134.

88 Ibid.

89 Ibid., 135.

90 See "Yto Barrada," Sfeir-Semler Gallery, Beirut, http://www.sfeir-semler.com/gallery-artists/yto-barrada/.

91 Nikos Papastergiadis, "Art in the Age of Siege," *Framework: The Finnish Art Review* (Helsinki), no. 5 (July 2006): 36.

92 Yto Barrada, "Talking Pictures," interview with Jennifer Higgie," *Frieze*, no. 142 (October 2011): 182–9.

93 In *Europlex*, videocassette. On Henri Lefebvre's understanding of space as neither inert nor neutral but, rather, always a product of social relations, see *The Production of Space*, trans. Donald Nicholson-Smith (Oxford: Blackwell, 1991).

94 "BIACS II Artists Guide."

95 Imre Szeman, "Remote Sensing: An Interview with Ursula Biemann," *Review of Education/Pedagogy/Cultural Studies* 24, nos. 1/2 (2002): 93.

96 In *Europlex*, videocassette.

97 Bal, "Heterochrony in the Act," 215. In this essay, Bal considers Biemann's video essay *Remote Sensing* (2001), about sex trafficking.

98 In Szeman, "Remote Sensing," 93.

99 Ibid.

100 Michel de Certeau, *The Practice of Everyday Life*, trans. Steven Rendall (Berkeley: University of California Press, 1984).

101 "Desire line" is the term used in landscape architecture to refer to the paths that pedestrians create as short cuts linking roads and sidewalks.

102 Jenny Edkins, "Remembering Relationality: Trauma Time and Politics," in *Memory, Trauma and World Politics*, ed. Duncan Bell (New York: Palgrave Macmillan, 2006), 110.

103 Ibid., 110–11.

104 Kristeva, *Strangers to Ourselves*, 97–8.

105 On the flash mob phenomenon as a set of collective practices that foster "new forms of sociability," see Virag Molnar, "Reframing Public Space through Digital Mobilization: Flash Mobs and Contemporary Urban Youth Culture," *Space and Culture* 17, no. 1 (2014): 43–58.

106 Basualdo, "Launching Site," 39.

107 See Ruud Kaulingfreks and Samantha Warren, "SWARM: Flash Mobs, Mobile Clubbing and the City," *Culture and Organization* 16, no. 3 (September 2010), who argue that mobile clubbing produces a form of inoperative community that "emerges like a swarm and develops in the plurality of differences it engenders" (224).

108 Said, "Reflections on Exile," 365.

Index

Ægis (Wodiczko), 23, 43, 74–8, 86
Abdul, Lida, 104–5, 112–13, 136
Abu Ghraib, 64, 133
Acconci, Vito, 33, 56, 58–9
Ador o, Theodor, 32
Agamben, Giorgio, 8, 110, 116, 128, 154, 206n62
Alÿs, Francis, 89–90
anarchitecture, 53–5, 187n98
And Counting… (Bilal), 112–13, 132
archives, 108–13, 122–3, 125, 128, 130, 136
Armenian Genocide, 130, 200n65
Atrabiliarios (Salcedo), 197n26
Attali, Jacques, 137, 148
Autocar—Tangier (Barrada), 164–70

Bal, Mieke, 127–8, 198n26; and heterochrony, 159, 172; and migratory aesthetics, 149, 156–61, 172–3
Barrada, Yto, 153–4, 156–7, 160–72
Beecroft, Vanessa, 101
Benjamin, Walter, 32, 49–50, 128
Bennett, Jill, 17, 123–5, 135
Bhabha, Homi, 4, 14, 21, 22, 46, 61–2, 68, 70, 104–5, 125, 135–6, 181n59
Biemann, Ursula, 139, 146–7, 149, 154, 156–7, 159, 161, 169–73
biennial culture, 24–5, 29, 138–47, 149, 151, 153–4, 156, 161, 164, 170, 203n22, 203n24
Bilal, Wafaa, 43, 52, 112–13, 120–2, 132, 197n22
Bishop, Claire, 87–8, 96
Boltanski, Christian, 110, 134–5
Bourgeois, Louise, 31, 33
Bourriaud, Nicolas, 10, 110
Braidotti, Rosi, 143, 204n29
Brecht, Bertolt, 84–5, 117
Butler, Judith, 5, 12, 14, 16, 17–19, 43, 88, 111, 128, 147

Cahun, Claude, 31, 34
Caruth, Cathy, 12
La Casa Viuda (Salcedo), 118–21, 125
Cazdyn, Eric, 99
Colomina, Beatriz, 40, 61
Contained Mobility (Biemann), 146–7, 159
Covered Word (Sierra), 70, 72
Corbusier, Le, 30, 44, 158, 182n22
Cvetkovich, Ann, 122–3

Day Labor (Labat), 157–61
Deleuze, Gilles, 141, 202n14

Demos, T.J., 32, 154–5
Derrida, Jacques, 108–10, 113, 130, 136, 196n8, 200–1
Deutsche, Rosalyn, 36, 75, 83, 91
Didi-Huberman, Georges, 134, 200n74
Dis-Armor (Wodiczko), 69–71, 73, 78–9, 81–2, 87
Documenta 11, 149–50, 202n9
Doherty, Claire, 139, 203n22
Domestic Tension (Bilal), 43, 120–2
Duchamp, Marcel, 32

Edkins, Jenny, 162, 173
empathy, 24, 79–81, 86–7, 99, 106, 114, 116–18, 122
Enwezor, Okwui, 140, 143, 149–51, 153–4, 161, 173, 202n9, 203n24
Europlex (Biemann and Saunders), 169–73

flash mobs, 174, 208n105, 208n107
Floating House (The) (Phillips), 53–5
Foster, Hal, 108, 110–11, 113, 136, 141–2, 207n83
Foucault, Michel, 37–8, 79, 110, 112, 191n26, 197n21
Freud, Sigmund: "Das Unheimliche", 20–3, 47, 52, 70, 74–5, 90, 125, 180n51; melancholia, 12–13, 102; Nachträglichkeit, 159, 206n75; screen memory, 42; trauma, 79, 116–17
Friend, Melanie, 60–1, 63, 189n114
Fusco, Coco, 96

Glissant, Edouard, 16
Graham, Dan, 33, 47, 49–50
Guattari, Félix, 141, 202n14

Haacke, Hans, 33–7, 45, 100–1, 138, 195n98, 201n75
Halilaj, Petrit, 6–7, 13–16
Hatoum, Mona, 3–4, 7, 17–19, 136
Hebdige, Dick, 37, 39, 77
Heidegger, Martin, 32
Hirschhorn, Thomas, 110, 152
Höller, Carsten, 53, 139
Homelessness, 29, 34–9, 45–6, 77, 91–4, 137, 143, 184n42, 194n81
Homeless Projection: A Proposal for Union Square (Wodiczko), 35, 37, 77, 84, 90–1
Homeless Projection: Place des Arts (Wodiczko), 23, 37, 74, 93–4
House Beautiful: Bringing the War Home (Rosler), 29, 39–43, 60–1
House Beautiful: Bringing the War Home, New Series (Rosler), 63–6
Huyghe, Pierre, 53, 197n11
Huyssen, Andreas, 26–8, 50, 86, 123, 199n54

If You Lived Here… (Rosler), 38–9, 45, 66
I'm hungry to keep you close… (Halilaj), 15
In the House of My Father (Rodney), 5–7
In This House (Zaatari), 7–8
Interior Landscape (Hatoum), 17–19

Jaar, Alfredo, 60–1, 91–4, 96, 133, 139, 144–5, 147–9, 164, 204n33
Jacir, Emily, 130–2, 139, 154–6, 200n67, 200n70
Johannesburg Biennial, 140–1, 149–50

Kosovo, 7, 14–15, 60
Krauss, Rosalind, 31–2
Kristeva, Julia, 21–3, 70, 74–5, 103, 173–4, 180n52, 181n59
Kwon, Miwon, 141–2

Labat, Tony, 156–62, 164, 206n72
Lacan, Jacques, 121, 207 n83
LaCapra, Dominick, 116–17, 122
Laclau, Ernesto, 77, 80
Lanzmann, Claude, 200n74
Lee, Pamela M., 45, 48–9, 140, 191, 187n98
Lefebvre, Henri, 171, 207n93
Lighted Building (Sierra), 91
Lights in the City (Jaar), 91–4
Liverpool Biennial, 140, 142–3, 147

maquiladoras, 82, 97, 202n37
Masco, Joseph, 62
Massey, Doreen, 11
Massumi, Brian, 42, 204n35
Matta, Roberto, 31, 45, 186n75
Matta-Clark, Gordon, 23, 29–30, 34, 43–59, 68, 92, 116, 127, 174, 186n81, 187n98, 188n100,
Melancholy, 11–14, 16, 17, 27, 80, 88, 97, 101–3, 106, 111–14, 128, 130, 134, 135–6
Memorial culture, 11–12, 114, 123, 132–3
Memorial to 418 Palestinian Villages… (Jacir), 131–3, 199n70
Mobile Home (Hatoum), 13–14, 19, 136
Mosquera, Gerardo, 153
Mouffe, Chantal, 77, 80, 86

Nauman, Bruce, 116, 158–60
Neither (Salcedo), 128–30
9/11 attacks, 9, 38, 56, 58, 61, 127, 132, 135, 178n9
nomadism, 10–11, 31–2, 137–9, 141–9, 154, 176, 204n27
nostalgia, 26–7, 181n7
Noviembre 6 y 7 (Salcedo), 123–8

One Million Finnish Passports (Jaar), 144–5, 204n33

Palestine, 17, 130–1, 154–5, 200n67,69
Papastergiadis, Nikos, 164
Phillips, Paulette, 53–5
The places I'm looking for, my dear… (Halilaj), 6–7, 13–14
postproduction, 110, 197n11
Pruitt-Igoe, 43–4

Rancière, Jacques, 42, 84, 86–7
Reed, Christopher, 30
relational aesthetics, 10, 87, 138–9
Rodney, Donald, 5–7, 16–17
Rogoff, Irit, 9, 27, 100–1, 163–4, 188n30
Rosler, Martha, 23, 29–30, 34, 36–43, 45, 47, 50–2, 59–61, 63–7, 122, 184n42
Ross, Christine, 101, 181n14

Said, Edward, 143, 154, 176
Salcedo, Doris, 24, 28, 52, 105–8, 113–16, 118–36, 137–9, 164, 174–5, 196n6, 197n26, 198n32
Sartre, Jean-Paul, 26, 59
Schengen Agreement, 153, 215n57
Scott, David, 150, 154
Sekula, Alan, 161, 207n79
Selzer, Mark, 99

Semiotics of the Kitchen (Rosler), 36–7
Seville Biennial (BIACS), 149–50, 151–4, 156, 174, 205n52
Shibboleth (Salcedo), 127, 137–8, 174–5
Sierra, Santiago, 23–4, 69–70, 72–3, 87–92, 94–103, 106, 120, 122, 149, 163, 195n102
Silverman, Kaja, 99, 105, 117–18, 121
Simon, Roger, 16
Smithson, Robert, 29, 198n32
The Smuggler (Barrada), 160–4
Splitting (Matta-Clark), 29–30, 44, 46–53, 59
Stallabrass, Julian, 96, 145
Steiner, George, 137, 143, 183n33
Sturken, Marita, 42
sublime, 20, 47–8
Submission (Sierra), 97–9
Surrealism, 30–3
Szeman, Imre, 172

Tate Modern, 137–8, 174–5
Taylor, Diana, 109, 113
Tenebrae (Salcedo), 123–7
3000 Holes (Sierra), 89–90, 163
Tijuana Projection (Wodiczko), 82–5, 97
Tiravanija, Rirkrit, 53, 139, 147, 193n56
Trauma, 7–8, 11–12, 16–17, 19–21, 24–5, 26–8, 42, 49, 69–73, 78–82, 85–90, 97, 99, 102–3, 111, 113, 116–18, 122–4, 133, 159, 162, 173–5
Tzara, Tristan, 31

Untitled (Salcedo, Istanbul 2003), 24, 106–8, 128, 128–30, 132–6

Venice Biennale, 15, 70, 99–101, 140, 149
Verhagen, Marcus, 149
Vidler, Anthony, 22, 45

Wall Enclosing a Space (Sierra), 70, 82, 99–101, 149
Whiteread, Rachel, 7, 12, 22, 28, 114–16, 126
Wilding, Faith, 34
Winnicott, D.W., 70, 73, 80
Witness, 11–12, 16–17, 19–20, 25, 28, 79–80, 86, 92–3, 96, 99, 102, 105–6, 112–13, 116–17, 122, 131, 134–5
Wodiczko, Krzysztof, 21, 23, 35, 37, 39, 43, 45, 69–71, 73–87, 90–4, 96–7, 99, 103, 116
Womanhouse, 33–4, 37, 47, 49
Workers Who Cannot Be Paid… (Sierra), 24, 95–6

xenology, 73, 75, 77–9, 88

Yaeger, Patricia, 16

Zaatari, Akram, 7–8, 12
Žižek, Slavoj, 178n9

CULTURAL SPACES

Cultural Spaces explores the rapidly changing temporal, spatial, and theoretical boundaries of contemporary cultural studies. Culture has long been understood as the force that defines and delimits societies in fixed spaces. The recent intensification of globalizing processes, however, has meant that it is no longer possible – if it ever was – to imagine the world as a collection of autonomous, monadic spaces, whether these are imagined as localities, nations, regions within nations, or cultures demarcated by region or nation. One of the major challenges of studying contemporary culture is to understand the new relationships of culture to space that are produced today. The aim of this series is to publish bold new analyses and theories of the spaces of culture, as well as investigations of the historical construction of those cultural spaces that have influenced the shape of the contemporary world.

General Editor: Jasmin Habib, University of Waterloo
Editorial Advisory Board:
Lauren Berlant, University of Chicago
Homi K. Bhabha, Harvard University
Hazel V. Carby, Yale University
Richard Day, Queen's University
Christopher Gittings, University of Western Ontario
Lawrence Grossberg, University of North Carolina
Mark Kingwell, University of Toronto
Heather Murray, University of Toronto
Elspeth Probyn, University of Sydney
Rinaldo Walcott, OISE/University of Toronto

Books in the Series:

Peter Ives, *Gramsci's Politics of Language: Engaging the Bakhtin Circle and the Frankfurt School*

Sarah Brophy, *Witnessing AIDS: Writing, Testimony, and the Work of Mourning*

Shane Gunster, *Capitalizing on Culture: Critical Theory for Cultural Studies*

Jasmin Habib, *Israel, Diaspora, and the Routes of National Belonging*

Serra Tinic, *On Location: Canada's Television Industry in a Global Market*

Evelyn Ruppert, *The Moral Economy of Cities: Shaping Good Citizens*

Mark Coté, Richard J.F. Day, and Greg de Peuter, eds, *Utopian Pedagogy: Radical Experiments against Neoliberal Globalization*

Michael McKinnie, *City Stages: Theatre and the Urban Space in a Global City*

David Jefferess, *Postcolonial Resistance: Culture, Liberation, and Transformation*

Mary Gallagher, ed., *World Writing: Poetics, Ethics, Globalization*

Maureen Moynagh, *Political Tourism and Its Texts*

Erin Hurley, *National Performance: Representing Quebec from Expo 67 to Céline Dion*

Lily Cho, *Eating Chinese: Culture on the Menu in Small Town Canada*

Rhona Richman Kenneally and Johanne Sloan, eds, *Expo 67: Not Just a Souvenir*

Gillian Roberts, *Prizing Literature: The Celebration and Circulation of National Culture*

Lianne McTavish, *Defining the Modern Museum: A Case Study of the Challenges of Exchange*

Misao Dean, *Inheriting a Canoe Paddle: The Canoe in Discourses of English-Canadian Nationalism*

Sarah Brophy and Janice Hladki, eds, *Embodied Politics in Visual Autobiography*

Robin Pickering-Iazzi, *The Mafia in Italian Lives and Literature: Life Sentences and Their Geographies*

Claudette Lauzon, *The Unmaking of Home in Contemporary Art*

www.ingramcontent.com/pod-product-compliance
Lightning Source LLC
Chambersburg PA
CBHW020323270725
30045CB00008B/41/J

* 9 7 8 1 4 4 2 6 4 9 8 2 8 *